Justice and the Slaughter Bench

In this follow-up to *Law and the Beautiful Soul*, Alan Norrie addresses the split between legal and ethical judgment. Shaped by history, law's formalism both eschews and requires ethics. The first essays consider legal form in its practical aspect, and the ethical problems encountered ('law's architectonic'). The later essays look at the complex underlying relation between law and ethics ('law's constellation'). In Hegel's philosophy, legal and ethical judgment are brought together in a rational totality. Here, the synthesis remains unachieved, the dialectic systematically 'broken'. These essays cover such issues as criminal law's 'general part', homicide reform, self-defence, euthanasia and war guilt. They interrogate legal problems, consider law's method and its place in the social whole. The analysis of law's historicity, its formalism and its relation to ethics contributes importantly to central questions in law, legal theory and criminal justice.

Alan Norrie is Professor of Law and former Head of the Law School at Warwick University. He has held chairs at Queen Mary and King's College, London, and is a Fellow of the British Academy.

Justice and the Slaughter Bench

Essays on Law's Broken Dialectic

Alan Norrie

Routledge
Taylor & Francis Group
LONDON AND NEW YORK

First published 2017 by Routledge

2 Park Square, Milton Park, Abingdon, Oxfordshire OX14 4RN
711 Third Avenue, New York, NY 10017

a GlassHouse book

Routledge is an imprint of the Taylor & Francis Group, an informa business

First issued in paperback 2017

British Library Cataloguing in Publication Data
A catalogue record for this book is available from the British Library

Library of Congress Cataloging-in-Publication Data
A catalog record for this book has been requested

ISBN: 978-1-138-95511-0 (hbk)
ISBN: 978-1-138-56395-7 (pbk)

Typeset in Baskerville by
Keystroke, Neville Lodge, Tettenhall, Wolverhampton

In Memory of Roy Bhaskar

Norrie shows again why he is one of the world's most insightful philosophers of law with this award-worthy volume. His development of a legal architectonic elegantly organizes thought about the legal form, the paradoxical nature of legal autonomy, and the lurking dangers of abstract freedom.

–Jonathan Goldberg-Hiller, University of Hawai'I, USA.

An indispensable starting point for those interested in what a genuinely critical, philosophically-engaged and social-theoretical approach to law looks like. It is the most recent instalment in a far-reaching, illuminating and important project that seeks to chart both law's nature and its place in the ethical landscape.

– Professor William Lucy, Durham University, UK.

When in its turn [the law] has done to him just what he did himself, it then lets go, but it still withdraws to a threatening attitude; it has not lost its shape or been made friendly.

Hegel, *The Spirit of Christianity and Its Fate*

But even regarding History as the slaughter bench at which the happiness of peoples, the wisdom of States, and the virtue of individuals have been victimised – the question involuntarily arises – to what principle, to what final aim these enormous sacrifices have been offered.

Hegel, *The Philosophy of History*

Contents

Preface

The essays in this collection cover a range of topics in criminal law and legal theory. They view law as a social, historical and ethical phenomenon, but they also think about law as law. The central methodological issue is how we grasp law's specificity while seeing it as constructed out of what it is not. To be a lawyer is to walk a line between the need to see law as sufficient unto itself and the fact that law expresses social relations that are not 'it'. Lawyers need to be able to differentiate and use legal materials, yet when they ask what makes these materials legal, it is difficult to provide a compelling rationale.

I argue that the way to understand law is to see its specificity as having an 'as if', fictional, quality. Law is the place of a quasi-autonomy or quasi-rationality, where abstract theoretical concepts produce the idea of a modern legal subject. That subject, *homo juridicus* and its variants, operates to organise the legal field. So doing, it performs a number of social, political and ethical functions as required by time and place. In that regard, *homo juridicus* is not unlike its first cousin, *homo economicus*. Perhaps because of its apparent failures, we are able to see through the latter. What of the legal subject, what are we to make of it?

In criminal justice theory, it is common not to see the issue. A close link is forged with moral philosophy, so that the idea of legal responsibility is pursued as an illustration of applied moral theory. This allows lawyers to think of the legal subject as a modern instantiation of an ancient idea, sanctioned and normalised by wreaths of tradition. The responsible legal subject is a man (or woman) for all seasons, times, places, and in the further reaches of analytic philosophy, worlds.

Perhaps it is ideological blindness or lack of imagination that leads lawyers not to see beyond the legal subject. Alternatively, it is a testimony to the strength of legal practices that they sustain a sense of modern law's inevitability. These essays lean more towards the latter. They want to understand legal fictions, see how they work, find the devil in the detail. They seek to show that a critical approach is not a 'funky' alternative to the standard treatments. They claim that a critical approach, because it gets to the heart of law, gives a better understanding of what law is, how it works, how it judges.

The essays here develop the idea of law's *architectonic* to bring this out. In criminal justice terms, this is the structure of thinking and practice organised around the core form of the legal subject and its variants. The architectonic of criminal law articulates the ideas of a general and a special part, offence and defence, actus reus and mens rea, culpability, strict and corporate liability, and so on. From these core ideas there emanate a range of criminal justice practices, practices which also shape the legal ideas in a two way process.

The essays in the first part reflect on the devil and the detail in law's architectonic. Chapter 2 examines how the 1950s to the 1970s was a special time for the liberal legal subject, while political and economic changes from the 1980s pushed subjectivity to perform different tasks and begin to change its shape. Chapter 3 considers how a critical approach, focused on abstract legal subjectivity, can discern underlying problems in sophisticated attempts at law reform. Chapter 4 takes an urgent political issue, shoot to kill on the streets of London, and shows how it opens up the nature of legal citizenship, the dialectical logic of the law, and the role of the judges. Chapter 5 considers how law's abstract individualism can be used productively with regard to issues relating to the politics and morals of euthanasia. Chapter 6 rounds off the first half by considering the overall orientation of criminal law theory, and how different moral, political and critical methods view it.

If the first essays ask how law (the legal architectonic) judges, the second set ask how we judge law's judgment. If law is a specific way of making judgements, it opens a space for considering the specific nature of those judgements. The essays in the second part are grouped around an initial essay (Chapter 7), pursuing lines of thought from it. They are exploratory and unfinished. They take a problem in liberal legal theory, the connection between legal and moral responsibility, and they ask how it is possible for liberal law to judge acts of extreme moral wrongdoing.

Criminal responsibility has a difficult relationship with the idea of guilt. Guilt can be seen as a formal legal concept, or it can be seen as connected to deeper moral issues. When the defendant in a court of law is found guilty, this may only mean 'guilty according to due process and application of law'. But guilt also implies something more, moral culpability for wrongdoing, especially where the wrongdoing is egregious. These essays probe the connection between legal and moral guilt.

They take as their starting point Hannah Arendt's assertion that the crimes of the Nazi genocide 'explode the limits of the law' and so call into question the relation between legal and moral culpability. There is something both logically compelling and morally troubling in Arendt's claim, and these essays mainly seek to explore it. They think through the moral metaphysics of justice and their connection with modern liberal law. They are concerned with how we may think of legal judgment (Chapter 7), what it means to talk of good and evil (Chapter 8), and what kinds of responsibility, inside and outside law, there are (Chapter 10). They think about the roots of moral experience, and how we translate that into our understanding of law (Chapter 9).

The outcome is a sense of the way in which law and ethics relate to each other in law's *constellation*. If law has an 'inside', an architectonal sense of itself, then, even if that 'inside' involves 'as ifs' or fictions, it must also have an 'outside' with which it stands together in a social whole. Its architectonic, the 'internal' structure from which it looks 'out', must give rise to a set of 'external' links to which it is related. If we think through law's constellation, we can then judge law's judgment, in the whole of which it is a part. This is the subject of the essays in the second half of the book.

Acknowledgements

These essays were presented in various places to various audiences, and then and later, I benefited from the generosity of those who took time to comment. I will not repeat expressions of gratitude made previously, though they are now no less deserved. I will thank the following who have contributed generally to my thinking or the production of these pieces. They include Henrique Carvalho, Davina Cooper, Antony Duff, Lindsay Farmer, Dermot Feenan, Robert Fine, Mervyn Hartwig, Nicola Lacey, Bernadette McSherry, Peter Ramsay, Craig Reeves and Victor Tadros. I should like to thank Colin Perrin for his patience and thoughtfulness as commissioning editor at Routledge and Sanjeeb Hossain, who took time out from his doctoral work to prepare the text for publication. Thanks also to Laura Muir, Holly Smithson and Nicola Prior at Routledge who worked on the book.

I should also like to thank Richard, Stephen, Sachiko and Eleanor for being there, and for the pleasure they give me. I especially thank Gwen for her love and constancy in our lives together, and through a period of significant changes.

I take this opportunity to remember the late Roy Bhaskar, whose philosophy of critical realism underpins this book, and whose ideas emerge in various places in it. A brief sketch of the three phases of his thought is provided in Chapter 10, where his analysis of metaReality underlabours for my argument on the metaphysics of responsibility. The spirit of his dialectics pervades the work as a whole. The book is dedicated to Roy's fond memory, his human being, his absent presence – as he might himself have put it. The world is a greyer place without him.

With regard to previous publication: Chapter 2 appeared originally in B.McSherry, A.Norrie and S.Bronitt (eds), *Regulating Deviance: the Redirection of Criminalisation and the Futures of Criminal Law* (2009, Oxford: Hart Publishing) and is used by kind permission of Bloomsbury Publishing Plc. Chapter 3 appeared originally in *The Criminal Law Review*, copyright 2006 Thomson Reuters (Legal) Limited, and is reproduced by permission of Thomson Reuters (Professional) UK Limited. Chapter 5 appeared originally in A.Duff, L.Farmer, S.Marshall, M. Renzo, and V.Tadros (eds), *Structures of the Criminal Law* (2011, Oxford: Oxford University Press). Chapter 4 is republished with permission of the Regents of University of California from *New Criminal Law Review* 2010 vol 13; Chapter 6 is republished with permission of the Regents of University of California from *New Criminal Law Review* 2011 vol 14; Chapter 7 is republished with permission of the Regents of University of California from *New Criminal Law Review* 2008 vol 11; permissions conveyed through Copyright Clearance Center, Inc. Chapter 8 is published with kind permission from Springer Science+Business Media and was originally published in *Criminal Law and Philosophy* (2015) 9: 443–456 (as A.Norrie, 'Ethics and History: Can Critical Lawyers Talk of Good and Evil?'). Copyright Springer Science+Business Media Dordrecht 2013. Chapter 9 appeared originally in D.Feenan (ed), *Exploring the 'Socio' of Socio-Legal Studies* (2013, Basingstoke: Palgrave MacMillan). Chapter 10 appears in amended form in the *Journal of Critical Realism* (2016) vol 15 as 'Critical Realism and the Metaphysics of Justice'.

Chapter 1

Judging law's judgment

The essays in this collection range over issues of law, legal theory and criminal responsibility. They move from the practical to the theoretical. They consider such matters as homicide law reform, self-defence and shoot to kill, mercy killing and assisted suicide, and growing authoritarianism in the criminal law. They relate these issues to questions about the evolving historical shape of the law and whether it is susceptible to rational understanding, what we mean by good and evil, the nature of moral, legal and political responsibility, and the relationship between criminal justice, moral freedom and human solidarity. Some of these deeper issues are developed from considering the problem of war guilt. Their overall concern, however, is with understanding how law can be seen as a specific form of regulation that is at once social, political and ethical, yet remains at its core *legal.* That concern focuses on the relationship between the part (the law) and the whole (the social, political and ethical milieu in which it operates).

Amongst the questions this generates are these: how does law judge? And how should we judge that judgment? The first question arises from the sense of a specifically legal form of judgment. What does that mean, and what is the nature of the part that is law? The second arises from the observation that legal judgment is emergent from a broader context in which it continues to reside, so what is the relationship between the part and the whole?

Law, the part and the whole

To pursue these questions, the essays develop two themes, and are organised in two parts. The first theme is how doctrines of responsibility are framed in criminal law, addressing the question 'how does the law judge'? Law has its own way of thinking about and putting into practice ideas of responsibility. The result is a system and structure of concepts which is specifically legal. This involves both a legal account of responsibility and a specifically legal mode of organising that account, and their conjunction is understood as morally compelling. Responsibility is couched in terms of individual agency according to a set of concepts that is seemingly rationally organised and self-contained. We have an autonomous subject understood within a self-referential, self-contained and, therefore, also autonomous system. I call this conceptual system, which involves both form and method, law's *architectonic* of justice or judgment.

In law's architectonic, however, things are not quite as they appear. Law's concepts of responsibility are not necessarily compelling or self-evident, and nor is its composition rational or self-contained in the ways it thinks. Neither the legal subject (the law's form) nor the legal discipline (its method) are autonomous in ways that are claimed. Nonetheless, criminal law theorists and practitioners act on an 'insider' view of law's rationality and autonomy.[1] This becomes the way law presents itself and, since self-understanding is practical and powerful, the 'insider' view appears true. In reality, the practical and fictional 'as if' quality in this gives the legal subject and the legal system only a quasi-autonomy. Thinking about criminal law is then a matter of testing criminal law scholarship and practice against its own self-understanding, identifying the gap between that understanding and the way things are, and then explaining it.

The first set of essays in this collection explores this 'inside' view of the law. They work between the law's self-understanding, with its consequent practical effects, and a critical perspective that sees that understanding as partial, yet practically powerful. The 'inside' of the law, what makes it law and not simply another social, political or ethical phenomenon, is produced by establishing an 'outside' that is not law. Yet the relationship between the 'inside' and the 'outside' is always problematic, and this gives law its 'as if' quality, and the problem-set specific to it. The question 'how does law judge?' (since it is a specific form of judgment) is thus answered by reflecting on the nature of the legal architectonic.

The second theme concerns the overall relationship of the part to the whole. If criminal justice thinking and practice establish an understanding in which a particular model of responsibility and an internal logic (a quasi-logic) of law is established, that raises a question not just about what this 'inside' is, but also how it and its 'outside' relate overall to each other. Viewed in this holistic context, how do we judge law's judgment? Understanding it to be a specific part in a broader whole requires us to appreciate not only law's specific workings and problem-set, but also its place in the whole. In a legal world where an 'inside' and 'outside' are created, the ultimate standpoint is one that thinks how the two stand together, their *constellation*.

The second group of essays in this collection begins to look at this holistic relationship. If the first group concerns law's 'internal' problem-set, and how this is maintained in its environment, the second concern the necessary co-articulation, co-relation or constellation of an 'inside', and what lies 'beyond'. The first group start from the nature of law as a specific form of judgment created from a broader context, looking inwards, outwards and across, whilst the second

1 I give the terms 'inside' and 'outside' inverted commas because what is regarded as 'inside' the criminal law is not truly self-contained, but rather is intrinsically linked to what is thought of, from the 'inside', as 'outside'.

begins with the standpoint of the whole of which the specific form that is law is a part. If the question 'how does law judge?' is answered by considering law's architectonic, the question 'how is law judged?', as a specific form of judgment in a whole, is answered by reflecting on the nature of the legal constellation.

Law's architectonic and its constellation

A special relationship?

There is a standard way of thinking about the nature of law which privileges an immediate link between criminal justice thinking and moral philosophy. Most straightforwardly, it is argued that the idea of the responsible individual lies at the core of both law and morality, so the natural starting point in both disciplines is individual blameworthiness. Once that is established, it may be admitted that other considerations, say of a political nature, come into play. These may be the upshot of living in a social world where the general interest must override principles of individual responsibility. The resulting tension is referred to as a situation where considerations of policy override principle (see e.g. Ashworth and Horder 2013).

Theorists may add that there is a recent tendency to emphasise such general considerations and, indeed, to restyle the law around them. In the process, the abdication of principle may reach dangerous levels. If, on the other hand, one accepts the need for such general policy considerations, it may be necessary to establish further arguments of principle that can control their operation (Ashworth and Zedner 2013). Whichever position is taken, the moral idea of the responsible individual remains the core normative ideal of the criminal justice system, albeit this is endangered by the surrounding environment.

Another possibility in standard thinking is to argue that the moral category of the responsible individual is an inadequate starting point, linked to one particular philosophy. It might be better to think more about what moral philosophy can teach. If Kant (or, more broadly, 'Kantianism') lies behind the standard model, then other philosophers such as Wittgenstein, Aristotle or Hegel might have other things to say. In this line of thought, the immediate link between law and moral theory is preserved. With the partial exception of Hegel, the result of these different approaches, whatever they may be, is to cement the relationship between law's architectonic and moral philosophy (compare e.g. Duff 1990, 2007; Gardner 2007; Tadros 2005).

Hegel is a partial exception because one way of thinking about his philosophy of law and justice is that he is not only interested in the moral foundations of responsibility, but in the need for a political community in which a theory of responsibility is embedded (Brudner 2009). That means at least that the forms of criminal justice owe their existence to something more than a morally responsible individual. Criminal justice is then seen as not only moral but also political in its nature. Further, insofar as Hegel was an historical thinker, which he was after a fashion, this means criminal justice also has an historical dimension. Yet, Hegel used in this way is not so far from the orthodox tradition I have been describing (see Chapter 6). His political understanding of law emerges after he has established the idea of a responsible individual, so that the latter continues to structure his philosophy of law. The same is true with the historical dimension in his thought: historical evolution is at the service of rational individual subjectivity.

How does law become law?

Moral philosophy, politics, history: all these are crucial to understanding criminal justice, but a fuller understanding of the nature of law, its self-understanding and its account of responsibility, would have to delve more deeply into their interconnection. If law is reduced to any or all of them, it is hard to see what makes it law. My starting point here is what I call law's architectonic. I view law as sitting at the intersection of three different circles in a Venn diagram, where the three circles represent social relations, political governance and ethics. Law's location means that it has three different facets: it is socio-historical, political and moral all at the same time. At the same time, however, law is also law. So, to put it more precisely, we should talk of law as being constituted with three different dimensions: the socio-legal, the politico-juridical and the ethico-legal. The question then is how it manages to achieve its *own* existence as a discipline that appears to be sui generis, when it is co-articulated with other things in this way. How is law both itself and constituted by other elements? How does it maintain its *differentia specifica* in such a setting?

My answer is that the legal architectonic has at its core a 'morality of form', that is, a formalistic morality based on the abstract universal figure of the legal subject. That figure is what constitutes the sense of law's 'sui genericity', and it is the intersectional location of this figure that provides it with its central, legal, task, which is both to be itself and to negotiate with others – the social relations, the political forms, the ethical problems of law in the modern liberal polity. It is this essential character of the law that gives it its practical–fictional, 'as if', quality. This is because the law needs to assert its autonomy in a situation of heteronomous dependence on forces beyond itself (the social, the political, the ethical). In this setting, achievement of its practical–fictional, quasi-autonomy is a requirement that exacts a price. On the 'inside', the formal discourse of law that becomes possible is purchased at the cost of a conflicted, in tension, antinomial quality. On the 'outside', there is a difficult and generally opaque relationship to the world 'beyond' the law and, in particular, to practical ethical experience in that world.

What is an architectonic?

Let me develop this more by considering the nature of the legal architectonic, the morality of form at its core, and the resulting conflicted nature of law. Use

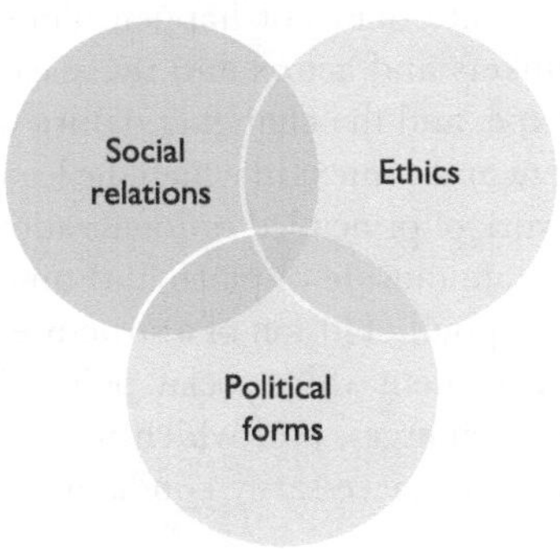

Figure 1

(i) Law's architectonic lies at the point of intersection of the three circles
(ii) It is constituted as socio-legal, politico-juridical and ethico-legal
(iii) Law's formalism has a practical–fictional quality

of the term 'architectonic' may at first seem surprising since it is associated with Kant, although my use diverges from his. Kant used it in a philosophical context to indicate a systematic series of metaphysical concepts, or 'the art of constructing a system'. Reason, he says, 'cannot permit our knowledge to remain in an unconnected or rhapsodic state, but requires that the sum of our knowledge should constitute a system'. This should take 'the form of a whole' in which reason determines 'not only the limits of its content, but the place which each of its parts is to occupy'. The unity is the end 'to which all the parts of the system relate, and through which all have a relation to each other'. In establishing this unity as 'an organism (*articulatio*) and not an aggregate', it may grow from within, but not by 'external additions'. The idea is of a 'schema', that is 'a content and an arrangement of parts determined a priori', and not from 'accidental aims and purposes'. It is this schema that forms the basis of unity, its constitution 'framed on architectonical principles' (Kant 1993: 532–33).

This captures well the sense of rational organisation and autonomy Kant desired for his philosophy. It also helpfully picks out what conventional legal theorists and practitioners find as law's sense of itself. I am arguing, however, that this involves a practical fiction, and therefore a quasi-rational, quasi-autonomous, understanding of law and the legal subject. My use of the idea of a legal architectonic accordingly reflects a second meaning, one associated with the idea of a building, of architecture, of something that has been materially constructed in space and time. I want to use the term to denote both that the legal architectonic has a sense of its own internal unity and that it has emerged from, and been shaped and structured by, an environment. It is a built form in an historical place so that its architectonic is both intellectual and material. Intellectually, it is understood as the work of lawyers and academics creating a system based on ideals of unity and reason, according to principles of justice.

Materially, however, this occupation of a practical and historical space means that the work of seeking to establish principled unity does not happen alone. Law sits between the intellectual work of its thinkers and actors and the socio-historical environment constructing its actual shape, and the changing nature of that shape over time. Importantly, the environment and context in which the legal structure emerges may not be conducive to the work of principled rationalisation attempted. Nor do legal thinkers and actors operate outside of place and time. The legal architectonic is accordingly the historical point of fusion of a structured set of concepts and practices in, and out of, an engagement with a social, political, economic and ethical environment from which it emerges, and which it helps constitute. It has a double provenance, and this is not necessarily conducive to principle or system.[2]

Legal subjectivity: antinomialism and the morality of form

What form does the legal architectonic take? It has different facets, but at its core there resides a universal model of a free individual as the key normative figure. This is the abstract subject of law who is responsible for his or her actions, independently of the social context in which he or she operates. It is this form that provides law with its own specificity. It is also the key bridging and negotiating point between the nature of law as social, historical and political and the idea of the legal subject as moral and subject to norms. The core theory of legal responsibility is in essence a 'morality of form' based upon the idea of the abstract legal subject (Norrie 2000: 7–10, 80–83). Consequently, the central ethical format is based upon evaluating the agency and mental states of a universally constituted, abstractly responsible, individual. The responsible legal subject lies at the core of the criminal justice architectonic.

This has two main consequences, the first being law's antinomialism, explored in Chapters 2–7. Law, as I have said, is constituted at the conjunction of the social, the political and the ethical dimensions of life and is, accordingly, socio-legal, politico-juridical and ethico-legal in its form. Such a constitutive setting is a recipe for conflict – emerging in the social sphere, generating political struggle, producing competing ethical demands. The legal architectonic adjusts to this environment and negotiates its tensions by virtue of a form that is abstractly universal in its terms. Each human being is treated as a legal person and actor, and this sense of abstract identity is able to play a key legitimating function in modern liberal society. The abstraction of the human being as a legal actor grounds the key ideas of a legal order, the responsible subject under the rule of law. But it also establishes the

2 For previous discussion, see Norrie (2005a: chs 4 and 5; 2014: 229–33). Hegel (1952: 6) uses the term to denote 'the rich inward articulation of ethical life, i.e. the state, the architectonic of that life's rationality'. There is a sense of political construction here, but Hegel aligns the working of ethical reason to politics in the modern state, whereas my position is to maintain their ongoing separation given the nature of the state and modern social and economic relations.

particular nature of legal categories as conflicted, contradictory and antinomial. The 'external' conflicts of the social and political world, seemingly kept at bay by abstract universality, do not disappear. Rather, they are introjected into the 'internal' categories of the law. They animate those categories, shaping them and ensuring that their logic is partial, disturbed and oppositional.

This process of introjection of social conflict and contradiction is the means whereby the legal architectonic comes to take the form of antinomy. By antinomy, I mean a self-contradiction in which two one-sided elements in an opposition are both required and inadequate to address a problem. The introduction of one and its ensuing failure leads to the introduction of the other, which in turn fails. Neither can be adequate in itself (they are both one-sided), and their opposition entails they cannot operate successfully together (they are in competition). They are two halves that cannot make a whole. The nature of legal form leads to the positing of 'a', typically an abstract, psychological, statement pertaining to human psychology, which is then followed by 'not-a', typically a more concrete or contextual statement relating to the same thing. The legal argument proceeds by way of an unresolved dialectic juxtaposing 'a' and 'not-a', seeking to find a resolution that is not forthcoming (see also Norrie 2005a: chs 1 and 2). Legal journals are full of examples of this process in action.

However, this is only a basic form of legal antinomialism. Ultimately, legal antinomialism can reveal a complexity that is very hard to disentangle. Law builds up a structure of concepts. One opposition entails another until we find ourselves with an overall grouping of antinomies, a fusion of difficulties that must work together but cannot. This is a problematic in the Althusserian sense, or what Roy Bhaskar would call a TINA ('There Is No Alternative') syndrome or compromise formation (Bhaskar 1993: 116–119; Norrie 2010: 105–109), meaning a structure of concepts which is regarded as inevitable but that can, in truth, only function through its buttressing by other partial concepts in an otherwise conflicted whole.

One example discussed below is the law of mistaken self-defence (Chapter 4) where the overriding problem is the antinomial opposition between 'imperfect justification' and 'warranted excuse'. Unpacking this, we find a cluster of antinomies involving the more basic 'justification versus excuse', 'offence versus defence' and 'honest versus reasonable mistake'. Legal theorists must seek to rationalise this TINA, but its difficulties remain unresolved, because unresolvable. One argument is the repetitive introduction to its counter and the matter can only be resolved ultimately by an 'external' political decision.

The second consequence of law's morality of form, explored in Chapters 8–12, concerns the broader constellational relationship between law and ethics, which can be represented initially by the antinomy governing our discussion so far, that of the 'inside' and the 'outside'. Law sets itself up as a specific architectonic embracing the socio-legal, the politico-juridical and the ethico-legal, and its claims to autonomy are based on a formalistic version of ethics based on abstract legal subjectivity. This affects not only the nature of the 'internal' ethico-legal debate, where antinomialism governs, but also how it interacts with the broader environment of which it is a part. In particular, its ethical formalism establishes an intrinsically difficult relationship with our understanding of ethics more broadly, and this is considered in the second group of essays. If law's architectonic establishes a morality of form, that is the basis for an internally conflicted (antinomial) set of concepts that makes up criminal justice thinking. But a morality of form is also problematic in how it sits in the social environment as a whole.

For example, the formalism of legal morality entails both a gap and an overlap between legal morality and morality in the world beyond law. How do these interface in a wider understanding? Questions of responsibility in law do not necessarily match the way responsibility is experienced beyond it. How are these differences related or co-articulated, and how do we judge their overall consequences? Morally substantive terms, of good and evil, are eschewed yet required by law. How do we think of these and their relationship to law? Overall, we need to understand how legal ethics fit with ethics in the social whole. How can we configure that relationship?

All these issues require a different standpoint, that of viewing the legal architectonic in the social totality of which it is a part. It never stands alone, but always with the social, political, economic and ethical elements in the social whole. That standing together provides the place from which to judge legal judgment, and is caught by the idea of a constellational setting. I return to the idea of law's constellation after the next section, in which we consider the 'internal' nature of criminal justice as a legal architectonic.

Inside law's architectonic: how does law judge?

The essays in Part I consider various aspects of the legal architectonic. Chapter 2 considers its historical evolution and recent changes, whilst Chapter 3 considers how it responds to efforts at reform. Chapters 4 and 5 then reflect on how it deals with political conflict (the idea of a police 'shoot to kill' policy), or ethical conflict (euthanasia). Chapter 6 then considers a recent effort to revindicate its rationality as a morality of form.

Criminal justice's socio-legal foundations

We begin by considering the historical development of criminal law, and recent changes in light of political and economic developments. Chapter 2 focuses on the socio-legal and politico-juridical aspects of the law's architectonic. It considers the historical evolution of criminal justice forms and reflects on the recent growth of authoritarianism in criminal law. This leads the law in competing directions. Under neo-liberal political and economic conditions, there is on one hand an increasing emphasis on individual responsibility for social ills, and on the other an accentuation of 'us and them' understandings of dangerous, irresponsible, subjects. The former accentuates the basic conception of individual responsibility at the core of the law, whilst the latter moves against it by broadening the powers of the state and the forms that legal control takes, and diluting the law's forms of responsible subjectivity.

In considering the socio-legal environment and shifting politico-juridical relations, the chapter argues that a central element concerns the nature of liberal citizenship in a move from a social democratic form of government to one dominated by neo-liberal assumptions and practices. It draws on T H Marshall's analysis of different forms of citizenship – the civil, the political and the social – to argue that a *fusion* of these three forms after the Second World War provided the liberal, social democratic moment in criminal law of the 1960s and early 1970s. Thereafter, it was their *fission* under neo-liberal conditions that unravelled the balances that underpinned social democratic criminal justice from the late 1970s onwards. The resulting trends were towards authoritarianism through both increased 'responsibilisation' and the turn to dangerousness. A relatively unified liberal criminal justice system was broken up in favour of a more punitive approach, both in terms of the increase in punishment and the forms of control created.

Informing this historical account of the change in criminal justice, however, is a stress on continuity between the two periods. Against the analysis of liberal lawyers, the argument is that the legal architectonic with its abstract morality of form is itself complicit in authoritarian practices. Increasing emphasis on the punishment of individuals (enhancing 'responsibilisation') and increased reliance on the ideology of dangerousness draw upon assumptions immanent in abstract legal subjectivity. The antinomy between the responsible and the dangerous subject evolved in the late 19th century, but has its roots in early modern liberal theory. Its re-emergence from the 1970s onwards was made possible by the breakdown of the relationship between the different forms of citizenship under neo-liberal politics and economics.

At a deeper level, the chapter draws on Franz Neumann's analysis of law in Germany in the 1920s and 1930s to argue that the politico-juridical antinomy between liberal legality and sovereign rule means that liberal legality is always intrinsically connected to political, social and economic power. If the political direction of a society is towards authoritarianism, then it is as much in the nature of law's architectonic to be shaped by such a dynamic as to act as a control upon it.

Legal antinomialism in the conceptual core

Chapter 2 sets the scene for the collection as a whole in that it is grounded in a socio-historical analysis of law's architectonic (its socio-legal aspect). The next three chapters all concern recent issues regarding its reform, and the role the morality of form plays in structuring the debate and its outcome. Chapter 3 concerns efforts to reform the law of murder and manslaughter in England and Wales. It shows the highly complex ethico-legal conceptual system operating at the law's heart. The proposals discussed here negotiate that system, whilst being shaped politically by the demand that murder be seen as a crime of special symbolic import.

The central part is played by the definition of intention, and the relationship between intention as part of the definition of the offence (its mens rea) and defences such as necessity, duress and self-defence. Depending on how intention is defined, an unlawful killing may result in a charge of manslaughter or murder, with the latter involving a mandatory life sentence. In 2006, the Law Commission for England and Wales sought to narrow the scope of the mandatory life sentence by distinguishing between murder convictions in the first and second degree. The chapter is a detailed analysis of the Law Commission's reasoning, which hinges on a central tension between an ethically formalistic, psychological and factual understanding of intention (what did D actually intend or foresee as a virtually certain consequence of his actions?), and a morally substantive account of the ethical quality of D's purpose (what was D's practical moral attitude to an outcome she has brought about?).

It is wrong to claim that all murders are alike ('Murder is murder is murder'). Killings come in different moral shapes and sizes. The law of mens rea permits only a formalistic approach based on the factual question of intention or foresight. This makes it hard to attune the legal response to the moral quality of the killing. The result is a widespread understanding that the law needs 'moral elbow room' to deal with difficult moral cases. In fact it is unclear that the English law even has a definition of intention, and it may be that the reluctance to provide one is a result of this need. Being vague permits discretion. At the core of the law is a tension between a dominant formalistic account of mens rea (known as 'orthodox subjectivism') and morally contextual or substantive accounts, which are necessarily invoked by the limited moral purchase of law's ethical formalism. The opposition between a factual psychological approach and a morally contextual one represents a core antinomial tension between form and content in the law. Its presence invokes a further structural antinomy, between offence and defence, and how legal responsibility for killings should be allocated between these two domains emerges as a moment of unresolved difficulty in the Law Commission's argument. Legal antinomialism structures the reform proposal throughout, providing it with its difficulties and irresolutions.

Criminal justice and the politico-juridical

In Chapter 4, we witness again this formalistic structure coming into tension especially around the offence–defence line. Competing moral and political understandings of wrongdoing lurk in the background, in this case where the police shoot dead persons mistakenly suspected of serious crime under the law of self-defence. In law, the question is decided according to whether such a mistake should be viewed as a question of mens rea (i.e. as a question of whether an offence has been committed), or as a matter of defence, a criminal act having been established.

In law, this matters because the nature of the mistake required depends on whether it falls under the definition of the offence (an honest mistake will negate mens rea) or a separate defence (in which case the mistake may need to be a reasonable one). The former is more beneficial to the accused, and it is this rule that governs the law.

Offence or defence? Behind this opaque, yet central, legal question there lies the tension between form and substance discussed in the previous chapter. A formalistic, factual and psychological account of mens rea and actus reus requires a morally substantive set of defences to accommodate morally problematic cases, but the line between offence and defence is always blurred, crossable and self-deconstructing. Defences subdivide into justifications and excuses, and there is a strong argument that any justificatory rationale for a defence means equally that no offence has been committed – since the person has done the right thing. Accordingly, there is then an argument for saying that such cases should be resolved as a matter of mens rea, i.e. on the definition of the offence, which is in fact the position the law takes at present. The defendant did not intend to commit an unlawful act, so the proposed separate defence folds back into the offence itself.

Situations of *mistaken* defence particularly illustrate the problem. Such mistakes can be seen as essentially rightful in their purpose, but wrong in their execution, and therefore as 'imperfectly justified'. As a form of justificatory defence, the way is open for a slide back into the terms of the offence. Alternatively, it can be argued that the act of defence was wrong but done for a reason worthy of exoneration, that is, 'warrantably excused'. As an excusatory defence, the sense of a wrong act requiring a defence is maintained.

Imperfectly justified or warrantably excused? The argument goes both ways and can be expressed in the antinomial form of a chiasmus: 'doing the right thing for a wrong reason' versus 'doing the wrong thing for a right reason'. This may seem like a game of paradoxes, but it matters – legally, morally and politically. One reason for not charging police officers for killing in cases of mistaken defence is the application of the rule that an honest mistake is enough to avoid liability. This is based on the view that mistakes affect mens rea as part of the definition of the offence. Critics argue that the law is wrong and should adopt a contextual, defence-based approach requiring a reasonable mistake. However, there is no right answer: it could go either way on offence or defence.

The rights and wrongs of classifying mistaken self-defence as part of the one or the other depends not on the formal terms of the legal definition, but on how a killing is viewed morally and politically. If a polity wished to encourage active and robust citizenship, where people step forward to defend themselves and each other, it would see mistaken self-defence as a right act done wrongly (i.e. as imperfectly justified). If it wished to ensure that citizens, including (especially?) armed police, acted in a circumspect and controlled fashion, the same polity might wish to see the same actions as wrong acts done rightly (i.e. as warranted excuses). Whichever way the society goes politically affects the legal rule of mistake applied – whether it should be based on an honest mistake on the definition of the offence, or a reasonable one with regard to a defence. A political choice resolves law's antinomial irresolution.

It is usually thought that we should contrast the formal rule of law with political voluntarism on the part of the judges. Judges ought to apply the law, not make it. If, however, the judicial application of the law depends on a political judgment that could go either way, we can see how legal antinomialism undermines the distinction between making and applying law. Legal form is more incomplete, fluid and mobile than we might have thought. Judicial politics are a part of the rule of law, not something that takes place as a way of disturbing that rule.

Criminal justice and the ethico-legal

Chapter 5 looks at practical problems associated with euthanasia, and the role law's morality of form plays in dealing with them. Again, the focus is on the law's antinomy of form and substance, and the role that a formal definition of the offence plays in dealing with a difficult social, moral and political problem. That problem concerns the political impasse surrounding the law of mercy killing and assisted suicide. The division in the UK Parliament between those favouring 'sanctity of life' and rejecting euthanasia, and those supporting 'quality of life' as the criterion for sometimes permitting it, remains, whilst there is a popular majority in the country in favour of some forms of euthanasia. The way this impasse is dealt with in law is by working through the existing legal architectonic to produce results that appear to uphold the existing legal ban, whilst allowing leeway under cover of law in particular cases.

This takes us back to the territory discussed in Chapter 3, that of precisely what the law of intention is with regard to murder, and whether there is any 'moral elbow room'. In the case of physicians hastening the death of patients, the law of intention is left sufficiently open in that the law of indirect intention (the foresight of virtual certainty rule) is not enforced. A degree of discretion is deployed in decisions to prosecute, or in the way that a direction to the jury is formulated. In the case of close family, cases reveal a process of discretionary moral judgment on the part of judges and juries ('jury equity') reflecting on the good motive of family members.

With regard to assisted suicide, the issue of informal prosecutorial discretion has been forced into the open in recent years, with the publication of prosecution guidelines which take into account the moral purpose of the person assisting. The criminal law architectonic with its emphasis on abstract formal rules necessitates a measure of discretion among actors (prosecutors, judges, juries) in the system to judge conduct as good or bad, on which the law is silent. In this, they must depart from the law's direction in order to deploy discretion. This runs counter to the formal rule of law, yet is a constituent element of how that rule operates. Moral discretion, like political judgment, becomes an element of the rule of law.

The result is that society is able to preserve its formal political ban on different forms of euthanasia, whilst the law tempers its effects *sotto voce* through the conjunction of legal rules and discretionary moral judgment. Here we also begin to glimpse the bigger picture of how the legal architectonic works in the social whole. The social, moral and political conflict over euthanasia reflects not just different ethical views, but political worries about the 'slippery slope' and the dangers of euthanasia in a socially unjust world. A middle class 'good death' may contribute to human well-being but, amongst poor people, it might have a different effect. To yield the line officially might open the door that would be hard to shut. Law's morality of form allows that door to be opened, without appearing to be.

Re-rationalising law's architectonic

Chapter 7 rounds off the flow of thought and argument in the previous three chapters. It concerns a recent attempt to revindicate the modern legal architectonic through a claimed Hegelian method. Read critically, Alan Brudner's work is important for the light it sheds on criminal law theory and understanding the criminal law. Over the past 30 years, such theory has been strong and has been particularly influenced by an approach which aligns directly analysis of legal categories with moral ones. (This is the approach that I describe at the beginning of this chapter.)

My reaction is the moral approach is not straightforward. Moral analysis of the rights and wrongs of actions and intentions can shed appropriate light on how legal concepts operate. Whilst this is not my approach, I think it brings a moral sensitivity to the standard categories of criminal law. Often times, this approach acts as a way of legitimating and rationalising law. At other times, it challenges law's categories to develop beyond their narrow cognitive forms. The moral criticism is of the 'orthodox subjectivist' approach to legal form, that is, to what I have described as the formalist approach to the criminal justice architectonic. So doing, it opens legal formalism up to critical scrutiny.

Such an approach is, however, limited, and Brudner illuminates the limits by taking a different, political point of view. His argument is that judgment in criminal justice has a particular formal shape and does not simply reflect ethical categories. That shape is derived from the nature of the modern liberal polity, and reflects three different levels of freedom. These organise criminal justice forms, and give them their rationality and cogency. The three levels are formal freedom, real autonomy and communal belonging. This is an important argument in that it shifts attention from a direct relationship between moral judgment and legal form, and establishes the idea of a formal political structure that shapes criminal justice thinking and practice. In effect, this is Brudner's version of the criminal justice architectonic, although he gives it a grand rational design.

A critical approach is also concerned with the rational thought of the criminal justice system, but relates this to the sense of an historical, built space out of the structured social relations of which it is a part, producing a sense of its quasi-rationality. For Brudner, law's morality of form is taken at face value as a means of legitimating modern law. For the critic, it is a means of mediating social, political and ethical conflicts and maintaining in their face law's quasi-autonomy. The critical architectonic has antinomy, conflict and contradiction at its core, where Brudner sees a reassuring and legitimating rationality.

Chapter 7 is written against the backdrop of these differences in approach, but it focuses on particular legal questions in order to test the two different approaches. It works on the basis that the best way of testing Brudner's analysis is to ask it to make sense of some standard criminal law cases. I argue that the problems with them remain unresolved in his analysis. To his grand conceptual design, which rules *ex hypothesi* how the criminal law ought to work, I oppose a sense of the complexity, tension and contradiction in the law. The critical approach is seen to work between the 'moral' and the 'political' approaches, but to link these to a deeper socio-historical understanding to produce a critical phenomenology of the broken character of modern legal form, one in which antinomy rules.

In conclusion to this section on law's architectonic, the first set of essays is focused as a whole on the legal architectonic and the intrinsic relationship that legal forms have with what appears to lie beyond them. Legal form in the shape of a morality of form and abstract legal subjectivity establishes the specificity of law – what makes it law – as a particular form of mediation of a social, moral and political environment. This generates its multi-faceted quality, as socio-legal, politico-juridical and ethico-legal, but it retains an understanding of the legal at the core, as a quasi-autonomous form.

The legal architectonic reflects and mediates structural problems in the social sphere, shapes and is shaped by politics and, importantly, establishes a split between ethics 'in the law' and ethics 'beyond it', with which it must engage. The consequence of this 'inside–outside' relation is an ethico-legal world of splits, of the introjection of conflicts 'outside' the law into a world of 'internal' antinomies. The essays in this first part have considered the legal *differentia* in the complex 'internal' world of the legal architectonic and in relation to its 'outside'. It is now time to look at this 'inside–outside' relation from a different vantage point, that of the whole.

Law's constellation: how should law be judged?

When we make a judgment about the operation of law, we can do so at two levels. One is narrowly at the level of 'the law itself'. What is the law, has it been properly applied, what is its impact? Another is more complexly at the level of how a legal outcome emerges from a broader social field. What is the nature of the legal formulation, how does it fit with other forms of intervention available, what are the intended and, as important, the unintended consequences of intervention? In the former, formal stipulations of what law is and narrow understandings of cause and effect lead to seemingly straightforward judgments about the operation of law. In the latter, complex understandings of the nature of law and how it relates to the broader social and ethical environment permit a judgment of legal operations as they emerge from and feed back into the workings of the social whole.

This second, more complex, approach is present in the essays discussed so far. Left to its own devices (as in the standard debates), the law of mistaken self-defence remains unattuned to the broader moral and political contexts of which it is a part. These need to be coupled with the legal forms to produce a legal solution. With regard to euthanasia, it transpires paradoxically that it is the obtuse abstraction of the legal formulae that permit a working outcome. For a time at least, an informal limited permission operates under cover of its formal denial. Law's judgment must be understood not only in terms of a deeper structural analysis of how its architectonic works, but also holistically, as it is related to specific social, political and ethical contexts. In short, it must be appraised in depth (law's architectonic) and in the round (law's constellation). So much is already implicit in our discussion of law as both *differentia* and as a form of structured being that intersects the social, the political and the ethical with the legal. That the legal in itself is also always the socio-legal, the juridico-political and the ethico-legal bespeaks an entity that is both part and part of a whole. Ultimately, to understand how this works, we need a sense of the whole, and the complex place of the part within it.

To grasp this sense of the place of the part in the whole, I use the concept of the 'constellation'. This is the idea of the way in which things that are different and distinct nonetheless 'stand together'.[3] In thinking this relationship of part and whole, different entities, levels, forms and parts of being may be seen as co-embedded with each other, and this co-embeddedness enables their constitutional difference. The co-embedded terms retain their individual importance, whilst remaining dependent nonetheless on what they are not. A constellation involves the interlocking of distinct entities to provide a sense both of the autonomy of the parts and their co-dependence in the whole. There is a real, intrinsic, relation of the individual terms together with a real, relative, autonomy as between them. It is this sense of autonomy-within-dependence that generates the sense with law, stated previously, that it enjoys a quasi-autonomy, meaning exactly an autonomy in relation to that with which it is intrinsically connected (the social, the political, the ethical).

The essays in this second part treat law constellationally with regard to its ethical constitution. They consider the connected yet differential relationship between legal and ethical judgment more broadly. There is a constellational unity of the legal and the ethical. This view entails the possibility of a holistic understanding of the working of legal ethics in relation to a broader sense of ethical judgment. Such judgment needs a sense of how things work out as a whole. How does this constellational relationship between the ethico-legal, based on a morality of form, and the ethical, understood more broadly, work?

3 The term is used in the dialectical tradition by Adorno, but the use here is distinct and drawn from Bhaskar (1993: 114–115). He uses it to denote how one term is either contained within another or intrinsically connected to it. The former he describes as a state of constellational identity; the latter one of constellational unity. See Norrie (2010: 99–101).

Legal and metaphysical responsibility

The essays in this part mainly follow a line of thinking initiated in Chapter 7. The starting point here is an ethical problem that lies at the core of Western liberal criminal justice systems. It is a problem of judging the part in the whole. How do we reconcile the claim that criminal law produces justice, when it does so in a social environment that is structurally (socially and economically) unjust? There is a structural violence in modern capitalist societies, which impacts most on the most disadvantaged. It is they who form the bulk of processed criminality, of those to whom the law does justice. This is the problem of 'just deserts in an unjust society', which already troubled Kant and Hegel, and which remains today. It can be stated as one where there is a structural and systematic gap between law's judgment and judgment of the law in the wider setting. The chapter starts with this issue, but uses it to identify a parallel or homologous problem, in formal terms at least, in the problem of war guilt, as discussed by Hannah Arendt and Karl Jaspers.

After the Second World War, Arendt had raised with Jaspers the problem of moral engagement between the court and the perpetrator, as the basis for judging and doing justice. Where there was not simply individual culpability, but a fundamental and systematic gulf in the understanding of right and wrong, there could be no true punishment. A perpetrator could be punished in a physical sense, but the impossibility of moral dialogue or connection with those judging her meant she could not be punished in a legal or an ethical sense.

Reading Arendt's correspondence with Jaspers and her later *Eichmann in Jerusalem* indicates a formal or logical parallel between her argument and the problem of 'just deserts in an unjust society'. In both settings, there is a structural or systematic gap between the court and the offender. But morally, this is highly counter-intuitive. How could it be that conduct as wicked as that of the Nazis could not be brought to justice? Could it really be the case that the more systematic or structural the wickedness, the less it could be judged, because the less the possibility of moral dialogue between the court and the perpetrator? This seems wrong, but it focuses attention on how the moral issue is posed, and raises the question whether there is something in its *legal* framing that should be explored.

The chapter finds a moral answer to Arendt's problem through a critical reading of Jaspers's *Question of German War Guilt*, in the concept of metaphysical guilt that he developed there. That concept was contrasted by Jaspers with guilt in its legal, moral and political dimensions. For Jaspers, metaphysical guilt represented a deep, existential layer of responsibility that suggested human beings possessed a co-responsibility for the acts that had emerged from an historical culture of which they were a part. Perhaps there might be a universal responsibility – that metaphysically we might all share guilt for bad acts, which reflect upon the 'guilt of us all'. The chapter thinks through the implications of metaphysical guilt. Recognising that it raises issues that it is hard to resolve, it finds something important: a sense of a real, objective, 'non-actualist', conception of guilt that could exist, even where it might never be accepted by the guilty. Jaspers deploys it to think of the collective responsibility of bystanders, but it has a broader implication as the deepest and most foundational sense of guilt. It can be used to think about crimes that were committed without moral compunction, even with a sense of moral rectitude.

Such a metaphysical conception of guilt exists beyond the operation of formal law or individualistic morality. In terms of the relationship between the legal and the ethical, the law needs the connection between legal guilt and metaphysical guilt if it is to avoid the impasse in legal ethics identified by Arendt. The ethico-legal requires a further ethical level beyond law if it is to work. However, the chapter concludes that this deeper ethical basis then raises difficulties for the more narrowly framed conception of responsibility that drives the law. The constellational unity of legal and metaphysical guilt is not necessarily a comfortable one for law, because it leads us to think more broadly and systemically about the nature of responsibility.

Chapter 10 follows up the argument of Chapter 7. The deep concern there is the ontological validity of a conception of metaphysical guilt in a secular age. Jaspers's standpoint was religious and Christian, and the question animating the chapter is whether it might be possible to explore the existence of the metaphysical in a non-religious way. The investigation starts with the idea of survivor guilt and the intuition that there might be more to that idea than the psychological expression of a trauma. Might survivor guilt have an ethical dimension, that is, a metaphysical quality, expressing a sense of universal responsibility in a situation of survival where others perish?

Here, the reflections of Primo Levi on his experience in Auschwitz, and his later feelings of guilt are relevant, for Levi understands the psychological and ethical experience of surviving the camp in terms similar to Jaspers's account of metaphysical guilt. The argument of the chapter is that we can see here, in the thinking of a non-religious man, the way in which a sense of universal guilt and responsibility can be experienced. The idea of metaphysical guilt can be seen to be grounded in real human experience, under appalling conditions. The idea of the metaphysical in guilt, grounded in a universal ethical sense of human co-existence (our co-identity), is aligned with Roy Bhaskar's philosophy of meta-Reality, which articulates more fully the sense of a fundamental ethical identity undergirding human experience.

If metaphysical guilt is real and universally grounds our experience of wrongdoing, that is not at all to say that all are equally guilty. Victims are not perpetrators, and the existence of Levi's 'grey zone' of complicity between perpetrators and victims is important, but cannot become a means of dissolving specific responsibilities. As in Chapter 7, the argument here goes on to consider the different kinds of guilt that we can identify: the guilt of perpetrators, complicit victims, bystanders, and also beneficiaries of the system under which crimes occurred. At the back of all these there is also the system that generates the different actor positions in which guilt may be experienced. But acknowledging the existence of a wicked system is no longer, as in Arendt's thought, a reason to discount the guilt of perpetrators.

Her 'either/or' (system or agent) becomes a 'both/and' in a view of ethics that can link together the assessment of individual agency and collective or systematic wrongdoing (cf Norrie 2000: 220).

Law, good and evil

Chapter 8 takes a different track out of the concerns of Chapter 7. It follows up on the problems of law's morality of form by considering how we understand issues of 'good' and 'evil'. Arendt's analysis of the 'banality of evil' raises the question in what sense evil can be 'banal', but an initial question concerns what we mean, in a secular ('post-metaphysical') world, by 'evil'. For law in its ethical formalism, the idea of 'evil' has little traction, acting only as the occasional rhetorical flourish for the judge in sentencing.

The argument also draws on Chapter 5, which raises a similar question in relation to understanding what we mean by 'good'. If the actions of a mercy killer can lead to a finding of not guilty because of a good motive, what does this mean? Prosecutors, judges and juries are forced by the ethical situations they confront to think in such terms, yet they must circumvent the law's morality of form in order to deploy them. Where legal formalism find a factual intention to kill, actors in the criminal process must use their discretion to say that the intention to kill was linked to a good moral purpose.

Thus, if the criminal justice architectonic pushes the terms 'good' and 'evil' to the very edge of its frame of reference, they nonetheless remain relevant to the process of practical ethical judgment, and law has an interest in that too. Two moral languages are at play: the (ethico) legal's abstract formalism, and the broader ethical need to express substantive terms of good and evil.

To think through the gap between the ethico-legal and practical moral judgment, the chapter seeks help from Bhaskar's work. One way of thinking substantively about good and evil can be derived from his dialectical theory, and his analysis of a meta-ethics of freedom and solidarity. Concepts of freedom and solidarity can be developed through a series of dialectical linkages. We can start from the most basic form of freedom, that which exists in any action (lifting my hand without hindrance, rather than it being lifted for me). From that most basic of possibilities, we can identify forms of freedom like negative and positive liberty, autonomy, emancipation, and well-being, and we can identify the various forms of solidarity that accompany these. For example, the positive freedom to do certain things may require the support of enabling others.

The ethical endpoint of these forms of freedom and solidarity is the possibility that each of us should ultimately be free to flourish, developing fully our powers, talents and capacities. This would require the solidarity of others so that we may flourish, and for others to help us to flourish would entail that they should do so too. The interconnection of the forms of freedom, flourishing and solidarity would thus entail that in the good (the eudaimonic) society, the full flourishing of each would be conditional on the full flourishing of all.

This meta-ethical logic of a potential dialectic of freedom and solidarity leading to universal flourishing is then related to the ideas of good and evil that are necessary to law, but exist beyond legal definition. What we call 'evil' are those actions or things that crush the most basic forms of freedom and solidarity. The concentration camp obliterates solidarity at the most fundamental level (for example, the mother who is forced to save one of her children by choosing the other to die), and it crushes freedom in its most basic forms (the freedom simply to act). Those things we call 'good' are actions which reveal a loving attention to the flourishing of another, including the case of assisting a 'good death'.

This is all the more the case where this may entail loss to oneself, or risk to one's own freedom by so acting. In other words, good and evil are located at both the beginning and the end of the deepening logic of freedom and solidarity, with evil acts suppressing that logic even at its most basic levels, and good supporting it at its most developed levels. Here a deeper understanding of the ethical forms immanent in the powers of human being are a necessary addition to our understanding of the ethico-legal. Law's morality of form requires something more if it is to operate, and that 'something more' understood as a substantive ethics of good and evil sits uncomfortably alongside the legal in law's constellation.

A modern phenomenology of law

Chapter 9 strikes off in a different direction. It pursues this idea of an ethical dialectic of freedom and solidarity not just to think substantively against law's formalism, but also to think about the characteristic ways in which legal ethics are understood. It identifies three different approaches to the ethico-legal that are shaped by the way that law operates in Western societies. Relating law's architectonic to the problems generated by social, economic and political relations, the chapter thinks holistically about the characteristic ethical shapes we find in analysing law today. These have an internal logic so that one leads to another, and they express what one can call a modern legal phenomenology, based around the relationship between the 'ideal and the actual'.

In the first characteristic position, the ideal in the actual, law is seen as expressing individual freedom in society. This is the classic Kantian mode. An agent possesses the freedom to act, to pursue her interests through her actions, to be autonomous, and therefore to be responsible for her acts. It turns out, however, that modern society is never able to provide the setting in which individual freedom can be articulated fully. Social structural problems of inequality and exploitation impinge systematically on the possibilities of freedom and solidarity. This generates the problem of repetition, in which the claim that modernity can instantiate individual freedom is constantly repeated, but always fails or remains at best radically under-actualised.

This problem of repetition invokes different responses. The theorist may simply accept that there is a problem, but remain in the ideal in the actual position. The ideal is seen as retaining a validity even though it may never be achieved and, it is hoped, it may act to regulate in a limited way how actuality works. The ideal remains an important, influential, constituent element *in the actual*, although the key psychological note is one of disappointment.

A second response is as follows. The problem of constant repetition leads to the view that the claim of individual freedom is in fact unsustainable. In its promise, failure, repetition mode, it becomes a claim so threadbare that it no longer looks supportable. Modern society promises something it constantly fails to deliver, and this failure leads the theorist to rethink the relationship between the ideal and the actual. What happens in a relationship where a partner promises always to change his or her behaviour (for example to stop drinking), but never does? Eventually, it may be accepted that it is not within that person to be able to change, that the promising is a constituent element in an overall behavioural pattern and, importantly, that the relationship itself is supporting the inability to change. To promise to change while not changing represents a holistic state in which the partner is complicit.

Instead, therefore, of seeing the ideal of free, self-determining, subjectivity as law's promise of freedom in a world that structurally and systematically denies it, one possible deduction from the problem of failure and repetition is that the promise of freedom is part of an overall package by virtue of which a world *without freedom* is made possible. To continue to believe in it is to be complicit in this state of affairs. This view moves from seeing the ideal as a critical constituent element in the actual to seeing it as an element dominated by it. The promise of freedom becomes the means by which unfreedom is maintained. This can be expressed as a relationship in which the ideal is subsumed and turned against itself. This is the critical position of post-structural theorists in the line of Nietzsche, as well as the early Frankfurt thinkers, although both may find room for the third position to which we come shortly. This second position is an ethical state of being in which the ideal is dominated by, is in but *under the actual*.

The third position accepts the failure/repetition problem of modern freedom, but still holds onto the possibility of freedom as a utopian moment directing us to a different future. Holding that modern society seems to be incapable of delivering on its promises, this position still holds that the ideal expresses something that is ethically important, even if it cannot be instantiated under present social arrangements. The view may be that the utopian must always remain at a distance from what is present or possible, but is important nonetheless, or may claim, for example, that under different social conditions, the ideal could indeed be instantiated. Whichever position is taken, the ideal as a utopian element remains an ideal *in, against and beyond the actual.*

Reviewing different critical positions on the relationship between the ideal and the actual, Chapter 9 characterises these three as the broader, holistic ways of understanding how law's morality of form stands ethically (constellationally) in the modern social totality. Law's architectonic provides a key moral narrative that must be reviewed and interpreted according to how it stands in the broader ethical whole of which it is a part. Different theoretical approaches see the relationship differently, but they all must take some view of how law's architectonic is to be viewed in the social totality. Whether an Aristotelian, a Kantian, a Hegelian or a Nietzschean, an early Frankfurt theorist or a post-structuralist, one must think about the part and the whole, that is to say law's architectonic (how it judges) in law's constellation (where it is judged). With their different perspectives, they also reflect something of the dissonant, different and historically changing nature of that reality. There will be times and places where each strikes a chord.

Law's broken dialectic

The essays in this collection address an unresolved split between legal and ethical judgment in the modern legal system. The split is created by the socio-historical shaping of law as abstract and formal, that is, a morality of form which represents the core of law's architectonic. On one hand we have law's abstraction and formalism; on the other, law is constructed in a social, political and ethical environment. The former (its abstraction) is the way in which law is able to mediate the conflicts, contradictions and struggles of the latter, but the mediation is possible only at the cost of opposition and antinomy inside law's form. Law must eschew broader substantive judgments, but also requires them to fix or decide a formal outcome. The essays in the first half of the book consider legal formalism in its practical aspect, and the moral and political difficulties thereby presented. Given the nature of the legal architectonic, how does it deal practically with reforming the law of homicide, with the problem of mistaken self-defence, with different kinds of euthanasia? In short, how does law's architectonic judge?

The essays in the second half look at a more theoretical level at the underlying, suppressed ethical connections that cannot ultimately be denied. Implicit in law's co-location between a morality of form and a social, political and ethical environment is the idea that law never stands alone, but stands with these other entities. They operate constellationally, and this not only provides the legal architectonic with the political and ethical supplements required for it to decide, it also establishes the broader setting in which we may judge law's work. The legal constellation represents the whole within which the part that is its architectonic can be judged.

In Hegel's dialectical philosophy, the part and the whole, legal and ethical judgment, the rational and the real are connected by synthesis of the different elements in a rational totality. What is rational (or ideal) is real, and what is real (or actual) is rational. In the analysis presented here, that synthesis remains unachieved. The promise of a rational synthesis of the legal part and the social whole is belied by the very nature of the legal architectonic, its structural location and its core forms. Law must live with and through antinomy, not by way of its dialectical resolution. It is on this terrain that justice must be fashioned in the difficult ways described in these essays. Equally our understanding of law's place in the world reveals how, overall, the idea of the synthesis of the ideal and the actual (the rational and the real) must give way before an understanding of how complex the relationship between the ideal and the actual may be. In place of their rational integration, we must understand their difficult relationship, how it may change in history and how it may even be turned upside down under modern social conditions.

These are essays in 'broken dialectic'. They seek to show how a method designed to reveal the rational coherence of a modern institution such as law should be reinterpreted in the light of our knowledge and experience of how things are: how law is made, how the world is and how law acts in it.

Part I

Law's architectonic

Chapter 2

Citizenship, authoritarianism and the changing shape of the criminal law

In this chapter I want to think about the changing forms of the criminal law, and to seek to identify those structural conditions, forces and developments which predicate its shape and form. I plan to sketch some general elements and to provide some ideas towards a 'structural history of the legal present' (Garland 2001). My aim will be to problematise the relationship between 'law' and 'authoritarianism' by suggesting that what is often seen as an opposition in liberal legal theory in fact involves a relation of mutual implication or co-entailment. Liberal law possesses authoritarian dimensions along two axes.

To make my argument, I propose to return to the two ideas underlying my book, *Crime, Reason and History* (2001, 2014), concerning the nature of legal individualism and the conflicts which inform it. They were in their original form schematically presented, and I hope to develop them in order to help understand the complex structures that shape recent developments in the modern criminal law. These ideas focus on the 'psychological' and the 'political' aspects of the law's individualist core. It is these two aspects which constitute the axes along which law's authoritarianism can be analysed.

This chapter will take two different directions and then I will try to bring them together in a discussion of the present. One direction is to explore more concretely the historical trajectory of legal individualism canvassed in my previous work to take account of T H Marshall's analysis of three different forms of citizenship and rights within modern liberal society: those pertaining to the civil, the political and the social spheres (Marshall 1992). I will argue that the key to the development of the post-war criminal law was the *fusion* of these three forms of citizenship in the period of consensus that began after 1945 and came to an end in the 1970s. I will then suggest that one way to understand developments over recent years is in terms of the unravelling of the post-war consensus. This involves an unravelling of the three forms of citizenship and a resulting reconfiguration. In their newly *fissile* condition, new possibilities, conflicts and contradictions for criminal law and justice emerged. In the process, the authoritarianism at the core of legal individualism becomes more evident. I deal with this in the second part of this chapter.

Thinking about the changing configuration of legal forms also involves thinking in a second direction: that of exploring the relationship between liberal criminal justice and forms of authoritarian government. In the third part, my focus will be on Franz Neumann's often neglected essay on the 'Change in the Function of Law in Modern Society', which was originally published in English in 1939 and then in his posthumous volume *The Democratic and Authoritarian State* (1957).[1] I think that if the history of the legal present is to be understood, the nature of state authoritarianism as a structural force in modern law needs to be taken seriously. My overall argument will be that the unravelling of the different forms of rights and the way they are reconfigured owes much to their being placed in the general context of a form of state power that can be characterised as authoritarian and a form of (liberal) law that enables this. However, I want to stress that what comes out of this is a sense not of a single direction or shape to the criminal law, but a set of complexities in which legal forms habitually reveal different aspects, and in which one can talk of hybridity[2] or many-sided inflection within a structural context.

Three developments in modern criminal justice

If the major focus of this chapter is the historical structuring of legal forms, I want to anchor the discussion in the particular. In this introductory part, I will outline three broad developments in recent criminal law and justice, which will represent a tentative preliminary focus for the discussion that follows. Then, in the final section, I will return to these and think specifically about the changing shape of law today.

The three broad developments I have in mind are:

(1) an increasing emphasis on the retributive understanding of criminal behaviour, which is seen in the stress upon the responsibility of individuals for their actions. This involves a decline of rehabilitation as a significant ideology of punishment, an emphasis on notions of moral right and wrong particularly in the recognition of the role of the victim in the system, and an increasing reliance on imprisonment as a mode of punishment, even if it does no good. Let us call this a tendency to increased *responsibilisation*, noting, however, that this denotes a different use of the term than that deployed in some recent literature.[3]

1 See also his belatedly published doctoral work (1986). Quotes in the text below are from the 1957 text. For a recent analysis of criminal law with parallel implications see Dubber (2005).

2 Compare Lacey (2007), and my accompanying comment (2007).

3 For example, Garland (2001: 124) discusses responsibilisation as involving indirect forms of social control relying on individuals policing themselves and their environment. This reading of responsibilisation in terms of a Foucauldian 'governmentality' thesis is very important, but I want to emphasise the increased reliance on the formal legal invocation of individual responsibility here.

(2) an increasing emphasis, in conjunction with, but also in some ways in opposition to (1), on notions of dangerousness for a minority of criminals, for whom exceptional forms of punishment or control are necessary. This is seen in an increased reliance on mandatory forms of punishment for repeat offences of certain kinds, but also in the development of new categories of offender such as the 'terrorist', for whom new forms of control and surveillance are required alongside severe forms of punishment. Let us call this a tendency to increasing *dangerousness*.

(3) the development of new forms of criminal justice alongside traditional ideas of crime and punishment such as the development of new forms of control, as mentioned in (2). These include control orders for terrorists, but also new hybrid forms of control and punishment such as the anti-social behaviour order (ASBO) and other forms of preventative orders concerning, for example, sexual conduct that have sprung up. Such forms of control can be seen as net-spreading activities, but they invoke new forms of criminal justice in the process. Let us call this a tendency to increasing *regulation*.

I will return to these developments in the final section. With these introductory comments in mind, I now turn to the two ideas from *Crime, Reason and History* that I wish to develop. These concern the conflicts that are contained within the 'psychological' and the 'political' dimension of law's individualism. Considering how these ideas should be developed helps in thinking about the changing historical character of law and the citizenship contexts in which it operates. Both disclose, although in different ways, liberal law's relationship to authoritarian governance.

Citizenship and legal form: T H Marshall

In this section, I begin by outlining the oppositions that pertain to the psychological and political aspects of the form of legal individualism at the core of modern law. I then identify important limits on the way I addressed those forms in earlier work. One problem concerns the historically differentiated nature of modern legal forms and the need to periodise more adequately their development. These matters are considered in the context of an engagement with Marshall's three forms of citizenship. A second problem identified in this section concerns the co-existence of oppositional elements of freedom and political power within the modern law. The first problem relates to what I have called the law's 'psychological' individualism, the second to its 'political' individualism, although it should be noted that these are dialectically connected aspects of the same thing: the modern form of law. I will now outline these two aspects of modern individualist law and then contextualise the idea of the responsible subject in terms of Marshall's threefold conception of citizenship.

Psychological and political individualism in criminal law

One way of understanding criminal law, I have argued (2014, chs 2, 13), is to see its doctrine as structured around the liberal form of the juridical individual, which emphasises individual responsibility as the basis for punishment through central categories of physical and fault elements and the defences. However, law is essentially a relational phenomenon, mediating underlying social conditions, structures and relations, and these make the juridical individual the site of two basic oppositions which play out as contradictions within the law. Legal individualism can be seen to possess both a 'psychological' and a 'political' dimension. The first of these emphasises the importance of human agency through 'psychologistic' ideas of intention, voluntariness of acts and reason for finding that an individual is responsible for his or her actions. This was, in historical terms, as Adorno puts it, an 'assist to freedom' under modern conditions (1973: 238), but its morally progressive and expressive quality was immediately limited by the fact that the universal attributes of human freedom recognised in law excluded contextual and motivational conditions for action. As a result, the model of the juridical individual finessed substantive moral and political justifications and differences as well as the deep-rooted social conflicts that predicated them.

The psychological individual, I argued, 'is a political and ideological construction which operates to seal off the question of individual culpability from issues concerning the relationship between individual agency and social context' (2014: 367). If it operates in a morally *expressive* way, that is, by way of valuing individual freedom, as liberal theory tells us, it also possesses an important *repressive* function, albeit one that is articulated in a seeming paradox in the language of human freedom. This combination of expressivity and repression gives law its double-edged quality, and can be regarded as the 'cunning of legality': it is at the same time legitimating and coordinative.[4]

The nature, the significance and the value of this claim have been debated,[5] and I have sought to defend and develop its relevance for criminal law in different ways (2000; 2005a). I do not intend to pursue that ground here. What I want to do instead is to note the limits the argument has for thinking about the history of modern criminal justice. It is too schematic to pick up properly two issues (Ramsay 2006).

The first issue is the growth and impact of forms of regulative or welfare-oriented criminal law from the second half of the 19th century, which became the basis for those many strict liability offences which make up the bulk of the criminal

4 By the latter, I mean the way in which law forces and canalises action through power. There is a difference in the way the German and the Anglo-American traditions think of 'coordination': in the latter, it can be presented in anodyne terms as facilitating the smooth running of society, for example, through 'rules of the road'. In the former, it can be understood as involving the exercise of authoritarian force, of forcing people to conform their conduct to norms they might otherwise resist.

5 See Duff (1998) and Horder (2000).

law today (Farmer 1997). Psychological individualism is relevant primarily to those offences which are regarded, mostly, but not always, appropriately, as the most serious offences in the criminal calendar: those which 'count down' from murder. How can an argument which sees psychological individualism as core to the development of the modern criminal law account for the existence of strict liability offences?

A second related issue concerns historical 'periodisation'. *Crime, Reason and History* sees the foundations of the modern criminal law in the first half of the 19th century, in particular in the Bentham-inspired work of the Victorian Criminal Law Commissioners. It has, however, been pointed out that, whilst they may be the forerunners of the modern orthodox subjectivist approach that dominated English criminal law in the 1960s and 1970s, and to some extent to this day, it was not until the post-war period that orthodox subjectivism became dominant (Lacey 1998). For most of the 19th century and the first half of the 20th, the law was a mixture of different forms of objectivist as well as subjectivist elements (Horder 1997). It was only with the eminence of Glanville Williams, Sir John Smith and H L A Hart, and the impact of reform documents concerning capital punishment, homosexuality and prostitution in the 1950s and 1960s, that a recognisably liberal project with the responsible psychological individual at its core came into its own. The question is, then: why should there be this time lag? What else was going on, and what held things back? Why the fruition of orthodox subjectivism only 100 and more years after it was first thought of? Attempting to answer these questions indicates a better way of understanding the structural history of our present, and I will develop it below.

Just before doing so, however, let me say something about the limitations of my previous position on the law's *political* individualism. Turning from the psychological to the political dimension of the legal individual, here the original argument is also truncated. Essentially, what it does is to observe that legal individualism claims the freedom of the individual as its starting point, but individual legal freedom is organised within a political system and with regard to a need for social control that limits its possibilities. Criminal law is not just about the moral relations between individuals; it is also the basis for a system of state control over individuals and, as such, there is a constant possibility that arguments based upon state necessity will kick in to negate ideas of individual right and responsibility.

This is seen in the criminal law in the frequent resort to 'policy' concerns over those of 'principle', and this, I argued, is a structuring opposition *inside* law that flows from the conflict between individual freedom and political power it embodies. Again, however, this is a rather limited view of the matter and further thought needs to be given to precisely what is the nature of this overriding political power. Plainly, the idea of such a power intervening against individual rights suggests an authoritarian element within the law, but how does it work, and does it have different effects in different periods? Are communities more or less prone to authoritarian interventions today and, if so, how does authoritarianism shape legal forms and responses? In the third section of this essay I will consider this question in discussing Neumann's work.

My overall aim is to argue that developing a sense of the contexts in which legal individualism is embedded, in both its psychological and political aspects, provides a better understanding of the structural forces that give us our legal present. In particular this will involve relating the idea of subjective right contained in the law's *psychological* individualism to the development of citizenship forms in modern society, and this is discussed immediately below. Thereafter, it will involve thinking about subjective right as a liberal *political* argument in the context of what it means to call modern societies authoritarian. The goal is to reflect on where modern Western societies are in terms of how they deploy ideas of subjective right in legal practice today.

Three forms of citizenship and their dynamic

An effective way of dealing with the problems I have identified in a psychological individualist account of criminal law is provided by Peter Ramsay's work (2006). This focuses on the differential impact of three conceptions of citizenship identified by T H Marshall (1992) as emerging from the 19th century onwards.

The earliest form of modern individual citizenship for Marshall is the *civil* form, which involves rights necessary for individual, primarily economic, freedom. This is particularly linked with individual property rights, and came into existence in England in the 18th century. Whilst this form of citizenship is associated with the rights and interests of the property-owning citizen, it provides a foundation for thinking about political freedoms more generally and therefore about criminal justice and the rights and responsibilities of citizens as a universal category. Such a conception of civil citizenship is a necessary, but not a sufficient, condition for criminal law to be based upon the idea of the free individual subject. For this to happen, the second form of what Marshall calls *political* citizenship[6] is also necessary.

Political citizenship involves a further commitment not just to individual rights and liberties but also to a universal order in which every individual has the right to participate in political decision-making. Once that is introduced, the basic form of the responsible individual introduced by a civil conception of citizenship can be generalised politically to all relevant areas of social life, including criminal law. Of course, the introduction of the rights of political citizenship took many years to be introduced for both men and (particularly) women, but the British utilitarians, in conceiving of society in universal terms as based upon the pursuit of individual interest, took a first step in that direction. In so doing, they laid the

6 Note that Marshall's use of the term 'political' to denote the move to public and universal notions of citizenship is distinct from my use of the term to denote one contradiction – that between individual freedom and state power – within the law's individualist core.

groundwork for a subjectivist account of criminal law and responsibility, and it was this that was introduced in law reform documents in the first half of the 19th century by the Victorian Criminal Law Commissioners.

What, however, of the time lag noted above? As stated, this model only came to practical fruition in the second half of the 20th century, whilst political citizenship rights date from the end of the 19th and early 20th centuries. This was after a government had come to power committed to a radical opening up of channels of political citizenship in the wake of the Second World War and resulting social expectations. But the advent of civil and political citizenship rights per se was insufficient by itself to determine the modern development of the criminal law. Something else was needed to push this through.

Marshall's third form of citizenship – *social* citizenship – was introduced from the late 19th century onwards and had the effect, amongst others, of introducing standards of social and economic welfare into penal measures across a range of aspects of life. One effect of social citizenship was to produce those forms of regulation that generate alternatives to subjectivist, capacity-based approaches to individual responsibility, and which focus more on the control of outcomes than on fault and blame. The growth of regulatory offences from the late 19th century can be explained according to the rise of this third form of citizenship, which, slotted in alongside the first two, provides for the juxtaposition of two rather different forms of criminal law regulation in modern society: one outcome/strict liability based, the other capacity, fault and responsibility based.

Marshall's account of the three forms of citizenship is helpful in terms of explaining the gaps in my previous analysis. It helps explain, as I have just noted, the first problem identified above, the co-existence of strict liability alongside forms of individual responsibility in the modern criminal law. If civil/political citizenship generates the conception of the responsible individual, social citizenship generates the conception of strict liability. How, though, does it help explain the problem of time lag, that it was only the period from the 1950s to the 1970s that represented the fruition of the capacity-based, orthodox subjectivist, liberal project based on the psychologically free, responsible individual? Why was *this* in particular the time of these ideas' dominance, when universal political citizenship had been around for a much longer time? Was it just the political radicalism of the post-war government? My suggestion is that this was the period in which the three ideas of citizenship – civil, political and social – came together, and that the historical fusion of a social conception of citizenship rights with an already existing civil/political conception gave real impetus to the civil/political conception.

The dominant liberal conception of the criminal law is shaped by the civil commitment to personal freedom and the political commitment that this should be universalised and generalised. What the new post-war social welfare commitment did was, in combining with the civil and the political commitments, to add a drive to 'perfect' the existing commitments to civil and political freedoms, to insist that they should be actualised in practice. Whilst earlier individualistic freedoms of a civil and political form were not sufficient for the social welfarist vision, they were nonetheless a necessary component of the good society that would be completed by the introduction of social welfare measures. For example, the poor not only required welfare benefits; they also needed rights and access to legal services to achieve those benefits and to emancipate themselves before the law and the state. The universalisation of legal freedoms invoked by political citizenship would have to be actualised fully in any world in which social citizenship also played a significant part. Pushing beyond the civil and political, social citizenship of necessity included implementation of these other, in a sense 'lesser', forms of citizenship, and the legal freedoms they embodied.

To be sure, this historical fusion of different purposes also resulted in tensions between civil and political conceptions of citizenship and the newer social conceptions, as seen, for example, in conflicts between lawyers, social scientists and proponents of the 'psy-disciplines' of the period,[7] but the drive beyond civil and political citizenship notions still gave a new thrust to their development and actualisation. If the post-war welfare state were not also a state committed to civil and political liberties, it would not have been true to the underlying, although complex and conflicted, inter-relation between the different forms of citizenship.[8] Under the aegis of a commitment to social citizenship, there was a joint thrust of the different kinds of citizenship rights, and the criminal law model of the responsible individual flourished as one deduction from the form of citizenship (civil, political *and* social) within an overall liberal–welfarist, social democratic project. The time lag was, then, due to the fact that it was only after the Second World War that this fusion of rights-based purposes occurred.

Three forms of citizenship today

I have elaborated the place of a liberal theory of responsibility in modern society because I think it helps to understand what is happening to the law today. If the post-war period involved a coming together of civil, political and social forms of citizenship so that the growth of the political was encouraged under the aegis of the social, the relationship between these forms has proved more problematic from the 1970s onwards. What has occurred over the last 25 years or so has been a series of attacks on the idea of social citizenship in its post-war welfarist form in the name of neo-liberal economic, social and political policies. This has tended to set the different strands of citizenship in Marshall's vision against each other so that conflicts between forms of rights, which had been less apparent previously, have surfaced. The underlying dynamic has been an attack on social citizenship in the name of civil citizenship, with political citizenship caught in the middle. By this, I mean that the core idea of the economically

7 See Hart (1963: ch 2); compare Lacey (1998).

8 This is why the Western welfare–liberal polities of the 1960s were also engaged in struggles for basic democratic rights, in the southern states of the USA and in Northern Ireland. The broader liberating dimension pulled the narrower, more basic one along in its wake.

self-interested individual, *homo economicus*, which originally animated the idea of civil citizenship, has become the core idea legitimating the stripping back of welfare measures, and therefore an attack on social citizenship. A neo-liberal polity sets civil (individualist, economic) citizenship *against* social citizenship, challenging the latter in the name of the former. The dynamic relation between the three forms of citizenship has changed.

What of political citizenship in this context? In the process of the civil attack on social citizenship, political citizenship comes to play a dual, complex and contradictory role. On the one hand, since the political individual is seen as reflecting the interests of the ('private') economic individual in the ('public') sphere of state activity, the political rights and freedoms of the individual are portrayed as an important element in the neo-liberal economy and polity. 'Freedom from state intervention' and 'under the rule of law' become legitimating slogans associated with the critique of the welfare state.

To be a libertarian in civil or economic terms is also to be one in political terms. In the sphere of criminal justice, this is observed in the increased weight placed upon libertarian ideas of decriminalisation, the idea of 'doing justice' through the criminal process and on a retributive philosophy of punishment based upon the responsibility of the individual. The increased responsibilisation strategy referred to in the first section of this chapter is rooted in this development. Until the 1980s, something of a balance was sought between individual and social conceptions of responsibility and justice. Thereafter, more weight was placed on individual responsibility, in opposition to demands based upon a social conception.

On the other hand, political liberty comes under attack in a neo-liberal polity as the drive to restore economic or civil liberty, or the 'discipline of the market', encounters social opposition. As a result, conservative and authoritarian modes of governance are deployed to secure the (civil) market order against the demands of political citizenship for freedom. In the neo-liberal world, civil citizenship tends also to split off from its fractious political bedfellow, and the latter is placed in question. Without the protective cover social citizenship gave to it, political citizenship operates both as a legitimating rhetoric for neo-liberal change and, contradictorily, as a barrier to such change, to be overcome where necessary. In sum, where the sense that the state should support and protect the individual in socially substantive or welfarist ways is lost, political citizenship is both held up as crucial to individual liberty and seen as a threat to it.

To summarise this broad history of the present, my argument is that the overall political and historical dynamic from social democracy and welfare to neo-liberalism has reconfigured the relation between civil, political and social forms of citizenship. Fusion of form and purpose is replaced by fission in a way that brings out more clearly the latent conflicts between these forms, and sets them against each other. This is seen in a conflict in the treatment of political citizenship under modern conditions. This is the form of citizenship most relevant to the classic form of the responsible legal individual within the criminal law, and it means that the present period treats that law in an ambivalent way.

On the one hand, it prioritises law and responsibility as a primary legitimating device for the neo-liberal polity; on the other, it looks askance at its claims on behalf of individual freedom where social order appears, or is presented as being, under threat.

I will return to this issue of the evolving relation between different citizenship forms and their impact on the changing shape of the criminal law in the final section. For now, I want to move to a discussion of law and authoritarianism, for neo-liberal strategies on citizenship are closely aligned with authoritarian state responses to opposition to change. So doing, we move from considering the nature of the law's psychological to its political individualism.

Law and authoritarianism: the work of Franz Neumann

Turning now to the second, 'political', conflict of legal individualism, between individual right and social power, I want to consider this in the context of what it means to talk about an authoritarian state. Such a concept may in recent years have seemed surpassed in light of the depiction of authoritarianism present in everyday life inspired by Foucault's work on 'discipline' and 'governmentality' (Foucault 1977; 1991). Developments of new capabilities and technologies, including technologies of the self, have focused attention away from the state and onto the ways in which power operates through a variety of individual, informal, non-state (but also state-sponsored) media (Garland 2001: 124–27).

Notwithstanding these important arguments, I think it is still helpful to return to a discussion of state authoritarianism, for two reasons. The first is that recent developments indicate clearly the ways in which the state remains at the core of significant developments of an authoritarian kind. The second is that, whilst it is of course true that the life of the law is lived and experienced across a society, it nonetheless has a crucially significant formative locus in the institutions of the state.

In thinking about authoritarian law, it is hard to avoid considering state authoritarianism. For these reasons, I have gone back to Franz Neumann's work (1957) on the changing functions of law and the state in modern society. Neumann in fact wrote this essay shortly before the Second World War, as a refugee from German fascism. It considers how law changed from classic 19th-century forms concerning the *Rechtsstaat* to those interventionist forms associated first with the Weimar Republic, and then, on an increased scale, with fascism, totalitarianism and authoritarianism in Nazi Germany. Because of its specific historical context, and the fact that Neumann associates the authoritarian state with fascism, his analysis needs to be treated with some caution. It would take a fair imagination to describe – other than rhetorically – a society such as Britain today as 'fascist'. Nonetheless, there are components of the authoritarian state that are generic. If Neumann is taken to be describing the extreme case, his analysis can be used to see how things work in an intermediate case such as is provided by the fading, authoritarian democracies of the West today.

Between liberal–legal right and the arcanum domintionis

The starting point in understanding Neumann's work is his account of the liberal-legal polity, and its *intrinsic* linkage to authoritarianism, before getting to the idea of the authoritarian state per se. Thinking of the classic liberal state generally brings to mind the 'negative state' or the Lockean 'night-watchman state': a state with limited functions and forms of power. However, Neumann notes that there is a serious mistake in associating 'negativeness' with 'weakness'. The liberal state, to the contrary,

> has always been as strong as the political and social situation and the interests of society demanded. It has conducted warfare and crushed strikes; with the help of strong navies it has protected its investments, with the help of strong armies it has defended and extended its boundaries, with the help of the police it has restored 'peace and order' (ibid: 22).

In short, the liberal state has 'been a strong state precisely in those spheres in which it had to be strong and in which it wanted to be strong' (ibid). Accordingly, the image of the liberal state as one resting on 'right' as opposed to 'might' is from the beginning a false one. The liberal state – and its law – work *through* oppositions they embody, between law and force, freedom and sovereignty, *ratio* (the articulation of freedoms) and *voluntas* (the expression of power), between 'subjective right' and 'objective right' (the last in the German legal context). Intrinsic opposition is reflected from the very beginning of liberalism in Locke's philosophy, for whom the state rests upon the rights of the people, but who also recognises state prerogative powers reflecting sovereign necessity.

To these constitutive oppositions, I would add the one that informs *Crime, Reason and History* – individual right versus state power – to argue that liberal criminal law contains *both* individualist legal form *and* a power that over-reaches or surpasses it: what one might call an 'extra-legal power'. This formulation is not, however, quite right, because what is constitutive of law must be already within it. That law embodies 'extra-legal power' already indicates that what is described as 'extra-legal' is no such thing. The vision that liberal lawyers endorse of the possibility of regulating or taming power through law is a false one, for liberal law already entails, indeed is 'contaminated' by, that which it would control. Modern liberal law *combines* in its form individual right and political necessity.

This generates an important question. If the authoritarian dimension *within* liberal law is recognised, is it nonetheless possible to think of a development *beyond* liberal law, to a more authoritarian form of rule? The answer for Neumann lay in the way in which the axis constructed by the polar oppositions of liberal law moves increasingly towards one pole as a liberal society becomes more authoritarian. Law comes increasingly to support force over law, sovereign power over individual freedom, will over reason and objective over subjective right. Under the extreme case of fascism, law becomes 'nothing but a technical instrument for the execution of certain political objectives; it is nothing but the command of the ruler' (ibid: 61). Accordingly, the legal theory of the achieved authoritarian state is 'decisionism and law is nothing but an *arcanum dominationis*, i.e. a means serving the stabilisation of power' (ibid), and this occurs through a progressive shifting towards one pole in an oppositional form.

It is important to pursue Neumann's analysis a little further into his account of the distinctions between a liberal and an authoritarian legal order. In order to get to law as pure *arcanum dominationis*, those features of liberal law associated with freedom, reason and subjective right have to be discarded. What are these? Neumann suggests three special features of liberal legal form: that law must be formulated in general terms, and not be specifically addressed to individuals; it must at the same time be formulated with a high degree of specificity so that discretion in its application is removed; and it must not be retroactive. One could, I think, add more: a fourth feature would be that law must to a significant extent respect the freedom of individuals in ways associated with Marshall's account of civil and political rights. Liberal legality operates where these elements are held in balance or tension alongside matters of sovereign power and will.

Despite the emphasis on oppositions, this seems a fairly positive account of liberal law, but Neumann is no wide-eyed supporter of the liberal state and its law. This comes out when he discusses the different functions of liberal law, of which he identifies three: 'All three functions of the generality of laws—obscuring the domination of the bourgeoisie, rendering the economic system calculable, and guaranteeing a minimum of liberty and equality—are of decisive importance' (ibid: 42).

The first of these gives Neumann's account its most critical quality. He argues that liberal law obscures domination in a conflicted and exploitative society. Second, it provides calculability for the economic system and therefore protects its functioning. Third, it guarantees minimum levels of liberty and equality across the board. In the second and third of these functions, Neumann's analysis aligns with Marshall's account of the significance of civil and political rights under capitalism. In the first, however, his position is more critical, and is aligned with the argument I sketched in the second section concerning the distinct yet conjoined 'legitimative' and 'coordinative' ideological qualities of modern law. To speak of the domination achieved through law in a conflicted and exploitative society refers back to the repressive function of modern law with regard to the law's psychological individualism. It is important, I will argue, to hold on to this function in order to grasp fully what is significant in modern law.

Despite this inherently repressive, exploitation-masking function of modern law, the fact that it also guarantees calculability and minimal liberty and equality entails that a contrast must still be drawn between a liberal and an authoritarian system, where the functions and the form of law both change. Neumann associated the rise of fascism in Germany with the onset of the period of monopoly capitalism, in which cartels and big business dominated social life. In such a society, the economic function of calculability was less important because business wielded power through its size rather than through law, and the general guarantee of liberty and equality was also rendered otiose.

Domination also assumed different forms, through the emphasis on the role of 'the leader' and the construction of 'the enemy' either within or without, or both (ibid: 193). In this situation, 'new auxiliary institutions' arose to promulgate and enforce the direct commands of the sovereign, or, as it was called, 'Leader' (*Führer*) state as administrative acts 'which directly protect the interests of the monopolist and restrict or abolish the old guaranties' (ibid: 58). Law itself undergoes a radical change in which flexible 'general principles' concerning 'good conscience', the 'will of the people' or the general values of the fascist polity take over from general rules. These lack specificity, becoming a broad licence to interpret actions according to a leadership principle. Under this approach, generality of rule and the specificity required for individual liberties are lost, and retroactivity becomes possible. As a result, in the authoritarian state 'all restraints are abolished which parliamentary democracy, even when functioning badly, had erected against the unlimited execution of the requirements of monopolies' (ibid: 59). Law, which should involve *voluntas* and *ratio*, ceases eventually to be law as it becomes associated purely with *voluntas*, an *arcanum dominationis*. This, then, is Neumann's sophisticated analysis of the changing functions and forms of law as they evolved from the Weimar Republic to Nazi Germany. I will now explore its significance for thinking about legal authoritarianism today.

Authoritarianism and legitimation pre- and post-war

Does Neumann's analysis translate to the post-war, post-fascist world? Neumann's account is bound up with a particular historical experience, but he did return to these themes in work produced in the 1950s. Here he maintained the relevance of his discussion for contrasting democratic and authoritarian modes of government in the new socio-political context, but modified his position in one crucial aspect. In the post-war world, he identified the importance of the citizen's alienation from government in an 'I don't care' attitude, the shrinking from political matters, and the failure to offer alternatives as factors which 'play into the hands of demagogues, and . . . may lead to caesarism' (1957: 190). Underlying factors included the growing complexity of government, the growth of public and private bureaucracies, the concentration of power in private hands and the hardening of political parties into machines. This is plainly a set of descriptions that differs from, although perhaps in some ways overlaps with, the earlier 'monopoly capitalist' thesis. The growth of collective power and the marginalisation of law are both present, but their nature and circumstances are described differently.

One important change, however, is that Neumann became less hard on liberal law than previously. Where earlier he had viewed such law as rooted in the vectors of social and economic power, after the war, his position became more ambivalent. In his essay 'The Concept of Political Freedom', he maintained the view that 'within the scope of the juristic concept of liberty, escape clauses like the clear and present danger formula permit political power to prevail over individual rights' (ibid: 178), but he also wrote of law's 'traditional guarantees' and minimal liberties as being undermined not from within *but from without* by new socio-economic developments. He depicted law as involved in a democratic process whose aim is 'maximising the freedom of man', and whose integrating element 'is a moral one, whether it be freedom or justice'.

To this liberal conception of liberal law, the embedding of law in a dynamic of justice and democracy, and involving traditional minimal guarantees of freedom, Neumann now straightforwardly opposed the authoritarian (fascist) integrating principle that fear of an enemy, either within or without, is the key to legitimation (ibid: 193). Liberal law in this view becomes the locus of freedom and justice in opposition to power rather than itself the locus of their opposition. It is seen as on the side of right *against* authoritarianism, rather than as imbued with authoritarianism itself. In terms of analysing the relationship between freedom and power, freedom is regarded as inside law, whereas power is outside it.

In order to make this argument, Neumann also changed his view of the functions of law. It will be recalled that in his earlier essay he wrote of liberal law's different and conflicting functions of ensuring domination, calculability and freedom/equality. In this post-war work, the first of these functions becomes invisible when law's freedom is aligned with democratic process and the broadening of justice. I would argue against this that it is necessary to continue to think of the place of authoritarianism in modern law in terms of the more complex picture Neumann presented in his pre-war essay. There, his account of the dominatory aspect of modern law plus his account of law as containing both freedom- and power-related oppositions seems to me to be more profound and more helpful in terms of understanding law and authoritarianism today.

Shaping the criminal law: the authoritarian road

In this final part, I want to bring together the discussion of the two previous sections around the 'psychological' and 'political' aspects of legal individualism, the dynamic of citizenship forms and Neumann's account of authoritarianism in law. I will argue that the contradictory repressive/expressive quality of the law's psychological individualism, also caught in Neumann's analysis of the dominatory/freedom enhancing nature of law, is relevant to an understanding of the tendency to increased *responsibilisation* in modern criminal justice. As for the way that modern law contains as its two poles *ratio* and *voluntas*, freedom and sovereignty, the conflict between individual right and political power is relevant to the understanding of increased *dangerousness* and *regulation* more generally in recent times. These three tendencies are rooted in the law's conflicts of psychological and political individualism and are enabled at the level of the dynamic of citizenship forms by the fission where previously there was fusion between the civil, political and the social forms (in Marshall's terms) since the 1970s.

Increased responsibilisation: authoritarianism through legal freedom

If one way of understanding authoritarianism through law leads to the opposition within law between *ratio* and *voluntas*, a second way looks at the ideologically dominatory or repressive nature of individualist legal form per se. That is, it considers how law as *ratio* or as freedom is itself authoritarian in its effects. Here, I want to argue that criminal justice provides an authoritarian mode of legitimation through its emphasis on punishment as a morally proper social response to individual criminal acts. It establishes through the classical retributive discourse a sense of the justice or moral propriety of acting in an authoritarian manner. In this it provides a classical political legitimation of domination that is based on *ratio*, not *voluntas*, and is all the more powerful as a result.

This returns us to the discussion of increased responsibilisation in the context of the shifting relationship between the different forms of Marshallian citizenship under modern conditions. Increased responsibilisation arises out of the renewed emphasis on political citizenship as a mode of legitimation in an increasingly authoritarian neo-liberal polity. I argued in the second section of this chapter that aligning political and social citizenship in the 1960s and early 1970s meant that the classic 19th-century model of the criminal law was supported in its actualisation in the context of a socially progressive, welfare-oriented polity. In that context, the criminal law was seen as part of a generally liberal, social democratic project in which matters of individual and social justice were linked.

However, the model of political citizenship is subject to two contradictory pressures once the supportive overlay of principles of social citizenship is withdrawn. On the one hand, it retains its importance as a political legitimating device to stand alongside the demands of civil (economic) citizenship; on the other, it comes under attack as an unnecessary appendage and threat to economic efficiency and good order, that is, to economic policies pursued in the name of civil citizenship.

Responsibilisation in criminal law draws on the first of these two contradictory alternatives, for the classical, decontextualised, individual, psychological model of responsibility provides an alternative legitimation to social intervention. Responsibility and justice in the model of political citizenship rest upon individualist rather than social premises: it is up to individuals to act responsibly within the law and, where they do not do so, they may be appropriately punished under classical retributive principles of justice. Removing the contextualising manifold of principles of social citizenship, welfare and justice places renewed emphasis on individual responsibility as a primary legitimating and dominatory ideological device. Legal responsibilisation comes to the fore.

This fall back to principles of individual as opposed to social justice promotes the idea that individuals are criminally responsible for their action and helps divide society along class lines into the 'haves' and the 'have nots'. It does so, however, indirectly, through the mechanism of a strongly *universalising* sense of moral justice for punishment. That is its special power. This helps explain the emphasis on increased punishment as the state relies more for its sense of moral vindication on its retributive, rather than its redistributive, function. Increased punitiveness follows increased responsibilisation and is one reason for the increasing numbers of people being sent to prison. The return to legitimation through the decontextualised and remoralised psychological individual of the criminal law, without the tempering cover of social citizenship principles, presses remorselessly on the punishment button. In so doing, authoritarian legitimation relies upon the dominatory or repressive nature of legal individualism in its psychological aspect. Such legitimation takes place not because of a shift between the poles of freedom and sovereignty *but by virtue of the concept of legal freedom itself.*

Increased responsibilisation is also linked, I think, to the increasing role of victims in the system. At the same time as the neo-liberal state invokes punishment with greater regularity, it loses some of its own moral standing in the matter of redressing wrongs. Under the older welfare–liberal model of the state, a clear line was drawn between the role of the state and the role of the public, and in particular the victim, with regard to crime. Crime was the infraction of a public norm and it was the state, as the representative of the general will, which was effectively the injured party. Punishment should therefore be both its right and its responsibility.

The current emphasis on the victim in the criminal process arises out of the sense that it is a moral relationship between individual citizens that punishment addresses, and that it is the private person who is centrally the wronged party. As social interventionist provisioning decreases, the moral role of the state also decreases, and it becomes less able to absorb the moral passions invoked by crime. As it represents itself as a formalistic 'night watchman', its substantive moral authority is reduced. As the state takes less of a moral stance, moral passions find their home among victims and their families in a reallocation of the moral economy. Increasing the role of victims accompanies increased responsibilisation of perpetrators just because the repressive side of law's psychological individualism is relied upon for legitimation purposes.

Increasing dangerousness: authoritarianism within/against legal freedom

Turning now to the second tendency, that of increasing dangerousness, it is necessary to consider both the 'politically' and the 'pathologically' dangerous offender. As regards the latter, penal policies of bifurcation into 'normal' and 'abnormal' or dangerous offenders have a long history, and reflect different underlying structural elements. The idea of a dangerous offender who lacks qualities of civil and political citizenship can be traced to the turn of the 19th century when, under the influence of doctrines of social intervention, certain groups of people were subjected to special measures of control because of their residual deficiencies.

Whereas I have heretofore focused on the progressive qualities of a model of social citizenship, it should be noted, and this is part of the overall complexity of thinking about the criminal justice system, that such citizenship itself involves its own distinct undertow of authoritarian intervention. Ways of treating the mentally ill, inebriates, habitual prostitutes and persistent offenders reveal what can happen to those in whom it is thought that 'the essentials of citizenship' do not reside, as the turn of the (last) century philosopher Bernard Bosanquet put it (1919: 210). For such people, the promise of social citizenship in recompense for their own failings as civil and political citizens was always a hollow one. For them, law was already an *arcanum dominationis* before the concept was generalised under totalitarian rule (cf Norrie 1991: ch 5).

Such people may be said to experience psychological conditions that make it hard for them to conform their behaviour to law, although it is usually underlying social conditions that are deficient. In a social world that relies increasingly on an authoritarian sense that the state should be in control of everything, ever greater emphasis is placed on identifying groups of persons who must be controlled by law where their conduct is in some way threatening. Sexual offenders convicted of committing offences of an 'abnormal' kind are an obvious case in point, but the general rise of punishments of an indeterminate form is also relevant here. A general sense of the pathological or abnormal dangerous offender comes to the fore as a special class to be treated according to rules tailored to their dangerousness. In this move, authoritarian state intervention does not affirm a juridical model of the responsible citizen (as in increased responsibilisation) but rather cuts against it, seeing political citizenship as an obstruction to the demand for control and the legitimation benefits that control brings. Control becomes a matter of state will and bureaucratic determination rather than the juridical allocation of rights and responsibilities.

Alongside the increased targeting for control of those who are seen as dangerous in the sense that they are pathologically unable to conform their conduct to law, there are those who are seen as at war with society in general. Here, the idea of a split between 'them' and 'us', foe and friend, in more classically authoritarian terms emerges, where being one of 'them' involves being treated as outside the law and denied rights associated with political citizenship, for example to normal criminal justice or due process requirements. To the extent that the state ceases to treat certain crimes of violence as part of the normal criminal calendar and re-categorises them as part of a 'war against terror', it legitimates the denial of legal rights to those involved, and itself as a strong state.

In considering the logic of this development, it is important to note the shift away from the aspect of domination through legal freedom to the moving between poles enabled by the law's political individualism, for here the form of law is pushed towards political power, sovereignty and *voluntas* and away from individual right, freedom and *ratio*. The pathologically abnormal offender and the political offender, constructed as a terrorist, are both cast beyond the citizenship pale, and submitted to a general regime of control that resembles Neumann's *arcanum dominationis*. Here it can be noted that increased dangerousness can also align – rhetorically at least – with increased responsibilisation, for the person who undertakes dreadful acts of violence either as a pathological or a political offender becomes precisely the most heinous kind of criminal, for whom increased punishment is justified. Dangerousness and culpability both point in the same direction in practice, towards the likelihood of increasing prison populations. But the main thrust of increased dangerousness stems from the reshaping of legal form towards authoritarian interventions and away from principles of individual right. Where dangerousness is in issue, it is that conflict in legal form that is brought to the fore.

Increasing regulation: the forms authoritarianism takes

Finally, there are the legal phenomena associated with increasing, and new forms of, regulation. Many could be mentioned here, including special laws governing terrorists, drug dealers and sex offenders. I will, however, only briefly consider the United Kingdom's anti-social behaviour order (ASBO),[9] and here I am beholden to Peter Ramsay's work (2004; 2006). The key to understanding the ASBO is the way in which it reflects many of the different issues canvassed in the above discussion.

First, it involves pursuing a dangerousness strategy, and therefore undermining the juridical model of the political citizen in favour of authoritarian ordering principles. As Neumann points out, the classic political citizenship doctrine of the rule of law involves both generality of law and specificity in its application (1957: 28). An instrument such as the ASBO undermines legal generality since it represents in effect a criminal law specifically tailored to particular individuals with regard to forms of conduct that would not be criminal were anyone else to do them. An order on X, for example, not to meet with Y at a particular place where it would be otherwise lawful to do so because this elicits a sense of fear in the bystander, leads by another route to Neumann's idea of law as *arcanum dominationis* within the authoritarian state.

Second, the idea of the ASBO also reflects the idea of state intervention as a means of achieving moral legitimacy and consensus by deploying authoritarian measures, for it is in essence a way of dealing with the bad behaviour of problem families on council estates, of controlling the 'rough poor' for (what are presented as) morally valid reasons. Third, the idea of the ASBO plays around with the concept of citizenship to establish moral legitimation in terms of the individual in that it stresses the duties owed by the citizen to the community as well as the rights

9 Under the Anti-Social Behaviour, Crime and Policing Act 2014, the ASBO was replaced with a system of civil injunctions and Criminal Behaviour Orders and other orders designed to rationalise the previous regime. One particular problem was that the ASBO had become a badge of honour for some of those required to wear it.

and privileges he or she enjoys. In a way, it represents a new form of social interventionism after the demise of welfare-oriented forms of social citizenship, and one that bases itself on a revised (communitarian) vision of the political model of citizenship. But it uses that model as a means of denying the core idea of citizenship *rights* that the political model itself implied.

Conclusion

In conclusion, even from this brief and preliminary discussion of how the dynamic of citizenship forms interacts with a ratcheting up of state authoritarianism to favour increased responsibilisation, dangerousness and regulation, it will be appreciated that what is at stake here is not an easy one-to-one matching of underlying developments with particular forms of law and justice. Many variables are at play, so that a fuller identification of structural forms would have to be aligned with a more finely grained understanding of particular forms of criminal justice to achieve a satisfactory analysis.

My comments above are only a beginning in a complex task. Alongside this pluralism, it is necessary to understand how individual developments can display different facets, feed into and off each other, and satisfy different agendas at one and the same time. For example, although the ASBO can be seen as a form of attack on the basic ideas of liberal political citizenship, that is, the idea of the individual as an abstract, general member of a liberal polity, it at the same time can be presented, as my third point above makes clear, as a way of getting individuals to measure up to the responsibilities of being a member of such a polity, that is, as a way of renovating political citizenship for more legitimating work in authoritarian times. It seems to me that it is often the case that an 'idea whose time has come' is just the kind of idea which can serve a number of different and conflicting agendas just because of its multi-faceted quality. What needs to be aimed for is a sense of how legal measures or forms are shaped by their structural contexts, but are not reducible to them. Herein lies what might be called their 'relative autonomy'.

More broadly, what I have sought to develop is a sense of the *implication* of liberal law in the evolution of authoritarianism within criminal justice. It is too tempting to seek to oppose authoritarian developments in the criminal law by resorting simply to a liberal conception of justice. If that conception is itself imbued with authoritarianism, it is necessary to be reflexive about the nature and limits of legal freedom. Law is too complex a phenomenon, embodying moments of partial freedom within a socio-economic matrix that shapes and conditions its overall possibilities, to be the source of easy answers to problems posed by an authoritarian state.

At the same time, it would be foolish to throw the baby out with the bathwater, as Neumann's contrast between liberal legality and the *arcanum dominationis* makes clear. By analysing liberal criminal law as co-constituted by elements of individual right and authoritarian power in its political individualist moment, and by depicting its model of the responsible individual as entailing both repressive (freedom-denying) and expressive (freedom-enabling) elements in its psychological individualist moment, I have argued that its own contribution to authoritarianism in terms of increased responsibilisation, dangerousness and regulation must be acknowledged. If we are aware of these implications of liberal law, we may be more alert to the complexities involved in identifying legal solutions to the problems of authoritarianism today.

Chapter 3

Between orthodox subjectivism and moral contextualism: intention and the Law Commission report

In the Law Commission's Consultation Paper entitled 'A New Homicide Act for England and Wales' (2006), the concept of intention plays a central symbolic and legal role. The symbolic role is that intention represents the most culpable mental state, and therefore is the most appropriate one to place at the heart of the law of murder, the most serious crime. In the Law Commission's proposals, this means that intention to kill, and only intention to kill, must be at the core of the new concept of first degree murder. The more directly legal role is seen in working out the nature of intention in Part 4 of the consultation paper, where two possible definitions of intention are proposed, and the doctrine of double effect is considered.

In this comment on the role of intention in the paper, I will focus on how these aspects interconnect, and I will consider some of the problems revealed as a result of the symbolic master role that intention plays in this area of the law. My comments will be organised in three sections. In the first, I will consider the main themes that structure the Law Commission's view and which accordingly place intention at its core. In the second, I will consider whether intention can have the primary role the Law Commission gives it by reflecting on the concept of practical indifference with which the Law Commission also works, but at the level of second, not first, degree murder. In the third, I will consider the two views of intention developed in Part 4 of the report, and their relationship to the doctrine of double effect.

In reviewing these matters, two linked themes emerge. The first concerns the relationship between the *political* and *moral* aspects of judgments about criminal responsibility for murder. Lawyers and legal theorists all too frequently think that there is a direct link between the moral understanding of an event and how it should be categorised in law. Legal categories should essentially reflect moral judgments of wrongdoing. However, legal categories only indirectly distil moral issues, which they mix with other considerations in a process of political, state-based judgment. In homicide law, this is particularly relevant given the existence of the mandatory life sentence for murder. Such a penalty, with its historical roots in the practice of capital punishment, operates as a highly contestable political vision, albeit in attenuated form, of the ultimate power of the state over the citizen.

Accordingly, to consider questions of a person's legal responsibility for an act is both to consider how such responsibility relates to underlying moral issues, and how it should be related to a political context shaping liability and punishment.

The Law Commission report is sensitive to this aspect of the politics of criminal responsibility in two rather different ways. First, it works with the mandatory life sentence as a reason to shape the division of murder into two grades. Recognising the significance of the penalty, it opts for a narrow first degree murder category, placing one form of responsibility that would now be subject to the mandatory penalty ('implied malice') within the second degree category. This narrowing of the practical impact of the mandatory life sentence is to be applauded (although it remains to be seen if it can be defended theoretically). Second, it not only accepts the government's remit to work with the mandatory penalty, but goes further by rationalising and legitimating it, and making it a justificatory foundation for its own particular take on intention to kill as the most serious form of responsibility. The link is from the mandatory life sentence as the gravest punishment to the sanctity of life principle as expressing an absolute value, and thence to the significance of intention as the worst mental state. In this sense, the mandatory life sentence becomes totemic for the report's theoretical structure (see next section).

The second theme concerns the ways in which political aspects of judgment directly inform legal categories of judgment. The Law Commission report comes at the end of a period in which the general principles of criminal law have been shaped by a highly successful political project: the liberal 'orthodox subjectivist' account of the general part associated with academic lawyers such as Glanville Williams and Sir John Smith (Dennis 1997). That approach, with its emphasis on cognitive conceptions of mental states and capacities, has in recent years been submitted to an influential critique from a 'morally contextualist' or 'substantivist' standpoint.[1]

The report reveals signs of both approaches, reflecting the Law Commission's historical commitment to orthodox subjectivism as well as the influence of the new ways of thinking. However, the orthodox subjectivist approach remains dominant, in that it structures the account of intention provided here, and downplays a more morally contextual approach. This leads to a mistake, I shall argue, in the understanding of the worst kind of mental state. The morally substantive approach is, however, not without its own problems: it may be too vague, and it may result in a more punitive approach in that it expands the categories of responsibility.[2]

To press this approach may therefore threaten to undo the Commission's commitment to limit the practical effect of the mandatory life sentence. The question is therefore whether there is a way of stating the mental state for murder

1 The most influential work amongst many is probably Duff (1990).

2 See my review of Ashworth and Mitchell (2000) in (2001) *Legal Studies* 679.

in the first degree that is not too broad or imprecise, and yet reflects the element of truth in a morally contextualist approach which the report otherwise misses (see second section). It also leads to some familiar problems in the area of indirect intention, where the supposed informal balance between cognitive mental states and the evaluation of moral contexts which appears to exist after *Woollin*[3] is thrown into question by a systematic attempt to define intention (see final section).

Before we turn to the Law Commission's report, it may be useful to outline three general points which inform its project. The aim of the Law Commission's proposals is to set out a structure for the law of homicide which is 'modern, fair and comprehensible' (at paragraph 1.47),[4] and which takes the law away from the centuries old common law foundation established by Coke. What would such a law look like? It would respect the principle of a 'ladder of offences', that is, a graduated hierarchy reflecting appropriate degrees of offence seriousness and defence mitigation (1.31–1.32). It would involve, for the first time, clear definitions of murder and ancillary categories (1.30), and it would reflect other important principles such as that of fair labelling (1.45–1.47).[5] In this spirit, it would divide homicide law into three categories (first and second degree murder and manslaughter), and it places an intention to kill at the apogee of this structure as the mental state required for first degree murder.

Such principles are important in themselves, but also reflect a concern about the relationship between the proposed new homicide categories and the sentencing structure for crimes of murder introduced by section 269 and Schedule 21 of the Criminal Justice Act 2003. Whilst this provision came about by happenstance (the anger of a politician, the then Home Secretary, having been triggered by a human rights ruling that he should no longer set the minimum term on an indefinite life sentence), it has become, says the paper, 'the main legislative pillar of the law of homicide' (1.124). In such ways does law reform occur. It has made 'perhaps the most important legislative changes to the law of murder since the final abolition of the death penalty in 1965' (1.126), and it presupposes 'clear and coherent definitions of murder and of the partial defences to murder' (1.127). Thus, the 2003 Act accentuates the need for law reform in this area by virtue of its effects on sentencing.

Finally, there are two important issues that structure the report. One of these, already noted, is the externally imposed one provided in the terms of reference that the Commission should 'take account of the continuing existence of the

3 *R v Woollin* [1998] 3 WLR 382.

4 All references to the report are to passages located by the paragraph numbers in it.

5 Interestingly, however, the report downplays this last issue, not wanting to get 'bogged down in questions concerning the appropriateness of particular labels for particular offences', yet the issue of fair labelling, with emphasis on the 'fair', is surely central to the idea of establishing a ladder of offences. As regards labels too, the report with its emphasis on first and second degree murder as well as manslaughter must feel that these are appropriate terms to reflect offence seriousness and offender culpability, so fair labelling does seem to be central to what it does.

mandatory life sentence for murder' (1.1), and the other is the internally chosen one that the report does not consider justifications for killing, which include necessity and self-defence, and which are excluded from the Commission's considerations. All three of these points are germane to what follows.

Intention's general significance

Three foundations: the life sentence, sanctity of life, intention

The significance of the crime of murder and its relation to the law of intention is addressed in Part 2 of the report. Here a link is forged between the idea that human life is sacrosanct, the mandatory life sentence for murder and the special significance of intentional killing. As regards the first premise, the report draws upon Judaeo-Christian doctrine (2.28) to argue that the importance of the sanctity of life is directly linked to the prohibition against intentional killing.[6] The latter 'best expresses the idea of the sanctity of life, the idea that life must be . . . "morally secured against (certain kinds of) interference"' (2.29).

Since murder 'is a crime centred on intentional or deliberate killing', it is 'a crime whose central definition connects it with the core ideal at the heart of the view that life is sacrosanct' (2.30). Further, this nexus between intentional killing and the sanctity of life underwrites the mandatory life sentence which the Law Commission not only accepts as its term of reference, but endorses. To abolish it would be 'seen as a signal that the law did not regard murder as a specially or uniquely grave crime', and 'the uniqueness of the mandatory life sentence . . . reflect[s] the "sanctity of life" ideal' (2.30). Not only is this a valid foundation on which to cast the law; it also chimes with public opinion, which, Barry Mitchell's survey reveals,[7] shows 'a very high level of agreement that an intent to kill is (subject to considerations of excusable motive) an indication that the crime was especially serious' (2.13). Thus, intention is central to the crime of murder, and this is placed in the context of a set of 'absolutes': the life mandatory penalty, the sanctity of human life, the special significance of intentional killing.

Questioning the foundations

The question is how much of this is really true. As regards the special character of the mandatory life sentence, the 2003 Act makes it clear that there are now in effect three kinds of murder: one with a minimum starting sentence of 15 years, one with a minimum starting point of 30 years and a third with a whole life tariff. Whilst the judicial reaction to this is to downplay the legally binding

6 It also expresses this view in a secular version (2.21).
7 See appendix A of the report.

quality of section 269,[8] and whilst it will be said that all sentences, no matter what their minimum, remain life sentences, it seems as if the 2003 Act provides the beginnings of a new 'functional' or 'shadow' law of murder – in three degrees of offence seriousness.

What this does is to undercut the notion that murder in itself is an exceptional crime and always one of exceptional seriousness for which only an exceptional penalty is required. After the 2003 Act, there is no longer officially one 'uniquely grave crime' (2.30). There is rather a very serious crime, which at its worst may warrant a whole life or 30 year punishment, but one which will most often warrant a term of 15 years' imprisonment subject to factors of mitigation and aggravation, and subject to release on licence. Without wishing to overstate the point, and recognising the continuing significance of licence arrangements, the 2003 Act has in symbolic terms chipped away at the notion of one, uniquely serious, crime possessing one, uniquely serious, penalty.

Alongside this we need to think about what the sanctity of life doctrine means, and how much society really accepts this as a foundational premise. To begin with, it should be noted that those who support the theological view do not in fact say that 'intentional or deliberate killing . . . best expresses the ideal of the sanctity of life' as the Law Commission has it (2.29). What they say, as the Commission also notes (2.27), is that 'It is always wrong deliberately to kill the *innocent*' (2.28, emphasis added). This is a different formulation since it raises the issue as to who 'the innocent' are. Is it against the sanctity of life to kill in defence the person who attacks you? Would the sanctity of life principle exclude the execution of the condemned man? Where does killing out of necessity fit morally here? Or killing in a war? Or mercy killing?[9]

It should also be noted that there are significant areas of social life where *sanctity of life* is weighed against *quality of life*. This is true of the way society deals with the intentional taking of life at both its beginning and its end. To some extent, we are shielded from this conclusion by a questionable distinction between act and omission, so that we 'let die' rather than intentionally 'kill', but this only goes so far. Doctors are allowed to hasten death by drug injections which they know will kill so long as it was not their 'purpose' so to do.[10] We are in short not as a society necessarily convinced of the sanctity of life. Some may regard this as a gross understatement in the light of the various ways we allow people to die, and how society acts in wars, but I make the point non-contentiously here. Recent newspaper reports suggest a clear majority of people believe that mercy killing is acceptable in appropriate circumstances. Mercy killing in effect places quality of life issues before sanctity of life issues.

Further, it should be noted that the nexus between intentional killing and the worst form of homicide in the popular view is nuanced. The popular view that

8 *R v Sullivan* [2005] 1 Cr App R (S) 308. For further discussion see Ashworth (2005: 116–118).

9 See Lacey, Wells and Quick (2003: 603–610, 677–95) for discussion.

10 *R v Cox* [1992] 12 BMLR 38.

intentional killing is particularly bad depends upon considerations of 'excusable motive' (2.13), so the badness of intentional killing is qualified from the start. The report also notes that one reason the public sees intentional killing as particularly wrong is that it associates such killing with premeditation, but premeditation is irrelevant to the legal conception of intentional killing. Premeditation is in fact one of those 'morally substantive' facts of killing that, according to the 2003 Act, aggravates it. It has little to do with the formal definition of intentional killing that the Law Commission wants to build its account of homicide upon.

So the value of all three initial premises can be questioned: the shape of the mandatory life sentence is changing, the sanctity of life principle is questionable and the centrality of intention is based on a false understanding of what it means. If we think about intention and its relation to the value of life, what alternative starting point might we have for the law of murder? One possibility is a less formalistic account of intention, to which the Commission in fact points when discussing the difference between intention and premeditation. The Commission quotes the Victorian Stephen (2.45), without seeing that what he had to say against the salience of premeditation also points away from the intention view it wishes to promote. Stephen's argument is that, whilst premeditation might be thought to be at the moral core of murder, some of the worst homicides cannot be said to involve it. Stephen does not, however, argue in the direction of a formal account of intention, but for something more morally substantive:

> As much *cruelty*, as much *indifference to the life of others*, a *disposition at least as dangerous to society*, probably even more dangerous, is shown by sudden as by premeditated murders . . . A man makes advances to a girl who repels him. He deliberately but instantly cuts her throat. A man civilly asked to pay a just debt pretends to get the money, loads a rifle and blows out his creditor's brains. In none of these cases is there premeditation unless the word is used in a sense as unnatural, as 'aforethought' in 'malice aforethought', but each represents *even more diabolical cruelty and ferocity* than that which is involved in murders premeditated in the natural sense of the word (emphasis added).

The italicised passages indicate a different way of considering the wrong in murder.[11] They point to the morally substantive attitudinal states which accompany intention or premeditation. Intentions, understood in a psychological sense, or premeditation may be informed by such attitudinal states, but they are not the same as them. Shorn of moral substance, the simple fact of intentionality does not tell us very much about what was wrong in a killing, and therefore what might be the underlying reason that some killings are regarded as morally serious enough to be classed as murder. In the next section, we will examine how the Law

11 This is not to say that Stephen's own position on the mens rea for murder reflected this standpoint; only that it reveals a different way of thinking about the wrong in the crime.

Commission deals with the notion of practical indifference, an attitudinal concept which Stephen's comments reflect, but which the Commission treats as relevant only to second degree murder, and not to first, where intention has primacy.

Practical indifference

Part 3 of the Law Commission's report concerns the structure of the murder/manslaughter divide and the creation of an intermediate offence of second degree murder, which pulls together three different forms of culpable homicide: where a partial defence exists, where the mental state was that of intending to do serious harm and where the mental state was one of reckless indifference. Second degree murder involves the demotion of 'implied malice' (intention to do serious harm) from the offence of higher/highest gravity and the promotion of a form of reckless killing from the offence of lower/lowest gravity to an intermediate position. Whilst killing with implied malice most obviously draws on an element of intention, it is killing with reckless indifference that I want to consider here first for what it can tell us about the report's approach to intention in the law. I will then look at the serious harm rule in the light of this discussion, and suggest a change to the Commission's proposal.

Distinguishing forms of recklessness

The report identifies two kinds of recklessness, namely reckless indifference and reckless stupidity, and argues that the former is a sufficiently culpable state for second degree murder. Reckless indifference is formulated as 'manifesting a "couldn't care less" attitude to death, when [D] realises that there is an unjustified risk of death being caused by his or her conduct, but goes ahead with that conduct, causing death . . .' (3.150).

This notion of a 'couldn't care less' attitude is drawn from the law of reckless rape,[12] and is thought to be a concept that the judges are sufficiently familiar with to be able to implement in the law of homicide. As the report says, it involves the use of an 'evaluative criterion', rather than the standard subjectivist form of a psychological cognitive mental state (intention, foresight, knowledge). My question of it is not whether it constitutes a valid means of determining culpability, but how it relates to both second and first degree murder in the Law Commission's scheme. The Law Commission notes that, prior to the decision in *Moloney*,[13] which narrowed the law, it was possible to argue that the old notion of malice aforethought had some substantive content in that it included both the intention to kill or do grievous bodily harm plus a degree of recklessness as to death. That degree of recklessness might not be expressed in the modern

12 *R v Satnam; R v Kewal* [1983] 78 Cr App R 325.
13 [1985] 1 All ER 1025.

subjectivist manner, but in terms of a general bad disposition, a 'willingness to produce the particular evil consequence', as Lord Diplock put it in *Hyam*[14] (3.40).

It is this notion that the Law Commission wants to resurrect, but not as part of the more/most serious offence of first degree murder. The Law Commission wants to 'lower the stakes' (3.43) by including reckless indifference as a form of second degree murder. In terms of the mandatory life sentence, this makes sense. In terms of culpability, however, why should recklessly indifferent killing be part of murder in the second degree rather than in the first? After all, Lord Diplock, and the older tradition in English criminal law going back to Stephen (3.40) saw it as being an alternative form of culpability for the most serious offence available. Might they, if they were here today, not see it as a candidate for culpability for murder in the first degree?

Different standards of indifference

The question about the moral status of reckless indifference is raised by the Law Commission's discussion of alternative ways of stating it in legal terms. Various alternatives are discussed. Scotland works with an alternative to intention in murder in terms of 'wicked recklessness imply[ing] a disposition depraved enough to be regardless of the consequences',[15] whilst the Model Penal Code speaks of 'recklessness under circumstances manifesting extreme indifference to the value of human life'[16] (3.163).

These, of course, are formulae designed to capture culpability for the most serious offence, not for an intermediate one, so why should the Law Commission think that its own formulation should apply to an offence of less seriousness? The answer is, first, definitional: the Law Commission thinks that an intention to kill stands out as the highest form of culpability, and everything else is at a lower level. But, secondly, compare the Law Commission's terminology, a 'couldn't care less' attitude of reckless indifference, with that used in Scotland or the United States, 'wicked recklessness', a 'depraved disposition', 'extreme indifference'. Are these the same? The Law Commission sees these approaches as reflecting the same kind of view as the 'couldn't care less' attitude (3.164), although the Law Commission criticises them for the scope they give juries to make subjective judgments (3.165). However, it seems to me that there is a further difference here that the Commission has not picked up, and that is that the Scottish and American language points to a more severely judged form of indifference. All three approaches are attitudinal, but there is significantly different moral colouring in the terms used. They are not all describing *the same* attitude. 'Couldn't care less' manifests a culpable attitude, but one that is presumably not so serious as 'wicked', 'depraved' or 'extreme' indifference, and therefore might validly be seen as giving

14 [1974] 2 All ER 41.
15 *Cawthorne v HM Lord Advocate* [1968] JC 32, 35.
16 Model Penal Code § 202.2(b).

rise to a secondary form of culpability. However, there are other forms of reckless indifference that are stronger and the question would be whether *they* are lesser forms of liability to that constituted by an intention to kill.

To consider this question in a practical context, take the two examples given by the Law Commission of the planting of a bomb in a city street intending to damage property, and wantonly shooting into a moving car or busy shop where there is foresight of an inevitable risk of death (3.168–3.170). For the Law Commission, these would be cases of reckless indifference, of a 'couldn't care less' attitude, and therefore cases of second degree murder. Yet these are the cases of 'indiscriminate malice' to which Lord Hope referred in *Woollin*[17] as if they might be a valid alternative mens rea for murder, and the question may be asked whether the appropriate description of their mental state is one of 'couldn't care less' indifference, or something stronger. By prioritising a concept of intention, however, as the most serious form of mens rea for murder, the Law Commission does not see the differences in gravity in the different attitudinal tests.

Indifference and the serious harm rule

A related issue concerns the Commission's proposal to separate out intention to kill, leading to first degree murder, and intention to do serious harm, leading to second degree murder. The Commission's proposal on 'implied malice' leads to a widespread and rigorous review of approaches to the serious harm rule, and the (correct) conclusion is that the rule has been unclear and is in need of tightening up. The Law Commission therefore proposes that where the guilty state of mind involves intending to do serious harm, there should be the rider that harm is 'not to be regarded as serious unless it is harm of such a nature as to endanger life, or to cause, or to be likely to cause, permanent or long-term damage to a significant aspect of physical integrity or mental functioning' (3.144).

However, having added this qualification, the Law Commission then queries whether such a version of 'serious harm' would not now be 'sufficiently blameworthy to warrant conviction for "first degree murder" and not just for "second degree murder"' (3.146). The Law Commission proposes to stick with the positioning of it in the second degree category, but gives no reason why this should be so in light of its query. What is at stake here?

The problem with the implied malice rule is that it 'does not necessarily connect the defendant's state of mind with the causing of death itself' (3.37) and is in breach of the correspondence principle (2.101). The argument for boosting implied malice to first degree murder might be that, on the Commission's restricted definition of serious harm, 'there is no significant moral difference between the intentional killer and the person who intentionally inflicts serious harm' (3.12).

17 *R v Woollin* (n 3) 394.

However, and this might be the Commission's rationale for not boosting it, an intention to do serious harm is always just that, and never an intention to kill. At best it will involve something akin to foresight of a risk of killing, but this would be insufficient for first degree murder. This then leaves open the question why the Commission might nonetheless think that a restricted account of serious harm could ever be considered an alternative to the intention to kill. Surely it must be a form of second degree murder, no matter what?

An answer to this tension might reside in something similar to the idea of reckless indifference with which the Commission has been working. A person who intends to cause life-endangering harm displays an attitude to the victim and to human life that is practically indifferent. But at what level? On the Commission's approach, such indifference cannot take the killing beyond second degree murder, yet here, the Law Commission appears to think that there is a viable argument for first degree murder. The answer must surely be that assault to the endangerment of life resulting in death displays precisely the kind of aggravated indifference that we see formulated in something like the Scottish and United States approaches. In its ambivalence about how to place implied malice in its restricted form, we see another consequence of the Commission's general reliance on an orthodox subjectivist account of intention, and its attendant restrictive principle of correspondence between intention and outcome.

A way forward

The Commission's support for orthodox subjectivism is most prominent in its argument that only an intention to kill will do for first degree murder. This leads to a narrow conception of the offence, which is to be welcomed in the light of the mandatory life sentence. However, it is hard to justify this in theoretical or moral terms because intention to kill does not possess the primal significance granted to it by the Law Commission. When practical indifference is opened up, it can be seen to reflect forms of culpability that are arguably as significant as intention. The problem with moral contextualisation of cognitive states, however, is that it leads to conceptions of responsibility that suffer significantly from vagueness, and are potentially over-inclusive. The Scots law notion of 'wicked recklessness', for example, relies on what a jury would consider to be a 'depraved disposition'. Such an idea is unlikely to be acceptable in England and Wales;[18] were it or an equivalent to be adopted, it would only broaden the category of first degree murder in a way that would be unacceptable.

One way forward in the light of this impasse might be to deploy the Commission's restricted definition of implied malice as a proxy moral contextualist addition to first degree murder. An intention to do serious harm, meaning to endanger life, is

18 But see Goff (1988).

of course couched in the language of orthodox subjectivism and, in the logic of that language, is regarded by the Commission as unacceptable for first degree murder. But it can be seen to work in a way that is morally equivalent to an intention to kill. Doing harm so serious as to endanger life can be regarded *substantively* as of the same order of culpability. It exhibits a practical indifference that is as bad as intending to kill.[19]

Could this formula operate as a place-marker for a conception of practical indifference? The Commission does point out (in the context of second degree murder), that the serious harm rule and reckless indifference are modally distinct (3.58). Where the former builds out of the subjectivist vision of intention, the latter is based on a substantive outcome and the accused's reflexive attitude to bringing it about. However, this difference does not rule out the possibility that the former, particularly in its new restricted form, gains its real moral significance from its ability to express, ventriloquially (Norrie 1999: 543), what is understood substantively in the latter. Moral substance is implicitly articulated within the formalism of the implied malice rule. Certainly, if one thinks of the two examples considered earlier as giving rise to the need for a supplement to the intention to kill rule (planting a bomb, firing willy-nilly into a car or busy shop), it seems to me that a jury considering whether a defendant intended to do serious harm *qua* endangering life would be able to make appropriate moral sense with such a rule. A restricted, but only a restricted,[20] implied malice rule would do real moral work in terms of supplementing the intention to kill rule in determining the culpability of such an act. The Commission is not of this view (3.169), but there seems room for further thought and argument here.

Defining intention

The Law Commission develops two positions on intention in Part 4, one based upon previous Commission attempts to establish a clear definition, the other based upon the existing common law approach established in *Nedrick*[21] and *Woollin*.[22] Most of the work has gone into the former of these two approaches, although the Commission states that it sees competing values in both. Whilst the definitional approach has the attraction of certainty, it has the disadvantage of rigidity and, whilst the common law approach allows for flexibility and 'moral elbow room', it has the countervailing disadvantage of a lack of certainty (4.1). Overall, however, the discussion is coloured by one major issue, the relationship between a cognitivist account of the mental state of intention and the moral work

19 Where, of course, intending to kill is linked to a context of moral badness. Intending to kill per se is neither good nor bad, it gains its sense of wrongness from its context. That is why there is a problem with double effect – see next section.

20 Without the restriction, the rule is too broad to reflect the moral issue.

21 [1986] 1 WLR 1025.

22 See n 3.

it must do in the law of murder. This is seen in the third and final section of Part 4 where the concept of double effect hoves into view.

The definitional approach

The definitional approach now has a long and detailed history of attempts to settle a definition of intention, and the Commission's discussion is hinged around two previous efforts (clause 18(b) of the Draft Criminal Code (1989), clause 1(a) of the Draft Criminal Law Bill (1993)) at codification. Pushed along by interventions by the late Professor Sir John Smith, a definition has evolved here that owes more to the original 1989 Draft Code in that the 1993 Draft Bill introduced the word 'purpose' to describe direct intention (4.37), and the new definition has discarded it for reasons discussed below. The precise details of this circular evolution are not so important as the final result, which defines intention either in 'direct' terms as involving acting 'in order to bring a result about', or indirectly, in 'knowing that it will be virtually certain to occur'.

A third possibility involves the situation where a person acts indirectly in relation to a result but, because there is uncertainty as to the outcome he directly intends, there may be a dispute about whether he foresaw the indirect result as virtually certain to occur. Here the question whether the person knew 'that [the result] would be virtually certain to occur' is linked to the condition 'if he or she were to succeed in his or her purpose of causing some other result' (4.30). Finally, there is a proviso that 'a person is not to be deemed to have intended any result which it was his or her specific purpose to avoid' (4.3).

Plainly, the main elements of the definition of intention here are based upon the common law, but they state as a rule of law what is regarded in the common law itself as something less, guidance to a jury as to how to find intention where it is not in fact defined.[23] This ups the stakes in terms of the potential for definitional argument in case law and, for this reason, the word 'purpose', which was favoured in the 1993 Draft, has been discarded at least from the main definitions of direct and indirect intention. 'Purpose' suggests a confusion 'between the purpose with which one may act in the sense of an ulterior motive, and the purpose with which one acts in bringing about an immediate result' (4.36), and is therefore omitted.

Yet 'purpose' may have had a hidden value and point in terms of moral flexibility,[24] and its absence raises the problem as to how, if need be, such a quality might be introduced into the law. Here the final proviso plays a role. What this is getting at is illustrated by the situation where a father jumps with his child from a burning building, and also throws a second child out. Whilst he and the first child are badly injured, the second child dies. The father knows that death is a virtual

23 *Matthews and Alleyne* [2003] 2 Cr App R 30.

24 As its use in medical cases makes clear: what Andrew Ashworth (1996) refers to as moral elbow room.

certainty for the second child, but that it is an 'absolute' certainty if they remain in the building. He hopes against hope that the child will be caught below, or otherwise saved, but it is not. Does he intend to kill the child in these circumstances? The proviso stipulates not, because this is a situation where the specific purpose was to avoid the actual result achieved, the child's death (4.21, 4.47–48).

The underlying rationale here is that the definitional approach 'leaves little room for any evaluative element' and could 'in an unusual case, lead the jury to make a counter-intuitive finding of intention, in order to honour their oath' (4.49). There is then 'the potential for causing injustice and/or nonsense in unusual cases' (4.50). The Law Commission says: 'To require a jury to reach a conclusion about a defendant's intention which defies common sense cannot be a satisfactory way of constructing the criminal law', and adds that this is so 'even if the law provides that defendant, in some other way, with a defence' (4.42). There are, however, two problems with this argument.

Inconsistency as between offence and defence. First, it is plain that the example of the father in the burning building, and others like it (4.48), could fall within an appropriately expanded necessity defence (4.50). The Law Commission says that it will not countenance this because it makes a nonsense of the law of intention (4.42–4.44),[25] but this stand contrasts with its view later as to how to deal with situations of moral double effect involving doctors. There the Law Commission says that 'Recognition of the doctrine [of double effect] can be made elsewhere in the law, under "Defences"'. It is hard to see why the Law Commission should change its position between these two similar situations, where an 'evaluative element' is required in both. Even if one accepts that there is one class of double effect cases where the law would entail both literal nonsense and moral injustice, this class is no more than a sub-class of the general category of double effect cases. It seems strange that it should be treated in so different a way, that a proviso should be required only when serious injustice intersects with syntactic failure.

Intention and motive. Second, the proviso deals with a very specific situation, where a defendant foresees a result 'which it was his or her precise wish to avoid' (4.44). It is wrong in language and in morals to say that someone intended to kill when in fact they intended to save the person that died. The precise formulation of the discussion in terms of the contraries 'to kill/to save' gives the proviso both its rationale and its apparently limited quality. The latter is important because, the Commission says, the proviso is close to the danger of admitting good motives into the law of intention (4.51).[26] It does not, however, stray so far. But is this true?

The example that is given is the case of *Yip Chiu-Cheung*,[27] where the undercover drugs officer was held to have the intention to carry heroin through customs, so

25 Does not the majority's view in *Re A (children)* [2000] 4 All ER 961, that the doctors possess the mens rea for murder, also involve a nonsense? Yet this case would seemingly not be caught by the proviso. The report in effect identifies two kinds of nonsense, but only treats one as relevant to the proviso.

26 Of course, this already happens: see Norrie (2014: 43–57).

27 [1995] 1 AC 111.

that the mens rea for conspiracy was established. Here, it 'cannot be said that it was [the agent's] purpose to avoid carrying heroin onto the plane. His purpose was to carry the drug onto the plane in order to expose the drugs ring. [He] intended to do the proscribed act. His purpose or motive in doing the intended acts (to expose the drugs ring) was a secondary matter' (4.53).

Note most importantly the problem with the word 'purpose', which the Commission itself has already identified (4.36). 'Purpose' is used in this passage in two different senses, as 'immediate aim', and as 'ulterior purpose'. The word invites exactly the problem the Commission wants to avoid: that juries will use the word to open up the definition of intention to accounts of motive. However, the problem is more than just one of the word used. Suppose the issue in *Yip* had not been the guilt of the co-conspirators, but the drugs agent himself. If the agent had been tried, would any jury equally not think it counter-intuitive both in language and in morals to say that he intended to smuggle the drugs onto the plane, no matter how the offence was specifically worded? Deploying the word 'purpose' thus makes the proviso broader than the Law Commission wishes it to be. Considering *Yip*, however, makes it plain that if the proviso were to work in a narrower way, by adopting a formula that did not use 'purpose', it would be too narrow to avoid the kinds of moral and interpretive distortion against which the Commission seeks to act.[28]

The underlying problem here concerns the relationship between a cognitive, psychological account of intention, the concept that it will be recalled is central to the Law Commission's approach, and the moral issues which any account of the law of murder must take into account. With regard to the first model proposed by the Law Commission, the possibility for moral flexibility is reduced by the attempt to define intention, and this throws particular emphasis on issues of double effect, to which we will turn shortly, once we have considered the second approach to defining intention.

The common law approach

The second approach is based upon the existing case law, and in particular the failure to provide a common law definition of intention. Instead of providing such, the drift of the cases from *Moloney*[29] onwards has been towards the creation and refinement of a set of guidelines to a jury as to when it may find intention. In its post-*Woollin* form[30] this involves the notion that a jury is 'not entitled to find' intention unless members of the jury feel sure that 'death or serious bodily harm

28 The *Yip* problem could be resolved by using a defence in the law of complicity, but that would not resolve the overall concern: that the proviso is either too narrow to do all the work it should, or potentially too broad to be acceptable.

29 See n 13.

30 See n 3.

was a virtual certainty (barring some unforeseen intervention) as a result of the defendant's actions, and the defendant appreciated that such was the case'.[31]

The second Law Commission proposal takes this formula up without alteration as a means of finding indirect intent, whilst direct intent is defined, as in the definitional approach, as acting in order to bring a result about. The argument in support of this approach is that it takes all the strain out of the first proposal. The fact-finder is not required to reach a particular conclusion, but is permitted 'the freedom to find, or not to find, intent, in the way the common law does at present' (4.65), and it therefore avoids 'creating the difficulty which calls for the development of a proviso' (4.66).

In a sense there is nothing new here, and therefore perhaps less to discuss. However, it is worth thinking about the precise status of the 'entitled to find' formula within the law. The Law Commission clearly thinks that this formula is the means whereby 'moral elbow room' is permitted in the law, but I wonder whether this is really the case. It is true that the cases culminating in *Woollin* and *Matthews and Alleyne* have as their direct ancestor Lord Scarman's observations in favour of a jury's judgment in the earlier *Hancock and Shankland*,[32] but is it the case that this formula makes a genuine moral difference in subsequent cases? If we take the Court of Appeal's judgment in *Re A (children)*,[33] a case where one might have expected consideration of what a jury was 'entitled to find', two of the three judges stuck to the view that the mens rea for murder was present, and that there was therefore the need for a defence. Robert Walker LJ did, it is true, query whether there was an appropriate intention, but he did so in terms of a discussion about intention and double effect, and made no mention of the 'entitled to find' formula in *Woollin*.[34]

Similarly, in the trial of Dr Moor (Arlidge 2000), a case of injecting drugs which would have the anticipated effect of shortening life, it is reported that the trial judge finessed the issue by instructing the jury in terms of two alternatives, one based on direct intention, the other on recklessness, avoiding consideration of the virtual certainty formula and the possibility of the jury being 'entitled to find' intention. In other cases involving doctors who kill, the formula of 'primary purpose' and the possibility of double effect have been called into service rather than 'entitled to find', although admittedly these cases predate *Woollin* and much of the speculation about how the law works. There is nonetheless an element of speculation in academic writing as to how, or if, 'entitled to find' works, although

31 See *Nedrick* (n 21).

32 [1986] 2 WLR 357.

33 See n 25.

34 It might be said here that the problem in *Re A (children)* was that there was no jury who could claim their entitlement to find (or not) intention. That did not however stop the judges from finding themselves 'entitled' to conclude that there was no breach of Article 2 of the ECHR. There was no intention to deprive of life according to the 'natural and ordinary meaning' of intention, and in terms of the doctors' 'purpose': see *Re A (children)* (n 25) 1050, 1068.

this is aligned with their appreciation of a real problem in the law: that it needs to find a way to deal with cases involving 'good motive'. Academics have put two and two together, but I am unsure that the judges have said that this makes four.

In any case, would it be possible for the judges to admit a substantial lacuna at the very core of the criminal law? Would they be comfortable to state in judgment that in effect the law runs out at this point, and juries are therefore entitled to make up their own minds according to their own moral perceptions? I suspect it is much easier to phrase the issue in terms of time delay, as in *Matthews and Alleyne*: the judges have 'not yet'[35] reached a decision on the law. The underlying problem remains one of how to deal with morally challenging cases alongside a cognitive definition of intention.

The Law Commission's first model does this through rules plus a proviso, but the proviso looks as if it will cause as many problems as it solves. The second model, based on the common law, muddles through in a way that perhaps permits some consideration of moral issues within the law by leaving matters ultimately at large, with the possibility of coded encouragement to juries to get the law's cognitivism off the hook in appropriate cases. Putting this more positively, in the case of doctors 'easing the passing', the common law approach can perhaps finesse the value conflict in society between doctrines of sanctity and quality of life in a way acceptable to most people. But this is to some extent speculative. Where it does take us, of course, is to the doctrine of double effect, which closes the Law Commission's account of intention.

Double effect

No doubt, double effect is a contentious doctrine. The Law Commission considers two versions of it: one in which the conflicting moral outcomes are taken to operate within one ethically broadened definition of intention (4.81), the other in which the different moral effects are distinguished as matters of primary or secondary intention (4.83). Whichever approach is adopted, the effect is the same, that responsibility for a bad consequence is avoided by treating the defendant's intention in the light of an alternative good consequence. Double effect identifies, in the case of two consequences and their attendant intentions, a moral threshold, wherein the good effect is permitted to override the bad by a moral accounting, which is then cast in terms of intention. Put another way, intentions, treated *in their form* as abstract cognitive mental states, are enriched through moral double effect doctrine by a *substantive* moral judgment of what the intention in its content was.[36]

Whilst the Law Commission notes the arguments in favour of double effect, it in fact eventually rejects it as part of the law of intention. It subscribes to the

35 See *Matthews and Alleyne* (n 23) para 43. Compare the discussion below, ch 5, at pp 91–2.

36 The first of these is from Finnis (1991); the second from Kennedy and Grubb, (1994).

Kennedy and Grubb view that, in the case of medical practitioners hastening death, the doctor intends the death of the patient, but it is a non-culpable intention that the law in effect permits. The Law Commission take this to mean that a defence is required (4.89). Certainly, this appears to conform to the legal situation as stated by the majority in *Re A (children)*, but I think the position is not as clear-cut as suggested here. There are, for example, discussions of double effect in other cases involving medical practitioners,[37] there is the 'primary intention' or purpose rule in some cases,[38] and there is the famous view in the non-murder case of *Gillick* that '[T]he *bona fide* exercise by a doctor of his clinical judgment must be a complete negation of the guilty mind'[39] on a charge of aiding and abetting unlawful sexual intercourse. These point in the direction of double effect and intention, even if it is hardly articulated in explicit legal rules. Furthermore, although the Law Commission set its face against double effect with regard to intention, it is arguable that the proviso to its definitional account is itself a version of double effect.

The Law Commission concludes its discussion with the contention that it is now 'an accepted part of the common law that a doctor may lawfully prescribe [pain killing] medication [to a terminally ill patient] and, thereby, have a defence to murder' (4.90). This statement needs further consideration. Is this part of the common law, and on what basis? The evidence of Dr Moor's case and the primary intention rule suggest that the lawfulness of such actions is not resolved as a matter of defence, but as a matter of mens rea. It is at this point that the Law Commission's reasoning becomes weak. It says that these cases should be resolved on the basis of defences (although it did not think this when discussing the proviso to the definitional approach, with regard to the father jumping from the burning building). The Law Commission takes refuge in its initial statement that the justificatory defences are not considered here (1.3, 4.91), and in a simple assertion that the relationship between offence and defence is one without substance (footnote to 4.89).

This is not the place to contest that claim in depth (see Norrie, 2014, 229–33), but I do think it requires some kind of backing in argument if for no other reason than that the Law Commission's whole report is premised on the possibility of distinguishing the definition of the offence of murder, especially intention, from defences. Since the Commission's resolution of the moral problems attaching to the definition of intention is based upon the assertion that these can be treated as defence elements distinct from the definition of the offence, it is surely problematic to conclude that the offence/defence line is without substance. Similarly, the initial declaration that the law can be stated without consideration of the justificatory defences looks strange.

37 See Brooke LJ in *Re A (children)* (n 25) at 1029 and Lord Goff in *Airedale NHS Trust v Bland* [1993] AC 789, 867.

38 *R v Cox* (n 10).

39 *Gillick v West Norfolk and Wisbech Area Health Authority* [1986] AC 112, 190.

It should, however, be noted that the issue of double effect becomes more urgent if the definitional approach to intention is adopted, since the common law informal approach can (subject to the questions raised above) admit double effect issues within its interstices. With the definitional approach, it is hard to see how they can be dealt with without seriously contemplating justificatory defences, as of course did the Court of Appeal in *Re A (children)*.

Conclusion

The Law Commission's review of the law of intention confirms the view stated elsewhere,[40] that the English law of intention for murder is based upon an understanding that lacks in two opposite ways. First, as regards direct intention, the law is morally under-inclusive in that it places too much moral weight on a psychological conception of the required mental state. It therefore fails to recognise properly the issue and significance of the concept of 'indiscriminate malice'. Second, as regards direct and indirect intention, the law is morally over-inclusive, failing to differentiate culpable and non-culpable acts. It therefore requires supplementing either with a conception of moral threshold or double effect, or with a full consideration of the offence/defence line, or both.

These issues arise because of the English tradition of orthodox subjectivism. They are thrown into relief as a result of case law and practical problems, and also recent writings taking a more morally substantive or contextual approach. In the Law Commission's report, the matter is also affected by the framing of the issues in terms of the prioritisation of one form of culpability (intention) and this is linked to the continuing significance of the mandatory life sentence in English criminal law. The question that lingers, and which the report does not address, is how different the law of murder might be if it did not take place in the shadow of that particular totem and its associated taboos.

40 See Norrie (1999).

Chapter 4

The problem of mistaken self-defence: citizenship, chiasmus and legal form

On 22 July 2005, officers of London's Metropolitan Police shot dead an innocent Brazilian, Jean-Charles de Menezes, on the Underground. They had mistakenly believed him to be a suicide bomber. Although the police force was successfully prosecuted under health and safety legislation for the death, no prosecution for a serious homicide offence was attempted against either the force or individual police officers. The shooting dead, seemingly without warning, of an innocent man on the London Underground by armed, non-uniformed, police officers has a chilling quality. It is no doubt the case that suicide bombing presents new challenges to policing, but there have been other cases of innocent people, such as Harry Stanley (Crown Prosecution Service 2005a), being shot dead. Even with suspected suicide bombers, the police cannot enjoy *carte blanche*, yet the fact remains that these cases have not been subjected to the check or oversight that serious criminal charges should bring.

The Crown Prosecution Service for England and Wales (CPS) declined to mount a prosecution in the de Menezes case on the view that there was not a realistic prospect of conviction (Crown Prosecution Service 2006). This essay considers why the CPS should have taken this position, and the state of the English law of mistaken self-defence that made it possible. In the process, attention is given to the law's underlying structure of offence and defence, and justification and excuse, and how it operates differentially in different moral and social contexts. This permits us in turn to consider the nature of citizenship in a modern Western society, as reflected in its legal categories.

The shooting dead of unarmed citizens raises concerns about the nature of police powers and the role of the state with regard to the citizen. In terms of modern critical criminal justice scholarship, it suggests the kind of development in criminalisation and citizenship that one associates with the shift from a social democratic to a neo-liberal form of government (Garland 2001; Simon 2007). It suggests, indeed, a weighting of citizenship concerns away from the classical model of the liberal rights-bearing subject and toward forms of state authoritarianism (Ramsay 2006; Ashworth and Zedner 2008). On its face, the decision not to prosecute police officers looks like an acceptance of current trends toward the diminution of citizenship liberties in favour of the recognition that there are individuals or groups, such as 'terrorists', who, lacking the essentials of citizenship,[1] are regarded as beyond the pale.

I do not want to deny the importance of such broader structural currents in the understanding of citizenship, or that these affect and shape the criminal law today. I do, however, want to sound a note of caution with regard to the analysis of cases involving police shooting in terms of a simple opposition between liberal and authoritarian terms. In such cases, it is difficult to prosecute on serious criminal charges, but not necessarily because of a shift to authoritarian legal standards governing the criminal law. Rather, it is the law of mistaken self-defence, reformed 25 years ago in what was then argued to be a principled *liberal* way, that is the problem. By 'liberal', I mean a form of law reflecting a sense of citizenship that is respectful toward individuals and socially inclusive in its form. The paradox is that it is this form of liberal-inflected, citizenship-respecting, law that informs the English law of mistaken self-defence and that has contributed to the difficulty in prosecuting police officers in these cases.

Accordingly, if we want to understand the failure of the criminal law to control the use of guns by armed police officers on our streets, it will not be enough to argue that we have shifted from liberal to authoritarian modes of governance, although that may be part of the overall picture. Rather, it will be necessary to understand the logic and dynamic of *liberal* criminal law, and its complicity in permitting the police use of firearms without proper checks. It is as much the classic liberal conception of citizenship as it is reflected in law that needs to be examined as shifts in a non-liberal direction. This essay is concerned, then, to provide a more complex understanding of the relationship between the classic liberal conception of citizenship and the nature of state authoritarianism insofar as the former informs the present law of mistaken self-defence in England and Wales, and permits the shooting of unarmed and innocent citizens to occur without an appropriate checking mechanism through the criminal law.

This chapter has four sections. In the first, I outline the debate in England concerning the proper test for mistaken self-defence and introduce the idea that a normative chiasmus lurks unattended at the law's core. Outlining the implications of this argument, I then proceed in the second section to explore attempts to deal with it. Arguing that these are inadequate, I then investigate why the chiasmus should exist, drawing on Kent Greenawalt's (1984) analysis of the 'perplexing borders' of justification and excuse in the criminal law. In a brief final section, I consider the implications of the analysis for our understanding of the law and its relationship to the idea of liberal citizenship.

1 An old formulation worth pondering today: see Bosanquet (1919: 210). This chapter works as an immanent critique of the law of self-defence, drawing upon the problem posed by the chiasmus at its heart. As explained in the next section, a chiasmus involves a contradiction, expressed rhetorically by means of parallelism and reversed, as in 'Do not live to eat, but eat to live'. For a fuller structured analysis of the law, see Norrie (2014: ch 10).

Mistaken self-defence and chiasmus

Amongst criminal law commentators, the consensus is that the present law of self-defence in England and Wales is inadequate (Simester 1992; Ashworth 2009; Leverick 2007: ch 2).[2] Under the law as it presently stands, an honest mistake is enough to avoid liability, and most commentators argue that in its place a standard of reasonableness, which can be attuned to specific contexts, is more appropriate. The honest mistake standard is too easy to meet, and includes examples of behaviour where a defendant can deny wrongdoing by claiming that he acted according to an honest, even if unreasonable, belief. Of course, members of a jury may not believe him and so convict, but if they do believe he made an honest mistake, they ought to acquit. With regard to police shootings, why would the police officers have shot Stanley or de Menezes[3] except for the fact that they honestly believed them to present a significant danger? In which case, as the Crown Prosecution Service found, there was little prospect of securing a conviction, even if there was little evidence for thinking that the police action was reasonable or well founded. The law, therefore, ought to be changed.

Behind the argument of the commentators in favour of a reasonableness standard lies a seemingly valid critique of the direction the law of mistaken self-defence took in *R v Williams (Gladstone)*[4] and *Beckford v R*,[5] cases following the so-called 'inexorable logic' of mens rea established in the earlier rape case of *DPP v Morgan*.[6] In the cases of *Williams* and *Beckford*, both defendants, a young man on a bus and an armed police officer, mistakenly believed that there was a valid ground for self-defence. Both were given a denial of mens rea defence based on their honest mistake in carrying out a lawful act. Extending the *Morgan* rule from the law of rape, the courts argued that there could be no crime where the person's mistake meant he did not intend it, and the lack of intention negated the offence.

Offences of violence require the intention to carry out an unlawful act and where this did not exist, there could be no crime. If there had been no mistake, the action would have been justified, it would not have been unlawful, and there would be no offence. Where there was a mistake, there lacked mens rea for the unlawful act, and therefore no offence. The weight of analysis shifted from the lack of actus reus (no unlawful act) to lack of mens rea (honest belief in no unlawful act).

2 But see Ormerod (2005: 331–32).

3 'The two officers who fired the fatal shots did so because they thought that Mr de Menezes had been identified to them as a suicide bomber and that if they did not shoot him, he would blow up the train, killing many people. In order to prosecute those officers, we would have to prove, beyond reasonable doubt, that they did not honestly and genuinely hold those beliefs. In fact, the evidence supports their claim that they genuinely believed that Mr de Menezes was a suicide bomber and therefore, as we cannot disprove that claim, we cannot prosecute them for murder or any other related offence' (Crown Prosecution Service 2006).

4 *R v Williams (Gladstone)* [1987] 3 All ER 411.

5 *Beckford v R* [1988] AC 130.

6 *DPP v Morgan* [1976] AC 182.

The critique contends that it is wrong in doctrinal terms to treat mistaken self-defence as involving, as *R v Williams (Gladstone)* established, an absence of mens rea and therefore a failure to establish the 'definition of the offence'. The law of self-defence, the argument goes, does not hinge on establishing mens rea, so that the honest mistake rule evolved in Morgan for mens rea should not apply. Rather, self-defence should be seen as a distinct defence, once the offence has been established. Mistakes as to self-defence, freed from the definition of the offence (mens rea plus actus reus) formula, should be seen to involve a separate defence and, removed from the sphere of mens rea, be subject to a reasonableness test reflecting the different contexts in which self-defence operates.

This argument rests on an understanding of the formal structure of the criminal law as involving meaningful categories of offence and defence and, I shall argue below, of justification and excuse. It is an attractive argument that, if followed, could perhaps permit a more circumspect form of control to be directed at those such as the police officers in the Stanley or de Menezes cases. Yet – and this is the nub of my argument – it is simplistic, for its foundation in the law's formal structure of offence and defence places more weight there than can be borne. The law's structural definitions of actus reus, mens rea and defences, leading to a definition of the offence/defence distinction, lack the fixity required to make the critics' argument stick. This is witnessed, I shall argue, in the case of mistaken self-defence, by the existence of irresolution and instability around a normative chiasmus, based on offence and defence and justification and excuse, at the law's theoretical core.

What is chiasmus, and how does it operate in law? In general terms, chiasmus is a rhetorical figure from the Greek to denote a contrast created by parallelism and reversal, as in 'Do not live to eat, but eat to live'. It is linked to other rhetorical forms such as antithesis, but antithesis is philosophical as well as rhetorical in its uses, and this is the clue to how I use it to illuminate the law. I want to consider whether the juxtaposition of opposing, reversed formulae might indicate something more profound than an effect in speech or for the purposes of persuasion.

In the chiasmus of living and eating, the rhetorical purpose is plain in that the contrast is weighted to favour the second term – but does chiasmus always operate in this way? Consider for example Dr Johnson's more legal effort to distinguish nature from custom, as 'that which is established because it is right from that which is right only because it is established' (Cuddon 1992: 47). Dr Johnson appears to favour the first term in this contrast, but it might be pointed out that, in a legal world where custom and nature are both relevant as sources of law, the contrast picks out a conflict in legal sources, an antithesis (opposition) or antinomy (contradictory law) or aporia (impassable path) for law. So we can think of chiasmus either as a nice way of contrasting two different routes, where the contrast persuades us which is the correct route, or we can think of it as designating a site of conflict or opposition, where the contrast helps bring out the oppositional character of what is at stake and suggests *neither* route might be entirely correct or passable.

What of chiasmus and self-defence? I suggest that the law of mistaken self-defence can be expressed in terms of chiasmus. Where a person makes a mistake about the necessity for self-defence, she can either be said to have done an act that is objectively right, but for some subjective reason was wrong, or she can be said to have done an objectively wrong act, but to have done so for a subjective reason that is viewed as right, by herself, or by society.[7] However, the point is precisely drawn: a chiasmic contrast can be expressed in non-technical terms as 'doing the right thing for a wrong reason' versus 'doing the wrong thing for a right reason' or, perhaps, using broader and more capacious language, 'doing an acceptable thing for an unacceptable reason' versus 'doing an unacceptable thing for an acceptable reason'. The contrast can be expressed in the terms, in other words, of chiasmus.

Is this then a matter of legal rhetoric, or are deeper issues and consequences at stake? Behind the inversionary logic of propositions, one can glimpse such issues for the law of mistaken self-defence. If one follows the line of the initial proposition in the chiasmus, doing the (objectively) right thing for a (subjectively) wrong reason, we are in the realm of mistaken self-defence as a form of *justificatory* defence, for doing 'the right thing' overall has the normative strength to carry the mistake. The justification may be imperfect, but justification it is. On the other hand, if we follow the second proposition, doing the (objectively) wrong thing for a (subjectively) right reason, we are in the realm not of imperfect justification but of objectively non-justified action for which an acceptable subjective exculpatory ground is required. We are in the realm of *excuse*, for the act is held to be wrong and so we have to look at the exculpatory reasons why the person did it to see if she has a defence. Thus, the chiasmus rests on the division between justification and excuse within the criminal law.

More than that, however, it also reflects on the distinction between offence and defence. If we think of mistaken self-defence in terms of excuse, then an offence has been committed, and a separate defence is needed. If, however, we follow the line of argument that mistaken self-defence carries us into the realm of imperfect justification, then it signifies that no offence has been committed, and no defence, in the logical (as opposed to procedural) or 'true'[8] sense, is necessary. The underlying point is that matters of excuse and justification sit differently with regard to the definition of the offence. With the former, an offence has been committed and a defence is required. With the latter, logically no offence is committed and therefore, strictly, subject to an argument below, no defence is required.

If we pursue the argument, it has implications for the cases on mistaken self-defence. It could be argued, for example, for reasons I elaborate below, that *R v Williams (Gladstone)* was rightly decided as a case of imperfect justification, and

7 The precise formula, and what it accepts, will of course vary between jurisdictions.

8 Cf the discussion of duress in *R v Hasan* [2005] UKHL 22.

therefore bearing on the 'definition of the offence,'[9] but that the slightly later case of *Beckford*, which involved police officers shooting an unarmed suspect in the Caribbean, should have been seen as a case of excusatory defence, the offence having been established. This argument hinges on two things. First, it concerns the modal difference between questions of justification and excuse, and the sense that justificatory defences ultimately entail that no wrong, and no crime, has been done. Second, it depends on a socio-political judgment of the different rights and wrongs of active citizenship in *Williams* in comparison to those of bad armed policing in *Beckford*.

We may be more likely to construe the former as imperfectly justified than the latter. In consequence, some cases of mistaken self-defence can be validly analysed as entailing a standard of honest mistake because they do indeed go to mens rea and the definition of the offence, whereas others should be analysed as requiring that the mistake be based on reasonable grounds because they are properly based on a separate category of excusatory defence. The critics, because they cannot grasp that some cases lead in one direction, whilst others lead in the other, are unable to grasp fully the nature of the problem in this area of the law.

The chiasmus thus has implications for the lines drawn in law between offence and defence and between justification and excuse, and for the moral work that theorists want these supposedly clear categories to do. The underlying issue concerns how cases are socially, morally and politically perceived, and such perceptions rest in turn upon particular normative expectations of how citizens should act in different circumstances. Different perceptions would pertain where the mistaken citizen is for example an active and responsible member of the public, a householder threatened by an intruder, a woman in a violent and abusive relationship or an armed police officer or soldier on duty.

These perceptions affect the normative appreciation of what is done as either *right* but misconceivedly so, or *wrong* but excusably so. If the former, we are in the area of imperfect justification. If the latter, we are in the realm of wrongdoing requiring an excuse. Whereas the latter permits self-defence to be seen as a defence in opposition to the definition of the offence, the former is more problematic. Imperfect justification opens up the possibility that the mistaken act of self-defence negates the mens rea. In this way we see how visions of citizenship and norms of citizen conduct work to produce the moral chiasmus at the heart of mistaken self-defence and produce irresolution in the law's formal structure. In the process, I shall argue, we see the irreducible moral and political choices that law, even (especially) in its core formal concepts, entails.

9 Bearing on the definition of the offence because of the requirement that the offence involves intention (mens rea) to perform an 'unlawful' act (actus reus). I assume here what I argue for below: that the category of justificatory defence is harder to justify theoretically than that of excusatory defence because it involves claiming there can be a criminal act where a person has acted rightly in an objective sense.

Offence and defence: the prima facie argument

Commentators generally want to see mistaken self-defence as a matter of excuse, the definition of the offence having been satisfied. Working out why, however, causes problems. Andrew Ashworth, for example, sees self-defence in general terms as justificatory, and as negating the commission of an offence: 'Where the defendant's act is regarded as justifiable (e.g., self-defence), the act is not wrongful' so that justifications 'negate criminal conduct' (Ashworth 2009: 97–98). If self-defence negates criminal conduct, there is no actus reus, so where does this leave mistaken self-defence? The problem is that if one analyses justified acts in terms of absence of actus reus, one is committing to a mens rea – actus reus (definition of the offence) analysis of self-defence. Yet Ashworth opposes the extension of *Morgan* to self-defence cases. He contends that the law should be founded on 'considerations of moral fault rather than dictated by an abstracted "logic"', and his means of distancing himself from the abstracted logic of *Morgan* is to question the key assumption in *Williams* and *Beckford* that 'unlawfulness is a definitional element in all crimes' (ibid: 217).

It is not clear how this can be reconciled with the claim that self-defence is justificatory, and that justifications negate criminal conduct. The approach Ashworth would prefer looks at the moral context in which people act, rather than simplistically at what they honestly believed, but how to evade the logic of *Morgan*? The proposed answer lies in the idea of prima facie wrongfulness, which involves reflecting that there is after all *something* wrong in an act of self-defence: 'Using force is prima facie wrongful and should put a citizen on notice to examine the grounds for doing so' (ibid). The argument draws on the distinction between 'prima facie' offences and 'supervening' defences elaborated by Andrew Simester and John Gardner, amongst others (Simester 1992; Gardner 2007: ch 5). This argument seeks to sustain the possibility that an act can be justified, yet still brought within the terms of an offence, and therefore needs to be exonerated by the application of a separate defence. Andrew Simester, for example, has written that a prima facie offence is one that 'is considered sufficiently reprehensible to warrant its proscription' (Simester 1992: 303) for a wrong is inflicted on a victim. The supervening defence is then 'oriented towards the *defendant's circumstances* in which he commits the prima facie offence (and thereby wrongs the victim)' (ibid: 303–304).

The problem with this is that, where a justified act has been carried out on another person, there is in fact no wrong inflicted on him. There is initially what may (or may not) *look like* a wrong, and it may of course be experienced as such by its sufferer, but it turns out on further specification to be something else. There may be a seeming wrong, which a process of criminal investigation should examine, but if investigation or trial finds no wrong was done, there never was a wrong in terms of legal logic that a 'supervening' defence needs to cure, and 'prima facie' has its proper 'at first sight' meaning.

The distinction between prima facie offences and defences point has been elaborated by Gardner. He has written that there is a sense of prima facie wrongdoing that contrasts with an 'all things considered' judgment of the same events. The former is the domain of the offence, the latter of the defences. In this framework, all reasons for criminalising an action may have been defeated in the final analysis, so that it was all right for the defendant to act as she did, but it does not mean that the initial reasons fall from the picture: 'That a reason is defeated does not mean that it is undermined or cancelled. It still continues to exert its rational appeal' (Gardner 2007: 96–97).

My counter-argument is that this is a distinction without a difference, for how could a reason be 'defeated' without being 'undermined or cancelled' (Norrie 2000: 153)? Of course, a reason such as 'Thou shalt not kill' retains its rational appeal *in the abstract*, but it fails to deal with situations where it is justifiable to kill – for example, in defence of oneself or one's family, or in time of (just) war. In general, killing may be wrong, but saying so casts no legal shadow on the person who kills in self-defence. As soon as it is applied to these situations, it is appropriate to say that the rule is defeated both in the instant case and in all cases like it. Its defeat in such cases means that it is indeed undermined and cancelled, even if it retains its overall attractiveness, unapplied, in the abstract.[10]

Moral judgments require a degree of concreteness, and they establish their rational appeal in the situations to which they are applied. Ashworth is right in his initial claim that matters of justification function in criminal law differently than do excuses. They establish the rightness or wrongness of conduct, but this means that they are problematic for the line between offence and defence. The prima facie argument trades on a conflation of questions of evidence and appearance on one hand and moral substance on the other. Whether an act is prima facie one thing (right) or another (wrong) is neither here nor there, for what matters is not its prima facie quality at all. What matters is whether it *is* right or wrong, in which case either the logic of justification or excuse will be invoked *mutatis mutandis*.[11]

10 There is a deeper point on which Gardner and I agree. We both argue that the complexity, moral depth, and, I would add, social and political conflict expressed in moral reasoning makes it and precise legal rules uneasy bedfellows. However, the question is how the relationship between legal and ethical form is understood. Gardner, in my view, misunderstands the nature of a critical analysis of law when he suggests (2007: 253–5) that a critical approach is essentially Kantian and lawyerly because it probes the limits of legal formalism. The space for critical enquiry lies between law's formalist practice (the Kantian need for the rule-of-law virtues of coherence, certainty, generality) and an understanding of the fluidity, conflict, and depth in moral judgment. Hence it is important from a critical point of view to consider the different modalities of ethics *and* law, and to measure law immanently, against its expectations of itself. To test law against its own Kantian principles is to pursue an immanent critique, not to become a Kantian, or to adopt a 'legal' approach.

11 Gardner has produced an intriguing argument in response (Gardner 2007: 253–55). He suggests one should set a classical Greek understanding of right and wrongdoing in opposition to a rationalist Enlightenment sensibility. In the latter, the question of right and wrong is closed off by a rational principled judgment. In the former, wrongdoing has depth and retains its moral power, whatever rationalism may ordain as right. Life is tragic and fateful, so that we may do the right because it is the rational thing, yet our actions may be stained by wrongfulness. I find this idea morally

The matter is not resolved here.[12] Suffice it to say that there is good reason for arguing that justifications are differently placed from excuses in the criminal law. The former set the contours of wrongdoing, whilst the latter are dependent on such contours having been established. Accordingly, if conduct is regarded as objectively right but subjectively mistaken, it stands logically in a different place in the law than conduct that is objectively wrong but carried out for a subjectively good reason. These comments suggest that the rhetorical device of chiasmus may have something to tell us about a particular problem in the criminal law and about its underlying structure.

Chiasmus at the border

Further insight as to what is at stake here is provided by George Fletcher and especially Kent Greenawalt (Fletcher 1998; Greenawalt 1984).[13] Fletcher describes 'putative' (mistaken) self-defence as a problem 'at the borderline' of justification and excuse and suggests that the law deals with it in three ways. The first two point in the direction of justification. First, the problem is assimilated with the case of actual justification, as happens in the United States Model Penal Code, where a reasonable belief in attack is treated as equivalent to an actual attack. Fletcher notes that it is not clear why in this position the mistake needs to be reasonable, and that voices 'are often heard for the so-called subjective view of justification' (1998: 88). This is of course precisely what happens, as we saw, in England and Wales. Alternatively, second, a mistake about the conditions of a justification can be taken to be like a mistake about the object of the required offence; that is, it can be taken to be a mistake about actus reus.

Although Fletcher does not say so, this is in effect an approach licensed by the first approach and applied to the formal structure of the law. What the first spells out as a form of moral equivalence, the second confirms in the language of mens rea and actus reus. Precisely why one would treat the legal status of an act of violence as conditioned by the mental element (mistake) on the actus reus could only be because the act was seen as being lawful, and lawful because justified, even though it was the outcome of a mistake. Again, this is just what happens in England and Wales under *Williams* and *Beckford*.

Both the first and second approaches thus involve justificatory logics. A third alternative, however, is to bring the law of putative self-defence under the law of excuse and 'genuine' defence as focusing '. . . on the possibility of excusing rather

compelling, but still wonder how it relates to law and legal judgment. There, institutional closure is precisely what is sought, so to pray to tragic judgment in aid of law and legal understanding seems a stretch. There is nonetheless a compelling, but uneasy, relationship between a metaphysical conception of ethics and legal justice. See chapter 7, below.

12 For recent discussion, see Tadros (2005) and Duff (2007: ch 7).

13 For criticism of Fletcher's general analysis of the offence/defence line, see Norrie (2000: 155–65).

than justifying the use of force. The argument is that a mistake about the conditions of justification constitutes an excuse parallel to the excuses of insanity, personal necessity, and duress. The mistake allegedly negates the voluntariness of the act . . .' (ibid: 89).[14]

Why favour this third approach? Fletcher wants to argue that it may be important for victims and the public that the law distinguish in cases of putative self-defence whether an act is justified from whether it is excused. In cases such as the police beating of Rodney King or the vigilantism of Bernard Goetz, the public wants to know that, if the defendants are acquitted, their actions are not justified even if they are excused. The victim too appreciates the difference between an acquittal that says that the defendant's actions were 'justified and therefore not wrongful or whether they are treated as excuses bearing exclusively on culpability for wrongful conduct' (ibid: 90). It would be much better to deploy the language of justification and excuse so that a jury could find that 'conduct was unjustified, that [putative self-defenders] had violated the rights of the victim, but that they were personally excused' (ibid).

Setting aside the point that the public and the victim might prefer that their attackers in these cases were found guilty, and given neither justificatory nor excusatory defence, Fletcher has a point about the appropriate marking or fair labelling of offences and defences. However, is he right to say that putative self-defence should be resolved as excuse, as doing the objectively wrong thing for a subjectively right reason? If the different approaches he identifies reflect the chiasmus, is he correct to favour the one side over the other? Or, are the English law and the Model Penal Code on the better line? Or, a third alternative argued for here, might both be right, but in different circumstances?

In making his argument, Fletcher takes as his foil Kent Greenawalt's essay on the complex boundaries (the 'perplexing borders') of justification and excuse. He takes Greenawalt to be suggesting that the issue of justification or excuse is resolved as a matter of social utility. It is not a question of whether the invasion of a victim's interests was justified but 'whether the risk that the actor took – regardless of the impact on the victim – was reasonable and therefore justified' (ibid). Greenawalt's argument, however, is more complex than this, and involves an understanding of the shifting boundaries of justification and excuse within the law and, underlying the law, morals. It is an argument about the moral sensitivity of the borderline, so that judgments of right and wrong can go either way where mistakes about rightful action are concerned. Two examples from Greenawalt will illustrate.

First, in a non-legal situation, Al refuses to speak to Bruce because Bruce has betrayed his confidence (Greenawalt 1984: 1904–905). We may say that Al is within his rights in not speaking to Bruce but that, in an ideal world, he would

14 This argument requires a distinction between physical and moral in/voluntariness, because a physically involuntary act negates actus reus on most analyses. Fletcher does indeed provide such a distinction.

have responded to Bruce in a better way. He might for example have approached Bruce, engaged with Bruce's betrayal and sought his apology, for which Al in turn would have given his forgiveness. So is Al justified in not speaking to Bruce? Maybe, maybe not. Perhaps Al occupies a middle ground where we would not say that his action was justified, but nor would we say that he was in need of an excuse. What we have here 'is a claim in defence of action that may not fit smoothly into either of the two categories' (ibid: 1904).

Nor is this simply a borderline issue: Greenawalt indicates how the classification of Al's conduct as justification or excuse depends on the kind of morality we deploy, and how high we set the moral bar. From a perfectionist view of ethics, for example, we would be more inclined to say that Al's behaviour has been deficient because he has not reached the appropriately high standards required for friendship. He should have been open to Bruce, so his conduct reveals a blameworthy failure for which he needs to be excused. Perhaps he was, for example, emotionally harmed as a child and finds friendship very difficult. In contrast, a more prosaic quotidian morality may find that Al's conduct is well within the range of normal moral reactions to betrayal, and he is to be judged against that range. In that context, his reaction is quite justified.

Second, moving to a legal situation, Greenawalt discusses inter alia a case of self-defence, the rule concerning retreat in one's own dwelling from an intruder (ibid: 1906). He imagines a legislative drafting committee in which one member thinks refusal to retreat is positively desirable since it symbolises the importance of the home and endorses a 'forfeiture' view of rights vis-à-vis intruders. A second member thinks it better to retreat where this is possible but that refusal to do so is nonetheless permissible. A third thinks it is definitely wrong not to retreat where possible, as a duty is owed *ceteris paribus* even to an intruder. Taking these three different positions, one can see that where one stands on the *moral* issue of retreat affects how one casts the *legal* defence, as justification or excuse:

> The first plainly thinks failure to retreat is justified, the second regards it as justified only in the broad sense of morally permitted, the third thinks the actor who declines to retreat when he knows he can do so safely has only an excuse . . . based upon common human weakness (ibid).

As with Al and Bruce, the different moral standpoint affects significantly how one sees the issue, so that a decision between justification and excuse is not, *pace* Fletcher, a question of placing a general social value against an individual victim's rights, but the general way in which one achieves a moral and political balance between a number of relevant factors in a decision on a particular case. In this more complex situation, there is considerable room for a plurality of, and conflict between, moral and political views, and these establish in a fluid context whether a set of facts give rise to a situation of justification or excuse.

How does Greenawalt's argument affect the chiasmus of justification and excuse in the law of mistaken self-defence? Its logic is to suggest that one could go either way depending upon how one calls an issue morally and politically. Take *Williams.*[15] The court held that he was not guilty because he had the intention to do a lawful act, and therefore could not have the intention to do an unlawful one. His actions were brought under a rule of justified action, and therefore he did not need an excuse. Was this reasoning itself justified? Imagine two countries. In the first, a state and its police force govern through the law and rely upon a high degree of consensus between governors and governed. In such a situation, much emphasis is placed upon the links between the citizenry and the police, and therefore, to a degree, on citizen participation. In the second country, less emphasis is placed upon policing by consent; the police are seen as an arm of government who are given latitude in applying the law to a population that is regarded as subservient. Participation is frowned upon since it gets in the way of authoritative and authoritarian determinations of wrongdoing, and disrupts the clear lines between citizen, police and an overarching state.

In terms of mistaken self-defence and whether it operates as justification or excuse, it matters which state one lives under. In the first case, where citizen participation is encouraged, the citizen is likely to be supported in making a citizen's arrest, and is also likely to be given latitude where she makes a mistake. In such a case, the citizen has done what was best, but not got it right. She has sought to do the right thing and, in so seeking, even though getting it wrong, has still done the right thing overall. That she has done it wrongly is brought under the moral and political wing of the primary moral fact that it was right to become involved in the first place. The basic overall rectitude of what she did 'carries' her mistake. It would have been better to get it right, but doing it and getting it wrong was still the (imperfectly) right thing to do.

In the second case, it is different. Where citizen participation is frowned upon, the initial presumption is that one does not intervene personally or directly. One may, but only with extreme caution, under the maxim 'Citizen Beware!' Admittedly, one might have had a good purpose in making the arrest, but this must be understood in the context of seeing that this is the sort of thing people should not do. It was essentially improper to intervene, and this negatively colours any mistake in the terms of moral judgment. If someone did intervene mistakenly, she would need a secondary reason why she is not to be adjudged a wrongdoer, relating for example to her ignorance of the rule or the necessity of the situation. Alternatively, it might simply be a case of saying that a person acted wrongly, but her mistake is to be excused. Thus, depending upon the overall ideology of the society, Gladstone Williams could be said to have done the objectively right thing subjectively wrongly or the objectively wrong thing subjectively rightly. In the former case, his action would be justified and, in the latter, excused.

Similarly, considering *Beckford*,[16] whether his actions as an armed policeman are regarded as justified or excused depends upon how one regards the position of an

15 See n 4 above.
16 See n 5 above.

armed police officer facing an unarmed citizen. Academic commentary tends to the view that the police officer is in a position of real power in having a gun and should have the training, the expertise and the character to use it appropriately (Ashworth 2009; Horder 1990). Where he mistakenly shoots an unarmed citizen, he fails to do this. He falls short in a situation where he ought not to, and the outcome is unacceptable. Therefore, if he is to have a defence it is one of (warranted) excuse. It is wrong to kill an unarmed person, so he must plead some special reason why he should be exonerated.

An alternative view would be something like this. The police are required to do inherently dangerous jobs on behalf of society, so society should uphold their bona fide errors as well as their correct actions. Beckford, given the overall context, still does the right thing, even though he gets it wrong. We should thank him for 'putting himself out there' and accept that accidents will happen. His actions turned out to be wrong, but he was (imperfectly) justified in doing what he did.

From Greenawalt, we get the sense not of firm boundaries between justification and excuse but rather that the line may be one that is fluid and changeable, depending upon political and moral viewpoints. Judgment involves a floating signifier, and the result is that one can go different ways on different cases. A clear analytical line must yield to the alternatives in the chiasmus and to an understanding of the mediating role of socio-political context. Thus, the same person might take the view that citizen participation favours a strong and inclusive sense of justification in the *Williams* case, even as the dangers of armed policing and the need for proper training point to the need for a strict sense of wrongdoing in *Beckford*, so that any defence there must be excuse-based.

Putting this together with the argument concerning the different placing of justificatory and excusatory factors with regard to the definition of the offence, one would then see that Williams did nothing unlawful, and that the matter was properly settled on the definition of the offence. Beckford, on the other hand, did something potentially wrongful and illegal and, if it turns out that his victim was unarmed, he needs an excusatory defence of mistaken self-defence, the terms of the offence having been established. *Williams* was rightly, and *Beckford* wrongly, decided. The Court of Appeal in England and Wales was right to extend *Morgan*[17] to *Williams*, but the Privy Council was wrong to extend it onward to *Beckford*, although it should be clear that this conclusion depends on how the court itself views the different moral and political contexts in the different cases.

Forms of liability, conceptions of citizenship, legal judgment

It is suggested by those opposed to the current state of the law of mistaken self-defence in England and Wales that the problem lies with the so-called 'inexorable

17 See n 6 above.

logic' of *Morgan*. This, like bird flu, is dangerous when it jumps the species barrier, in this case between offence and defence, lodging itself virally in the defence of self-defence. However, the analysis of offence and defence, its relation to justification and excuse, and the way justification and excuse work fluidly in relation to each other, all reveal that *Williams*, at least, may have been a legitimate development of the *Morgan* doctrine, whereas other cases of mistaken self-defence may not. Often the evolution of the law depends on the happenstance of cases, and it just so happened that one of the cases that followed on the heels of *Morgan* was heard by a judicial bench with a degree of sympathy for the overall context within which the defendant acted. The English grandees of orthodox subjectivism took this as an affirmation of the logic of legal subjectivism in their textbooks (Smith and Hogan 1983: v) and, once established, the law of precedent decreed that subsequent cases, in different contexts, had to follow suit.

If it had been understood that legal subjectivism won out in *Williams* not because it was in principle right, but because it looked right to the bench in the moral and political circumstances of the case, things might have gone differently. But to say simply that orthodox subjectivism and the ensuing 'inexorable logic' they promoted is at fault in the law of mistaken self-defence is to miss a large part of the story and to fail to see why *Morgan* might have had traction in this area in the first place. That the 'logic' of *Morgan* made legal sense in *Williams* did not, however, make it 'inexorable' in other such cases. The main problem now is that this underlying context for understanding the law of self-defence is not understood. To argue for the correctness of the current approach is to overlook that lines could and should be drawn, whilst to argue that the law in *Williams* went wrong in following *Morgan* is not to see that this was not necessarily the case. The underlying issue is that mistaken self-defence may be either a matter of free-standing defence or of the definition of the offence depending on the context. This is because of the instability of the line between justification and excuse. Grasping this leads us to the chiasmus of mistaken self-defence and the irresolution contained therein.

In the meantime, the law is allowed to carry on regardless in its undifferentiated attitude to mistaken self-defence. On the basis of the present law, England and Wales has moved to an over-subjectivised justificatory law of mistaken self-defence. This is seen in two areas. The first is self-defence with regard to intruders in the home, where, provided that there is an actual 'live' intrusion (that is, the ultimate victim is not clearly leaving the premises, or already restrained, or unconscious), then the householder has significant leeway to kill him. In 2005, the Crown Prosecution Service and Association of Chief Police Officers in England and Wales issued guidelines (2005b) that establish that the householder must use 'reasonable force', a broadly justificatory measure, but then added: 'So long as you only do what you honestly and instinctively believe is necessary in the heat of the moment, that would be the strongest evidence of you acting lawfully and in self-defence' (ibid). They then add that: 'as a general rule . . . the more extreme the circumstances *and the fear felt*, the more force you can lawfully use in self-defence' (ibid, emphasis added).

What we see here is subjectivism ratcheted up a notch to include not only the perceptions of the householder but the emotional circumstances accompanying those perceptions. This is entirely in line with the subjectivist direction of the law initiated by *Williams*, but no thought is given to the overall moral context nor to how society considers the duties owed *on both sides* when an intruder intrudes. Perhaps, it might be said, society's overall attitude would be that intruders get what they deserve, and little or nothing is owed the other way. Permitting honestly mistaken forms of self-defence on the basis of *Williams* reflects the moral sense that a householder is justified in her actions, and that her honest mistakes are justified, too. The justificatory cast of the defence is appropriate, and the subjectivist approach captures rather well the underlying moral and political sentiment.

As in the United States, we have moved to a sense that the intruder forfeits all rights.[18] If so, I suggest, it would be as well to say candidly that this is the overall context and understanding of citizenship in which we fashion our rules, and therefore permit subjectivism the scope it has. To do so would be to acknowledge a meaner, less inclusive, view of citizenship, but perhaps society should be honest and less hypocritical about these matters, and not hide behind the seeming neutrality of a rule of law whose form, the liberal subjectivist honest mistake rule, in fact embeds specific political and moral views.

The second area is the use of fatal violence by the police against unarmed suspects, as in the cases of Harry Stanley and Jean-Charles de Menezes. Neither of these cases led to criminal prosecutions for murder and, in both, the reason given by the Crown Prosecution Service was the honest mistake test for self-defence (2005a; 2006). That test weighs matters very much in favour of potential defendants, and depends on the validity of the reasoning in *Williams* and especially *Beckford*. Given such a test, it is hard to criticise the Crown Prosecution Service for failing to prosecute in these cases. To say so is not to accept that such cases are unworthy of the examination a prosecution would entail. If I am right, however, that the way we see these cases depends on how society evaluates the overall socio-political context, then the law should be based upon a proper consideration of how society *wishes* to view such cases.

If the government wants to argue that police officers should have the kind of leeway they now have, that would be one thing, but a proper debate about whether these are justified killings gone wrong or unjustified killings for which an excusatory defence is required would help to focus attention on what are the limits of appropriate police action and citizen liberties in a democratic society. The current slavish marriage of a justificatory defence with an open subjectivist mental element treats as a matter of unquestionable formal rule what should entail a measure of moral and political reflection by both government and judiciary.

18 Under the Crime and Courts Act 2013, a further step is taken in this direction in that a householder's force against a burglar in self-defence must now be 'grossly disproportionate' rather than disproportionate for conviction. See Norrie (2014: 284, 300) for discussion.

Appreciating the underlying moral and political issues that accompany *and constitute* the justificatory and excusatory chiasmus of mistaken self-defence helps us see why this needs to occur.

To return to my opening comments, part of the work of a critical criminal law today is concerned with charting shifts in authoritarianism and criminalisation and in the nature of criminal law forms, as these are shaped by changes in the social world that predicates them. In that context, it is appropriate to look for the new, the distinctively different and the qualitatively changed. However, at the same time a focus on continuity must be maintained, and on the ways in which existing, 'classical' forms of legal intervention are deployed in the new period. The mistaken self-defence doctrine in England and Wales that makes it so hard to prosecute in the shoot to kill cases discussed above is a product of the orthodox subjectivist tradition that emanated from the post-1945 social democratic political settlement (Ramsay 2006; 2012), rather than part of an effort to redesign law according to the needs of an authoritarian state. That it functions rather well in protecting state agents in such a context may be true, but it does so as an example of specifically legal evolution rather than conscious design, following a case that was paradoxically aimed to cement inclusive citizenship rather than encourage authoritarian division.

The honest mistake doctrine has to be seen in this light, and it is only in this light that the lines of criticism appropriate to the law become clear. *Williams* was a case reflecting liberal principles of citizenship and it made moral, political and *legal* sense in that context. From that same point of view, however, it made no sense to carry the decision over to *Beckford*. Uncomfortable though it may be for legal formalism to acknowledge, slavish pursuit of a false 'inexorable logic' was at fault here, but it was in the transition between *Williams* and *Beckford*, not between *Morgan* and *Williams*, that the fault occurred. At stake in acknowledging this is an understanding of how legal form is inextricably linked to moral and political judgment about the terms of citizenship today.

Chapter 5

Legal form and moral judgment: euthanasia and assisted suicide

In this chapter, I consider the way in which categories of legal responsibility in the criminal law's general part are used to finesse broader moral conflicts around questions of euthanasia. Euthanasia and its close cousin assisted dying represent extremely problematic areas for the criminal law, as the recent formulation of prosecutorial guidelines for assisted suicide testify (Crown Prosecution Service 2014). The effect of the guidelines is to make no formal change in the law, which continues to prohibit assisted suicide. The guidelines make it clear as a matter of official practice, however, that where the law on its face has been broken, there will be no prosecution if the defendant was motivated by good moral reasons.[1]

This is a form of criminal regulation that operates by the contradictory juxtaposition of legal rule and administrative discretion. The effect is to balance conflicting social, political and moral claims in a society where there is no consensus as to the rights and wrongs of helping someone to die. A pragmatic compromise reflects a moral impasse in a way that appears to give something to everyone. Thus, the 'pro-life' lobby can say the law has not changed, no symbolic succour has been given to euthanasia and no line has been crossed. Those in favour of assisted suicide can claim to have chipped away at the monolithic view that assisting death is impermissible, and exposed the law's 'hypocrisy', whilst still accepting it has not changed formally.

On the surface, this is the kind of balancing act that occurs when a legal rule is maintained while social mores have changed or are in irreconcilable conflict.[2]

1 For example, with regard to whether a person stood to gain from a death, it is stated that: 'The critical element is the motive behind the suspect's act. If it is shown that compassion was the only driving force behind his or her actions, the fact that the suspect may have gained some benefit will not usually be treated as a factor tending in favour of prosecution' (CPS, 2014).

2 Surveys reveal that around 80 per cent of the British public are in favour of euthanasia for persons suffering painful, incurable disease (Lacey, Wells, and Quick, 2010, p 619), and there have been a number of cases sympathetically highlighted of assisted suicide in recent years. At the same time, there is powerful opposition from religious groups against changing the law. On recent attempts at law reform on assisted suicide in England and Wales, see *ibid*, p 637. The position argued for below is that, from a non-religious moral perspective, both sides have a point.

Underneath, however, the issue of assisted suicide, together with that of euthanasia, tells us something more general about the nature of criminal law regulation and the formalistic conception of responsibility that lies at its core. In addition to the moral complexity surrounding euthanasia, there is a complexity in the criminal law form itself that enables the moral problems to be finessed.

A deeper view of the relationship between law and morals would be to say that the moral complexity in euthanasia and assisted suicide is mediated by the peculiar complex of form and substance that constitute legal categories of responsibility. This enables a deeply conflicted moral issue to be managed, temporarily at least, through the legal structure, the 'architectonic', of the criminal law's general part. It is such a complex vision of the criminal law's general principles of responsibility that I wish to develop here, in order to apply it generally to questions surrounding euthanasia.

In thinking about the criminal law's architectonic, I will be bringing to bear my previous analysis of the role of formalisation on the categories of criminal law, a development that begins to occur in the early 19th century, and which sets up a tension in the law between formal and substantive approaches to criminal responsibility (Norrie 2000; 2005a: ch 4; 2014). In thinking about euthanasia broadly, I will be examining two different situations: those of active killing, in the sense of actually bringing about or contributing to a person's death;[3] and of supporting or assisting a person to commit suicide. In both cases, I will be looking at how the law finesses the moral problem by permitting some forms of active killing or assisted suicide, despite both being officially prohibited.

The chapter has four sections. In the next, I elaborate an argument on the nature of legal form in the criminal law, considering three different approaches – the moral, the political and the critical – to the idea of legal responsibility. I argue for a critical understanding of a dynamic of form and substance at its heart. In the following section, I consider the nature of the moral impasse on euthanasia, arguing that there are moral reasons for accepting some forms of euthanasia or assisted suicide, and moral reasons for refusing them. Then, in two final sections, I consider how the law operates with regard to active euthanasia and assisted suicide, in light of the law's formal structure and the relevant moral issues.

Legal form: 'moral', 'political' and 'critical' approaches

It is necessary to understand the legal forms of responsibility in the criminal law architectonic in a different way than most liberal criminal law scholarship. In saying this, I realise the claim may require to be tailored for different theorists in

3 Euthanasia may be voluntary (requested or consented to), non-voluntary (where it is not possible for the person to consent), or involuntary (where death is contrary to a person's wish, or consent was not sought). It may also be active (killing) or passive (letting die). See McMahan (2002: 457). Here I focus on the active, voluntary or non-voluntary, forms of euthanasia.

the tradition.[4] Nonetheless, at the core of the liberal approach is a sense of a homology between moral rules and legal rules, so that, for example, the legal conception of intention shadows and is given its validity by a moral conception of intention. As Antony Duff emblematically put it: 'As with morality, so with law' (1990: 102). Such a conception may be open to quite different interpretations. For example, a Kantian individualist will shape the concept of intention differently from a communitarian of either a Hegelian or Aristotelian bent. Nonetheless, the underlying sense is that a moral account of responsibility holds the key to an adequate legal understanding.

This is not to say that a moral approach does not recognise that legal concepts are also importantly political and institutional, or that rules elaborated by a state may be different from rules elaborated by a moral philosopher. For example, in moral philosophy, there is the possibility of fine-grained tuning of judgment which is not possible in law. Equally, other political or institutional considerations may come into play in law that are not there in philosophy. But if that is the case, the position adopted tends to be that the 'other things that come into play' are post-hoc considerations which may temper, or even befoul, an otherwise adequate moral understanding,[5] yet still be accepted as necessary in a process of moral-to-legal translation. Then the question becomes one of monitoring or controlling the extraneous post-hoc considerations in favour of underlying moral–legal principles.

The moral approach to legal responsibility, however, is not the only way that liberal theory can go. Alan Brudner has recently developed an alternative approach that he calls 'political' (Brudner 2009). If we follow this a little, we will be able to draw out the nature of the legal architectonic at the core of law. Brudner argues against the moral view just described. He suggests that principles of responsibility, and therefore the general structure of criminal law, are founded on the classical liberal view of principles of *political* authority to be found in Kant, and then developed by Hegel. From Kant, Brudner takes the retributive idea of punishment as the coercion of the criminal's freedom, which is given in return for the initial coercion of freedom that was present in a crime. This provides a universal basis for political and legal obligation founded on the idea of formal freedom, that is, the claim that all human agents are in principle capable of acting on the basis of making choices, regardless of what those choices may substantively be.

It is important to see that this is an abstract, formal, as its name indicates, account of freedom, which is quite removed from the actual needs or desires of choosing agents. It is the simple ability to make choices, the agent as a 'choosing mechanism' one might say, that is relevant. Now, as Brudner indicates, this is a very limited, indeed a dehumanising, conception of human agency in that it says

4 See the recent discussion of the different approaches sailing under the 'moral' flag in Brudner (2009: 17). For the differences between individualist and communitarian moral approaches, discussing the work of Michael Moore and Antony Duff, see Norrie (2000: chs 5–6).

5 See e.g. the role that 'policy' arguments play in Ashworth (2009: ch 3).

nothing of the choices people actually make, or the contexts in which they make them (ibid: 297–300). It requires accordingly to be supplemented by richer conceptions of freedom, including a positive freedom to act in conditions which permit one to choose according to one's real interests ('real autonomy'), and a freedom to draw upon and find expression for one's life in a community ('communal well-being').[6]

The important thing to note is that to this tripartite and developing vision of the forms of freedom, there correspond specific distinctions in the general structure of the criminal law. The realm of formal freedom is reflected in the law of mens rea and actus reus, whilst real autonomy issues are reflected in regulatory or welfare offences, and some of the defences are justified by the sense of what a community feels about wrongdoing in the light of excuses that a defendant might make for a crime. What is the value of this tripartite, structural scheme for our purposes here? I do not argue that Brudner's political approach is correct and the moral approach wrong. My own view, from a critical standpoint, is that both positions tell part of the story, whilst misrepresenting the whole in which both play their part.[7]

I do think, however, that it is helpful in that it affirms something of the particular historical structure of the modern law that moral approaches tend to ignore, and that is the sense of an overall formal architectonic of the law. Brudner is able to argue that different forms of normative argument concerning different forms of freedom are located in the overall structure of the criminal law differently. In particular, his argument points to the abstract formalism at the law's core, in its principles of mens rea and actus reus. In going back to Kant, and in placing Kant alongside Hegel,[8] Brudner indicates that there is something in the abstract Kantian principles that is intrinsic to a politically formulated architectonic of the criminal law. Political or institutional design is not separate from and additional to moral considerations but rather lies at the normative core of the law, in a formalistic account of the abstractly free, homuncular, individual who makes choices whatever the substantive ends or values may be that he or she endorses. Broader moral considerations, such as those identified in the moral approach are not thereby removed from the law, but are allocated their place in it according to its overall politico-normative structure.

I highlight Brudner's approach because its insistence on a political structure to the law founded on the principle of abstract, individual freedom also reflects my own position, albeit I approach it from a critical and sociological standpoint. My view too is that there is a formal structure allocating normative issues differentially in the criminal law, but I see the resulting layout of issues of

6 It is in the move from the second to the third form of freedom that the influence of Hegel is seen in Brudner's argument.

7 See further discussion in ch 6 below.

8 This is not necessarily how Brudner sees it: see discussion in ch 6 below.

responsibility as unsuccessfully synthesised and as essentially contradictory. The argument focuses, like Brudner's, on the realm of formal freedom at the core of the law, but departs from him in two ways. I argue, first, that formal freedom or a 'morality of form' is the historical product of a particular kind of society in which abstract, formal legal subjectivity complemented marketisation, or the exchange of commodities, as central to the organisation of social relations.

Second, I argue that the formal freedom adequate to the market and instantiated in the legal subject existed in contradiction with and within a world that denied agents the context in which to translate their formal freedom into a realm of 'real freedom' or 'free community', in the terms of Brudner's tripartite schema (Norrie 2014: ch 2). The critical view, accordingly, agrees with the political view that modern social life can be represented in terms of a progressive grading of forms of freedom. It sees these forms of freedom, however, as existing in contradiction to, not as completing, each other under modern social conditions. The consequence is the essentially antinomial and contradictory nature of the modern criminal law. The dialectic of modern criminal law is incomplete and broken.

Focusing on that law, the argument is that social, political and historical considerations structure the abstract nature of legal form, providing criminal law with its architectonic of offence (mens rea plus actus reus) and defence. Modern law expresses a notion of human freedom that is abstract, universal and formalistic and, in its abstraction and universality, one that is important but also importantly limited. It is important because it articulates a general sense of individual political freedom, one that is associated with a basic idea of agential freedom. It is importantly limited because it operates by way of a formalisation of ethical categories that excludes substantive moral concerns that pertain in different social contexts (Norrie 2014). It works essentially by establishing a form/substance dichotomy at the heart of criminal responsibility, which means that basic criminal law forms are expressed in formal, neutral, factual, psychologistic terms. Why such terms? 'Formal' because of the account of freedom that lies at the core; 'neutral' because the abstract freedom of the legal subject is the same for all; 'factual' and 'psychologistic' because it expresses responsibility in cognitive terms of intention, foresight and voluntariness – terms that at least appear neutral because they are shorn of moral substance.

This is a prevalent and continuing way of doing criminal responsibility, and is seen for example in the 'orthodox subjectivism' of the textbook tradition in England and Wales.[9] It should be noted, however, that its consequence is that a formalistic way of doing responsibility is always subject to criticism from positions

9 A tradition emphasising the subjective, psychological, autonomy of the criminal that includes the work of Glanville Williams and Smith and Hogan, and more recently Andrew Ashworth, although the last argues for a 'welfare principle' alongside an 'autonomy principle' as lying at the core of the criminal law.

that adopt a more morally substantive approach to issues,[10] so that a form/substance dichotomy, albeit one with form in the driving seat, is generally to be observed in the criminal law itself. Thus it is that legal categories always tend to 'hunt in pairs': intention and motive, subjective and objective, offence and defence being three main ones.[11] The general point is that a formalistic conception of legal freedom is achieved by excluding substantive moral concerns, but these return to trouble the law. For example, the division of motive from intention is a classic piece of formalism, but issues concerning motive return to trouble doctrine in the law of intention (ibid: ch 3), and elsewhere.

That is the general argument. What, however, is specific and interesting in the case of euthanasia and assisted suicide is that it is this dichotomising procedure, the law's failure to achieve a synthesis in Brudnerian terms, that helps it out. Many of the oppositions set out above are central to how the law handles different kinds of euthanasia: the distinction between motive and intention is central to permitting certain kinds of active killing, as is the distinction between offence and defence; in the case of assisted suicide, it is motive, which plays no part in the legal definition of the crime of assisting a suicide, which animates the discretionary decision not to prosecute. In such cases, there is the appearance that legal categories are functioning normally in the euthanasia context, but there is a surreptitious play on those categories which permits outcomes that should not really be allowed on a standard interpretation.

The issue is complicated. At one level, one can only be struck by the law's moral ineptitude in its dealings with euthanasia. The abstract formalism of its categories fails to carry necessary and appropriate moral distinctions. For example, the contract killer and the mercy killer are on the face of the law both culpable and, equally so, under the general definition of murder. An illustration is the case of the doctors in the conjoined twins case, *Re A (children)*.[12] In intending to separate the twins, knowing that one is virtually certain to die, the doctors satisfy the *Woollin*[13] test for the mens rea of murder. The definition of the offence having been satisfied, doctors are murderers who require a defence, but do we think of doctors in such a situation as murderers?[14] At another level, however, this abstract legal formalism gives the law a certain backhanded ethical facility, in its ability to

10 This is why the moral approach developed by Antony Duff, John Gardner, Jeremy Horder and Victor Tadros operates as an effective critique of orthodox subjectivist positions in the law.

11 The first term in each opposition is developed in factual, psychological terms as central to legal responsibility, and the second is then *mutatis mutandis* the locus of additional, morally substantive, information. For a more ambitious list of antinomies, see Norrie (2005a: 183).

12 [2000] 4 All ER 961.

13 *R v Woollin* [1998] 3 WLR 382.

14 If it is said that doctors are not murderers because a murderer is one who commits the offence of homicide without a valid defence, this does not avoid the moral problem, for we do not think of doctors as having committed any offence for which they might need a defence.

manoeuvre under cover of form, and thereby to finesse social and moral conflicts around a contentious moral subject.[15]

Officially, it appears to uphold a general prohibition against killing, the 'sanctity of life' position, whilst permitting 'quality of life' and choice issues to have their effect surreptitiously. Thus, *Re A (children)* notwithstanding, the law of mens rea proves flexible enough, and perhaps self-consciously so, to permit the issue of mercy killing to be dealt with as a question falling under the general rules of mens rea. This allows some mercy killing cases to be filtered out and treated differently from the normal run of cases, whilst it appears as though the general rules of mens rea are applied in such cases as in all others. The formal legal categories dispose of the matter, without any public commitment or substantive declaration that mercy killing is permitted. The ensuing benign hypocrisy operates through formal law, and allows society to have its moral cake and eat it.

Underlying moral issues

Before coming to the law, I discuss the moral issues concerning euthanasia. As already stated, there is no agreement in modern British society, or indeed in many other Western societies, on this matter.[16] Disagreement expresses itself as a conflict between the 'sanctity of life' on the one hand and the 'quality of life' or 'right to choose death' views on the other. The former is associated with religious views, but also works as a shorthand for the moral claim that human life is paramount and has intrinsic value.[17] The latter is the view that quality of life issues may be more important in some situations, and that a person may choose to die where such issues exist. In this section, I elaborate a moral view that identifies something of the main positions and indicate what I take to be the difficulty in formulating a clear-cut position one way or the other. I begin by comparing sanctity and quality of life positions, and proposing that even if there is a good argument in favour of sometimes admitting the latter, society might not want to admit it in law.

If we start with a sanctity of life position, this affirms the value of human life in a way that trumps even claims to self-determination. Human life just is a morally foundational good, and is never to be attacked.[18] The best to be said for euthanasia is that it may be permitted in its passive form ('letting die') where a person is dying and life surrenders itself up to a 'natural' process.[19] In one form of

15 As we shall see, it does not work quite so well with assisted suicide.

16 However, compare the situation in Holland. See Lewis (2007).

17 See e.g. Glover (1977). See also Dworkin, Frey and Bok (1998) and McMahan (2002: ch 5). For an excellent overview of the area, see Lacey, Wells and Quick (2010: 618–42).

18 Although, as Jeff McMahan notes (2002: 466–67), those who argue for the sanctity of life often do so inconsistently, in that they do allow certain instances where a 'non-innocent' person can be killed, such as in self-defence, in war, or as punishment.

19 Although any death involves a natural, biological, process whereby life closes down, what it means for nature 'to take its course' is debatable in social situations involving, for example, hospital care.

the argument, there is a straightforward ethical validation of individual human life; in another, it is human being *qua* species or relational being that is valued. The latter is the view that there is an important sense in which a person's life is not just her own, but has value beyond what the individual perceives it to be. There seems to me to be something fundamentally important in both claims, and with them a general ground for safeguarding life from attack. At the same time, however, such an approach can have morally problematic results: people who suffer from terminal or degenerative illness, for example, who want to die must remain alive in great pain or discomfort until death comes 'naturally' to them.[20]

Similarly, people who suffer from long-term disability or paralysis which grossly diminishes their capacities for life and who cannot take their own lives, are not permitted to die. In such circumstances, the argument for sanctity of life may seem sanctimonious to the person who is not allowed assistance to end her life. There have been cases in the media in recent years where the moral difficulty in insisting on the sanctity of life in such situations has been made clear.[21] Although such cases will not disturb the position of one who believes fundamentally in the sanctity of life, they do lead others to accept that there may be exceptional cases where sanctity gives way to quality of life issues.

In an indirect form, the sanctity of life argument draws strength from what one can call the possibility of dystopian futures. There is a concern that once we move away from sanctity of life claims, we open the door to various dangerous possibilities. If life loses its sanctity for the terminally ill or the physically paralysed, it may also lose it for others where quality of life might be regarded as diminished, such as the long-term depressed, the mentally and physically handicapped, and so on. There may then be a 'slippery slope' as between different degrees of quality of life,[22] and then, further, between voluntary and involuntary forms of euthanasia.[23]Against this, those supporting the quality of life stance will say that where freedom of choice pertains, there is a check on a drift to authoritarian forms of euthanasia, but much would then depend on what is meant by freedom

Passive euthanasia relies on the problematic distinction between acts and omissions, a distinction that lawyers acknowledge is hard to sustain. See Norrie (2014: 152–6).

20 Although their deaths may in law be hastened by medical treatments administered for other purposes such as to alleviate pain: see the discussion in the next section below.

21 See e.g. the case of Daniel James who was paralysed in a rugby accident and was assisted to travel to Dignitas in Switzerland by his parents, where the Crown Prosecution Service determined it would not be in the public interest to prosecute (Crown Prosecution Service 2008), or the cases of two mothers charged with the murder or attempted murder of their disabled adult children, Frances Inglis and Kay Gilderdale, discussed below.

22 Where the line should be drawn between for example the terminally and degeneratively ill, the paralysed or badly disabled but physiologically stable, and the long-term mentally ill or depressed is an important question.

23 For recent discussions of the 'slippery slope', see Lewis (2007), who argues there is no evidence for its existence and Greasley (2010).

of choice and how it is ascertained. Such a view is reflected in concerns that people may be pressured by those around them to 'choose' to die, and that, where assisted suicide is permitted in law, it will be the poor and unwanted who will make that 'choice', for their life chances as elderly or infirm will be much less than those of the wealthy with similar conditions.

I return to this point shortly. Suffice it to say for now that, whilst there are good moral reasons of either a direct (that human life should be generally valued as of intrinsic worth) or an indirect (that allowing exceptions would lead to a slippery slope) kind for supporting a sanctity of life view in the case of the terminally ill and ancillary cases, there are also good moral reasons for allowing exceptions to it. The latter stem from a quality of life view and, linked to that, the possibility of choosing the time and place of one's own death.[24] The possibility of agency as a central element in what it means to be human is premised on the notion of human freedom, and freedom implies a number of different elements. These include a simple freedom to be left alone with one's life, as well as a positive freedom to become what we have it within ourselves to be. Such freedom then entails further conceptions of autonomy, emancipation and flourishing, insofar as human life reflects the potentialities in human being.

The ability to choose one's own death reflects many of these aspects of human freedom, from the simple sense that one should be left alone to do what one likes to the more complex sense that an autonomous life would include amongst its components control over one's death, and then on to the sense – that is surely there in the term 'euthanasia' (a 'good death') – that a flourishing life is one in which one is able to register the time to go. These are moral arguments placing choice and quality of life ahead of sanctity of life, and therefore for the validity of suicide and assisted suicide, and the killing of a person who is unable to take her own life but who wants to die for good reason. A good life means a good death, and it is this kind of argument that leads one to think that a categorical prohibition on voluntary euthanasia or assisted suicide is problematic.

Thus far, it might be thought that for anyone who does not have a fundamental commitment to the sanctity of life on, for example, religious grounds, a balancing of sanctity and quality of life issues will lead to the conclusion that euthanasia and assisted suicide should be available in certain circumstances, and this should be publicly declared as such. Whilst in principle such a position seems right, in practice I hesitate to take this route for a reason briefly mentioned above. This concerns the problem of the differential social impact that such a position would have on the poor and the well-to-do,[25] and because of the possibility that, in the

24 It can be argued, as does Ronald Dworkin, that the ability to choose the time of one's own death is so central to the nature of human life as to be crucial to a sanctity of life position (Dworkin 1993: 215–217). However, there may be more to the intrinsic value of life than this, even if it is a central feature.

25 See the argument by Sissela Bok in Dworkin, Frey and Bok (1998).

future, a society with a population that is ageing and impoverished might be inclined to convert the permissive 'can' into the persuasive 'ought' (and then the authoritarian 'should'?).

To talk of the freedom to choose one's death is not to talk of the specific conditions under which differently situated people will make their choices. The strongest arguments for a balancing of sanctity and quality of life arguments so as to permit some good deaths identify specific situations where the balance works in favour of honouring the choice of death over life. If we say that freedom of choice to die should be upheld in certain circumstances, we are saying that situations of free choice are available. It could be said, however, that such possibilities for freedom of choice are not available in the here and now, certainly not for all people. Wealth, poverty and class structure have a profound contextual effect on the choices people make.

Accordingly, there may be a tension between what should ideally happen and what might actually happen if various forms of euthanasia were legalised. In the case of assisted suicide, consider the deaths of individuals with terminal illnesses who have chosen to die, who plan their deaths and who are able to pay to travel to the Dignitas clinic in Zurich with their close family. Everything has a measured, respectful character. This kind of death is, however, only likely to be for a few, and should be contrasted with the concern that legalising assisted suicide would mean that many people who are poor, who are leading lives in straightened circumstances, and who feel themselves to be a burden on their families would then be pressured directly or indirectly to 'choose' to die.[26] Nor in a society in which dystopian and authoritarian features are already present can one rule out the possibility that the circumstances of choice will be worse in the future.

Accordingly, in these circumstances, one might say that even if each human being has the real potential to live a good life and die a good death, that does not lead to the conclusion that the law should be changed to permit this to happen. A door that was once opened would be hard to close. Just as one has to balance different arguments around sanctity and quality of life, so one has to measure different practical outcomes in the real world. At bottom, there is a question about how 'good death' works in society as a whole, specifically about the relationship between individual and collective human flourishing with regard to it. Thinking about the balance between the two may lead one to favour the sanctity of life position overall, even if one accepts there are good arguments for a limited quality of life exception.

The short conclusion might be that the moral balance is in favour of saying that the better off should not be allowed a good death until everyone is able to have the same. On an individual basis, however, it is surely problematic to suggest that the moral flourishing of some with regard to a good death may have to be checked

26 This is not to deny that the wealthy may also be pressured to choose to die by relatives anxious for their wealth, but I do not take this to be a structural condition on the possession of wealth.

in favour of the protection of the lives of others from bad deaths in a divided society. This means that we cannot individually be allowed to flourish until such time as we all are able to do so. But if this is so, it seems to be a conclusion that is both cogent and unacceptable. There is surely a moral conviction that those who really can decide to die at a time of their choosing in the here and now should be allowed to do so, and should not have to undergo pain and suffering for the general social good. There is therefore a major premise that the moral risks of permitting assisted suicide and voluntary euthanasia may be too great under modern social conditions to permit legalisation; and a minor premise that people should be allowed where possible to seek a good death under conditions that genuinely enable it. The problem is that the major and minor premises are in conflict. How to deal with this? Optimally, we should move to a society where social justice is taken seriously; until then, what is the answer?

A pro-tem solution might be to think about whether it is possible to maintain both premises: at the institutional level, a prohibition on the pursuit of good deaths coupled with, at the individual level, their informal acceptance through, somehow, the turning of a blind eye in appropriate cases. This would be a complicated and messy way of trying to deal with a difficult moral problem. How could it be achieved, and what role could the criminal law, with its emphasis on bright and clear lines of regulation, play in achieving it?

Legal form and moral substance: active euthanasia

The argument I began to outline in the first section was that the formalism of legal categories of responsibility initially makes the criminal law inhospitable to moral nuance. However, that very inhospitability generates a legal praxis that requires and enables lawyers subtly to negotiate moral problems under cover of inflexible law and legal form. There is an intricate interplay between what the law formally says, and how it reflects substantive moral issues in practice. In this section, I look at this interplay with regard to doctors ending life, the role of the law of intention and the relationship between moral and legal argument. I also consider why the defence of necessity is a problematic alternative, and conclude by considering recent cases of mercy killing not involving doctors.

Primary and secondary purpose

As regards intention, an early flavour of the way in which criminal law categories are maintained but also finessed is seen in *R v Adams*,[27] where it was held that a doctor may do 'all that is proper and necessary to relieve pain . . . even if the measure . . . may incidentally shorten life' (Lacey, Wells and Quick 2010: 705). But

27 [1957] Crim LR 365.

under the law of contributory cause, *any* shortening of life or hastening of death counts towards criminal causation. To avoid the problem, Lord Devlin resorted to what he termed a 'common sense' view of causation. Underlying this vague invocation, however, was a moral distinction about the different reasons why a life might be shortened, and this became crucial. The distinction was between medical intervention aimed to relieve pain, which incidentally shortens life, and intervention which is aimed to shorten life (ibid: 705). Here, the discussion moves into the realm of intention. In the later case of *R v Cox*,[28] a distinction was drawn between a doctor's 'primary' and 'secondary' purpose (intention) in administering treatment. As against the incidental hastening of death (a 'secondary' purpose) pursuant to a course of treatment with the primary purpose of easing suffering, it was stated that 'what can never be lawful is the use of drugs with the primary purpose of hastening the moment of death' (ibid: 706).

This analysis of primary and secondary purpose provides considerable leeway. We cannot normally know what is going on in the doctor's head. It is, however, challenged by the settled approach to intention formulated in a line of cases in the 1980s leading to *Woollin*,[29] where any secondary purpose that has consequences that are foreseen as virtually certain to occur is promoted to the same position and status as a primary purpose. That was the background to the judge's direction to the jury in *R v Moor* (Arlidge 2000).[30] There, the instruction was that the jury consider, first, whether the doctor's purpose had not been to give treatment to relieve pain. If it had not been, then the jury had to be sure that he intended to kill his patient, and intention meant purpose. If he did so intend, he was guilty of murder. If Dr Moor thought it only highly probable death would follow the injection, there would be no intention to kill.

The jury was offered an 'out' and took it, finding Dr Moor not guilty, but this direction failed to relay to the jury the essence of *Woollin*, that if the doctor thought it virtually certain death would follow, he would have the intention to kill.[31] The direction was, to put it mildly, highly favourable to the defendant. It led to a subsequent proposal suggested by senior counsel in the case that intention may be found 'if death was a virtually certain result (barring an unforeseen intervention) and his primary intention was not purely to relieve pain and suffering but to cause death' (ibid).

This is an attempt to splice together the *Woollin* direction and the primary purpose rule, but it is not clear that it would work, for the two parts of the test come from different moral backgrounds. One is the idea that a foreseen virtually certain consequence is ipso facto so tied to a direct purpose that it is a consequence

28 [1992] 12 BMLR 38.
29 See n 13 above.
30 [1999] Crim LR 568.
31 Subject to the potential proviso in *Woollin* concerning what a jury is 'entitled to find' discussed below.

that is owned by the actor. The other is that one's purpose is circumscribed by one's moral commitments, and one only owns those actions to which one is morally committed. In this second view, one may accept consequences which are not intrinsic to one's moral commitment, where those consequences are themselves means to the end of that commitment but, importantly, only where they are not significantly at moral odds with it. Doctors who inject a patient to ease pain and suffering are arguably in that category, for easing pain is a necessary and sufficient part of their work as doctors even if it hastens death. However, if that is the case, then one does not need the additional test of foresight of virtually certain consequences to resolve the matter: the purpose analysis will do all the work anyway. On the other hand, if one goes with the foresight of virtual certainty rule, then the question of purpose is in principle irrelevant. The primary purpose and indirect intention/foresight of virtual certainty tests are in conflict.

A loophole in the law?

As already intimated, there is a problem with the universalism and formalism of the law of intention here, but there is also a possible 'informal' solution to it, within the law. The problem with the law's formalism lies in the foresight of virtual certainty analysis, which lacks an adequate moral grasp of what is substantively at stake in cases like mercy killing. The problem with its universalism is that rules should apply in all cases. From a morally substantive or contextual point of view, however, things are different. Thinking in terms of the moral content of the conduct that occurs, a person only morally endorses those virtually certain consequences which are not at significant moral odds with what it is one seeks to do. This is the analysis of a 'moral threshold'.[32]

The simple view that one accepts the virtually certain consequences of one's actions regardless of their moral implications threatens to be over-inclusive. *Woollin*[33] reflects the problem, but it also has a possible way out of it, in the stipulation that a jury is 'entitled to find' an intention to kill where it finds that the defendant (D) foresaw a consequence as virtually certain. If it is 'entitled to find', then this is arguably permissive rather than obligatory, so it can also choose *not* to find an intention even where it finds foresight of virtual certainty. This seems to be the logic of 'entitlement', and it is seen in the analysis of *Matthews and Alleyne*,[34] which follows *Woollin* arguing it did not produce a law of intention, only a rule of evidence.

32 The term 'moral threshold' (Norrie 2014: 70–71) reflects an original argument by Duff. See e.g. Duff (1990: 84), where an example is the examiner who fails a student knowing it will upset her. Despite the upset being virtually certain, the examiner does not intend it. For discussion of Duff's position and its limits, see Norrie (2005a: 62–69).

33 See n 13 above.

34 [2003] 2 Cr App R 30.

Of course, it is bizarre to argue that the law has no definition of intention, both because it seems fairly clear that it does have a definition, albeit one that is too broad, and because, more generally, it is just strange that a central concept in the criminal law should remain undefined. But the claim may be an important one. It may do important moral work in cases where a jury does not wish to find intention. Note, however, that the judges in *Re A (children)*[35] declined to go down this route, preferring to claim that *Woollin* intention was satisfied in the case of the doctors in that case. This decision stands in contrast to the more flexible, 'evidential', reading of intention permitted by *Matthews and Alleyne*. What one sees in *Woollin* is a tension between a formalistic statement of the law of intention in factual, psychologistic terms (what did D foresee as a virtually certain outcome?), and a hidden, morally substantive, informal invitation to go another way (what additional virtually certain foreseen outcomes did D morally endorse through her actions, which she can then be said to have intended?). This tension is indicative of an underlying ethical–legal relation that is unresolved but always present in the criminal law (Fletcher 1975: 400–401).

Double effect and necessity

The law on intention reflects underlying moral issues in the active euthanasia cases. These operate as a 'shadow' on it, but they are not part of the law. Most significantly, there is the doctrine of double effect. This is the claim that 'one may permit the evil effect of his act only if this is not intended in itself but is indirect and justified by a commensurate reason' (Price 1997). This is drawn on in some medical cases,[36] but it is essentially problematic for the law because it in effect permits a citizen or group of citizens (such as doctors) to second-guess what the law is. It is a requirement of legal form that it apply universally in society, that it be clear as to the forms of conduct to which it applies and that it brook no challenge from any other source in its sovereign territory. Double effect challenges this because it permits an alternative ethical evaluation to compete with the official norm. Nonetheless, I think it plainly underpins the moral calculations that go into practical decision-making in this area of the law. It is closely related to the moral threshold, mentioned above.

A good example in a non-euthanasia setting is the case of *Gillick*,[37] where the doctors' intention to treat under-age girls by prescribing contraceptive pills was held to be an answer to any offence of aiding and abetting unlawful sexual intercourse. It could hardly be denied that prescription would enable sex, but it was not part of a doctor's role to do anything other than protect her patients' health. Such an open endorsement of a moral threshold position would be quite

35 See n 12 above. Compare the discussion of this point, above, ch 3, at pp 59–60.

36 *Airedale NHS Trust v Bland* [1993] 2 WLR 316, 370; see also *Re A (children)* (n 12) 1012.

37 *Gillick v West Norfolk and Wisbech Area Health Authority* [1986] AC 112.

problematic if it were to be extended more broadly, but somehow, it was permitted in this case.

One specifically legal analysis that can reflect the moral threshold or double effect arguments concerns necessity as a justificatory defence. The doctors in these cases, it may be said, are caught between conflicting duties, in that they must treat their patients even if treating them would bring them into collision with the law. They must negotiate a balance of evils, and hastening the death of a patient (or prescribing the pill in *Gillick*) may involve such a balance (Ashworth 1996). They are entitled to a supervening defence of necessity. Against this, however, it should be noted that any general balancing of a doctor's duty to treat a patient when compared with the duty not to kill would be hard to resolve in favour of the doctor's duty to treat. If the duty not to take life is, as the law claims, one of the most fundamental obligations imposed on citizens, then it is hard to see that a doctor's duty to treat a patient can be weighed in the balance against it.

Furthermore, the law of necessity makes it clear that this is a defence of very limited application, and not in cases of killing. It is true that *Re A (children)* muddies the waters here, but it is clear that the judges' intention in that case was not to extend necessity to cover situations of doctors causing the deaths of their patients, but was limited to the very precise circumstances of the conjoined twins. The general problem with the necessity defence is reflected in the judges' discomfort in *Re A (children)* in formulating it: a declaration that the law of necessity goes beyond the precise facts of that case would be too open a statement that the law *does* permit the taking of life in situations such as that of mercy killing. Extending the law of necessity beyond *Re A (children)*'s precise facts would establish the morally substantive proposition that mercy killing is allowed, but it is just that morally substantive conclusion that the law cannot draw, for it cannot go against the official position that states that killing is wrong.

As I have said above, there are both real political and institutional conditions that make it impossible to move forward and underlying moral-political reasons why this may be no bad thing. In a situation of real-political blockage and moral-political concern, the use of a morally substantive defence such as necessity is unacceptable and, arguably, undesirable. Better perhaps to stay with the formal account of mens rea and smuggle in the morally substantive position in the interstices of that law. In truth, we do not know how the law works in formal terms. The 'easing the passing' primary purpose rules seems to operate at some level, despite its conflict with *Woollin* intention. We may talk of 'moral elbow room' here but, in formal terms, its operation is mysterious and the law is clear.

Beyond doctor and patient

Turning now to recent euthanasia cases not involving doctors, the issue that hoves into view is the distinction between motive and intention, for motive is the 'home' of moral substance alongside the formalism of intention in the standard form/substance dichotomy at the core of the law. Of course the 'first rule' of criminal law is that the two should be kept apart.[38] Here we are back on the familiar terrain of comparing mercy and contract killers, and affirming their equal guilt. Nonetheless it is clear that, even if this is so, it is motive that makes the difference in practice in mercy killing cases.

The recent conflicting decisions in the cases of two mothers, Frances Inglis and Kay Gilderdale, who both killed their disabled adult children suggest that it is how a defendant comes across in terms of her overall character and the precise moral circumstances in which she acts, where these reveal her motives, that is relevant. Frances Inglis stated that she had killed her severely brain damaged son 'with love in her heart', yet she was convicted of murder and found by the judge to have undertaken a 'calculated and consistent course of criminal conduct' and to have 'intended to do a terrible thing' (Pidd 2010). Kay Gilderdale in contrast was found not guilty of attempted murder with the judge describing her as a 'caring and loving mother', and openly questioning why she had been prosecuted for attempted murder, when she had pleaded guilty to aiding and abetting suicide.[39] The Crown Prosecution Service was left to assert that 'the intent was clear on our evidence',[40] and it was probably right in so thinking.

What went wrong for Frances Inglis? It is likely that she came across as a person too caught up in her own emotional concerns to act fully in terms of what was right for her son. He had been unable to express a wish in the matter. This is borne out by the ground of her appeal that the defence of provocation in a situation of severe emotional stress should have been left to the jury. In dismissing this argument, the Court of Appeal noted that the defendant was in complete control of herself, was obsessive in her conviction that her son should die, had acted without regard for the views of other family members, and bore some responsibility for her son's condition owing to an earlier unsuccessful attempt to kill him. She might have been better placed had she claimed diminished responsibility, but had not done so because she wanted all the facts to come out.[41]

38 Is this just an obscure slogan? I think not: it is there for a purpose, which is to separate out a factual and a moral understanding of legal responsibility. It has significant effects in cases, e.g. *Chandler v DPP* [1964] AC 763. It is certainly a very problematic separation, so it does lead to 'obscurity' in the law, but it is a necessary obscurity based upon the formal structuring of the legal architectonic. The 'moral' approaches discussed in the first section have difficulty in grasping this because they do not see that law has a formal structure allocating moral issues in a distinctive non-moral way, based upon what Brudner calls 'political' grounds. The 'critical' approach which I advocate latches onto the failure of the political approach to organise the law in an overall rational manner, but it accepts that the political approach grasps something about the structure of the law. See Norrie (2000; 2014, 229–33) on the idea that the criminal law form involves 'false but necessary' distinctions.

39 For which offence she was given a suspended sentence.

40 *Guardian* (26 January 2010).

41 *R v Inglis* [2010] EWCA Crim 2637. On appeal the sentence was reduced from nine to five years on the mitigating grounds that she believed this to be an act of mercy, and suffered mental disorder as provided under the Criminal Justice Act 2003, s 269 and Sch 21. On both cases, see further below ch 8, pp 157–60.

Legal form and moral substance: assisting suicide

The same kind of interplay between formal law and underlying ethics is also at play in the area of assisted suicide, although the nature of assisted suicide entails a different arrangement for legal practice. It may, however, be helpful first to summarise what I have said in the previous section. With active euthanasia, the main work is negotiated between primary and secondary purpose, and the distinction between direct and indirect intent. It is negotiated in active euthanasia cases by the moral, motive-based assertion that, although a killing may have been intended, the fact that it was carried out with an accepted moral or professional intention deflects the focus from the intention to kill to an easing of suffering.

The position is slightly different as between the doctor cases and the case of a parent such as Kay Gilderdale. With doctors, it is possible to claim that treating the patient represents the primary purpose, or the moral focus of their intentional agency, or an alternative moral effect to death. With a case such as that of Mrs Gilderdale, what is the distinct primary purpose or focus of her agency that can be taken as the alternative to the intention to kill? It can only be a loving commitment to bring an end to suffering, but the problem here is that this is essentially a euphemistic way of speaking about what Mrs Gilderdale did. There is no doctor's obligation or practice to fall back on as the 'narrow horizon' for action which blocks the criminal goal from view. Ending suffering just is killing the daughter.

These are, in law, hard cases to decide in favour of the defendant and involve a fuller quotient of jury equity than the doctor cases, where a distinct medical purpose can be ascribed. Juries simply have to 'feel' their way to a decision without the prop of an alternative distinct intention to rely upon. Mrs Gilderdale was regarded as a model of self-sacrifice, and one whom the law should respect rather than convict. In formal terms, there was a case to answer, but judge and jury baulked at the law's logic. Whilst it continued to be upheld in general terms, it was evaded in the particular case before the courts.

How does it work with assisted suicide? It is also hard to see such cases as involving an alternative purpose under which what then becomes the secondary purpose of assisting another's dying can nestle. If a spouse helps his or her partner to travel to Zurich, or to take a dose of drugs *that will kill*, there is no possible alternative purpose such as alleviating pain, just as there is no plausible argument that travelling to Zurich will broaden the deceased's horizons. The irreducible intention to assist the suicide is all too clearly visible. Presumably, if prosecutions were brought, it would be open to the defendant simply to argue the moral issue in the open of the courtroom and say that she acted from the best of intentions, and with love in her heart. The criminal law, however, could only take so many of such cases, which presumably are more numerous than those where a parent actively kills a loved one, before a disparity between the law and the outcomes of such cases, or the scandal of the difference in outcomes between individual cases, brought the law into disrepute.

These are hard cases for the law to deal with because it is too clear that defendants intentionally break it, without an alternative purpose to hang on to,[42] and defendants have themselves got the message that this is so: hence their resort to the Dignitas clinic in Switzerland, which means that the main activities around the suicide take place in a foreign jurisdiction. Yet, this hardly lets the law, or the defendant, off the hook. Assisting a terminally ill sufferer to travel abroad to his or her death is a form of aiding and abetting in its own right, yet even before the new CPS guidelines, no one had been prosecuted for so doing.

Before the new guidelines were issued, the way in which the problem of assisted suicide was dealt with was by means of a discretion to prosecute, the grounds of which remained undisclosed. After the guidelines, the discretionary basis is disclosed. In the draft guidelines, two sets of factors were regarded as germane to the decision to prosecute. One set concerned the condition of the 'victim', the other the position and motives of the defendant. In their revised form, the condition of the 'victim' has been removed from the criteria, leaving the motives of the defendant as the main factor. This was as a result of arguments that identifying certain conditions as being likely to lead to suicide would place a degree of pressure on those suffering from such conditions to think of themselves as potential suicides. In that way, it raised the morally substantive concern that some lives were of less value than others.[43]

It is the argument of this chapter that one way of dealing with the problem of euthanasia is not to treat it in a way that confronts actual moral concerns about the value of life. Better instead to treat it as a matter of individual choice for 'victims' (but without reference made to their actual conditions) (Crown Prosecution Service 2014),[44] and as a matter of individual attitude on behalf of defendants acting out of care and love and without self-interest in relation to a person to whom they are personally connected.[45] Dropping reference to the quality of

42 An alternative route here has historically been available through the partial defence of diminished responsibility. Whether this route has been closed off by recent reform of the Homicide Act 1957, s 2 remains to be seen. See Mackay (2010).

43 An argument prosecuted in Greasley (2010).

44 Of 16 factors in favour of prosecution, the first five concern the ability of the deceased to make a sound choice. These include: that the victim was under 18; did not have the capacity to reach an informed decision; had not reached a voluntary, clear, settled and informed decision; had not clearly and unequivocally communicated a decision to commit suicide to the suspect; and did not seek the encouragement or assistance of the suspect personally or on his or her own initiative.

45 Factors relevant to prosecution concerning the suspect include that he was not wholly motivated by compassion, for example, he stood to gain from the death of the victim; that he pressured the victim; or did not take reasonable steps to ensure that any other person had not pressured the victim; that he had a history of violence or abuse against the victim; that the victim was physically able to undertake the act that constituted the assistance him or herself; that the suspect was unknown to the victim and encouraged or assisted the victim by providing information via a website or publication; that he gave encouragement or assistance to more than one victim; that he was paid for his or her assistance; that he was acting in his capacity as a medical doctor or other professional

specific kinds of lives is another means of finessing the substantive issues by focusing on intentions and motives, and here the permissible intention is buttressed, in the guidelines but not in the law, by heavy reliance on motive. Hence the resort to motive as the main consideration in deciding to prosecute leaves the law of assisted suicide in much the same place as the law of active euthanasia with regard to doctors and others who hasten death: it is ultimately a question of motive, regarded as a means for qualifying their otherwise clearly criminal intentions.

The principal difference concerns where and how the supplementing of the law of intention with motive occurs. In the medical euthanasia cases, it primarily occurs informally in individual decisions not to prosecute, whilst in the parental mercy killings, it is a matter of jury equity (or perversity). In assisted suicide it now occurs at the prosecutorial stage through a formal structuring of the discretionary process that stands in uncomfortable juxtaposition to the law that denies it. Whether the kind of balance this provides represents a long-term solution to the problems of moral principle and practice described above, only time will tell. The mere publicisation of the terms of discretion may in itself promote the practice with ramifications that are not yet known (Greasley 2010).

In suggesting that such a balancing exists and has been enabled by the formalism of the legal architectonic, I have not argued for anything other than an ad hoc, and therefore possibly a temporary, solution to the problem society faces. The underlying issue, especially in the case of assisted suicide at present, concerns the possibility of good deaths in a morally bad – economically unequal, structurally unjust – society, and *that* problem lies beyond the cunning of law and legal form to resolve.

Conclusion

In this chapter, I have considered how a critical analysis of criminal law can be brought to bear on the problems of euthanasia and assisted suicide. I began by contrasting 'moral', 'political' and 'critical' approaches to criminal law. Put briefly, a 'moral' approach to criminal law considers how a social practice ought to be treated normatively, and then how this should be reflected in the law. A 'political' approach, such as Brudner's, sees the law as possessing a formal quality, which reflects in a structured way how freedom and a person's belonging in a community are internally related within the ethical-legal totality. Against 'moral' approaches, it argues that the study of criminal law is not simply an exercise in applied moral theory. By itself, the 'moral' approach fails to grasp law's *differentia specifica* as a form of political morality. A 'critical' approach also acknowledges the formal structuring of law, especially around abstract ideas of freedom.

carer, or as a person in authority, where the victim was in his care; that he was aware that the victim intended to commit suicide in a public place; that he was acting in his capacity as a person involved in an organisation or group, a purpose of which is to provide a physical environment in which to allow another to commit suicide.

This gives rise to the idea that law's formal structure of 'general' (offence and defence, etc) and 'special' parts constitutes a specifically *legal* architectonic. But it also argues against the 'political' approach that the broader synthesis of freedom and community envisaged there is not possible in a socially contradictory and structurally unequal society. Law's formal conception of freedom, in an 'unsynthesisable' social whole, is from an overall ethical point of view a source of weakness, not strength. That is the case, and this is the main argument here, *except* insofar as it becomes indirectly or obliquely a useful resource in negotiating moral conflicts such as those we see in regard to euthanasia and assisted suicide.

The abstract formalism of law's architectonic emphasises legal form over moral substance, psychological intention over moral purpose (or motive) and a formal definition of the offence alongside a limited set of exceptional moral defences. This makes the law morally inflexible at one level, but oddly useful at another, when it comes to finessing practical, morally and politically contentious issues such as euthanasia and assisted suicide. A society such as ours finds it impossible to reach a consensus, or escape an impasse here, but is able to accommodate its conflicts under the cover of formal law. This is seen especially in the way the law of intention plays out. At the formal level, it operates as a law that is not a law, or one with a built-in capacity to self-cancel. With regard specifically to medical euthanasia, it is a law that slips in *sotto voce* an exceptional interpretation ('primary purpose') for just such cases. In other euthanasia situations, it is the basis for prosecutorial, judicial and jury-based discretion in particular cases. The greatest difficulty emerges in cases of assisted suicide, where there are no actors with a special status (i.e. doctors), or a 'primary purpose' that is (in a limited sense) distinguishable from directly helping to bring about death. This makes the informal finesse harder to achieve, and is evidenced in the recent emergence of a new *formal* contradiction, between a law prohibiting assistance and lawful guidelines enabling it.

Chapter 6

Alan Brudner and the dialectics of criminal law

Alan Brudner's *Punishment and Freedom: A Liberal Theory of Penal Justice* (2009) is a formidable contribution to the debates around punishment and criminal responsibility. It is systematic and thorough in its exploration of theory and its implications for the different avenues of legal responsibility. Brudner and I share some things in common and disagree on some other things. We hold positions that in some ways overlap and in other ways diverge. The latter will be the main focus of this paper, so it is important to acknowledge the strength and complexity of Brudner's account. It is also important to say that this is my first encounter with his book, and I am aware that I may have misunderstood some of its arguments. So this chapter should be taken as a first attempt to master the work and to think critically from my own perspective on it.

Brudner's focus on the criminal law and an account of it that is Hegelian in its inspiration places us in a similar intellectual space, although we have taken different views of what should be made of Hegel in interrogating the nature of modern criminal law. In Brudner's account, Hegel operates alongside Kant to, as it were, 'complete' him by showing how the core Kantian understanding of freedom needs to be seen in a broader context of concepts, which together establish a complex unity. In this way, Brudner achieves an understanding of liberal criminal law as essentially *political* in its foundation, and establishes a line of argument that works between two alternative approaches: one that is *moral* in its inspiration, the other that is *critical*.

I will explain these terms in a moment, but to introduce my own approach alongside Brudner's, my work has taken the form of a critique of modern criminal law theory, which traces its underlying problems to their rooting in core liberal ideas associated with Kant and Hegel, but sees dialectical method as essential to understanding the way criminal law works in society. I particularly like the Kantian element in Brudner's approach for reasons I will explain. Thus, although we use the Kant–Hegel tradition in different ways, there is a common core in our identification of this line of thinking as central to an understanding of modern criminal law. However, we come to very different conclusions.[1]

1 Brudner (2011) responds to my original essay. I briefly consider his responses below at footnotes 2, 7, 10, 11, 13, and 14.

Against the moral approach

To develop this, let us look at Brudner's distinguishing of political, moral and critical approaches to criminal law. The core argument of his book asserts that there is a political justification for punishment that underlies criminal law's doctrines, and this distinguishes his approach from moral approaches of either an individualist or a communitarian cast. The essence of the moral approach is that it argues for or against criminal responsibility on the basis of a direct relationship between what is true according to a particular moral account of action. So, if one is a theorist committed to an individualist account of moral choices, legal responsibility will reflect individual blameworthiness and if one is committed to an Aristotelian account of action, it will reflect a commitment to moral understandings of virtue or character.

Brudner rejects what he would regard as these superficial approaches by arguing for a clear distinction between legal and moral blameworthiness. He notes the morally counter-intuitive nature of many legal findings of responsibility, enshrined most emblematically in the distinction between motive and intention. He argues that a formalistic conception of mens rea in the general part is not a mistake to be overcome by better moral understandings; rather, it is a core truth of legal morality – what I call a 'morality of form' (Norrie 2000: 7–10), a term that he supports (Brudner 2009: 167). Note, this is not to say that criminal law lacks a moral nexus; only that it has it in a special sense, one that at its core is *abstract* and *formalistic*, and is consistent with a certain way of organising society's basic political-normative structure. Hence the idea of a *political* theory of punishment and criminal law.

Since I have fought a long campaign in favour of recognising the structural irreducibility of abstract legal form in criminal law, so that it is not related *directly* to an understanding of morality, in the face of the predominant assumption that it is, I welcome Brudner's account. My argument has been that there is something essentially Kantian about the criminal law (Norrie 1991; 2000; 2014), and that this is not susceptible to direct moral criticism because it is enshrined in the historical structure of modern legal form, which begins with an abstract, formal individualism. Its historicity derives from the historical connection between modern society as one that is structurally based on the formal exchange of commodities and a conception of a formally free individual as the rational exchanger of commodities: *homo economicus* complemented by *homo politicus* and *homo juridicus*. Mine is, ultimately, an approach rooted in sociology.

Brudner, however, does not see legal responsibility as shaped by a socio-historical understanding of legal form. His account starts from (but does not end with) a conception of liberal first principles, but those first principles are what historically from the time of the Enlightenment underpin modern Western societies and their criminal law, and they take the initial form of an abstract individualism, as in his philosophy.

So for both of us there is something intransigent about criminal law's formalism: for him, because that is the way that liberalism's first political principles take us;

for me, because that is how it is in a particular historical form of society in which legal, political and economic relations are structurally configured in favour of abstract individualism. In that sense, Brudner is closer to the moralistic accounts than I, for he is arguing for a specific form of morality as pre-eminent (abstract individualist normativity). I in contrast argue from a socio-historical account of the relation between legal morality and social structure. However, it is refreshing to see modern Kantian and Hegelian flesh[2] put on the bones of criminal law theory and the theory of punishment, and his challenge to moralistic accounts brings out something of the underlying normative, political truth about law in a way that the direct, unmediated relationship to morality cannot capture.

The critical approach

If Brudner and I find common cause in our approach to moral accounts, we are unlikely to do so with regard to the relationship between political and what I call critical accounts. Brudner calls my approach a 'debunking' strategy. I am sure there is nothing wrong with debunking things that need debunking but, as a general description, it is superficial. It suggests something shallow and a little too clever. The debunker lacks the 'humbleness', as Brudner puts it, that is appropriate before 'an objective rationality' (2009: 7). This last comment is to me an

2 From discussion with Brudner, it is clear that he would resist my view of him as bringing together Kantian and Hegelian themes, regarding his position as 'out and out' Hegelian. This is in part because he regards the dominant theme in Kant's theory of punishment as Hobbesian, i.e., that punishment is primarily external rather than self-imposed. We disagree on this, as indeed we do on Hobbes. I argue for an essential continuity between Kant and Hegel as metaphysical retributivists, so that something like the first two forms of freedom identified by Brudner lie at the core of the *Kantian* theory of punishment in the form of the will as naturally determined (phenomenal) and as morally and rationally legislative (noumenal). Brudner 'demetaphysicalises' the latter form of freedom in his account of real autonomy, but there is something essentially Kantian going on here. I also think that Brudner does not follow Hegel in the way he deals with the relationship between property right and formally free will. Brudner wishes a first moment of formal freedom untrammelled by any account of substantive aims, a truly Kantian strategy, whereas Hegel insists that formal freedom (abstract right) already necessitates substance and world. Brudner's Hegelianism is accordingly restricted to incorporating a third moment of communal belonging in the manner of Hegel's ethical life and a dialectical method of argument that seeks to show the connections across the three forms of freedom. See Norrie 1991: ch 2 on Hobbes, ch 3 on Kant and ch 4 on Hegel. It would be important to work through the implications of the demetaphysicalisation that goes on in North American appropriations of both Kant and Hegel, but that is for another day. The effect, I think, is to deradicalise them. Brudner (2011) responds at some length to my suggestion that there is something Kantian in his Hegelianism, but he does so by over-accentuating the difference between them (see note 7 below), while conceding that 'Hegel completes a development initiated by Kant' (2011: 501). It is the hypostatisation (maintaining the abstract separation) of the different moments in his account of criminal justice, with a foundational role for formal freedom, that I see as the nub of his Kantianism. He writes in response to my comments for example that 'The issue of criminal liability for a wrong is decided by the formalist paradigm alone' (2011: 505).

uncomfortable reminder of the authoritarian side to Hegelian[3] (Hegel, 1952: 147) liberalism,[4] but my main concern is that it discounts the commitment to an inquiry into the nature of justice, albeit a critical one, that is in my work. Perhaps some of the original North American 'crits' could be criticised for 'trashing',[5] but the criticism has a hackneyed feel.[6]

Debunking for its own sake is certainly not what the critical approach to law is about, and I use the word 'critical' advisedly: to show that one is working by way of an *immanent critique* of legal materials; that is, seeking to be honest as to what they say and the problems within what they say; of an *historical critique* to argue that the problems of law are rooted in historical circumstances; of a *dialectical critique* to argue for the underlying interconnectedness of things that appear analytically distinct and antinomial (e.g. concepts of motive and intention); and of an *ethical critique*, to argue for the relational quality of social problems and legal solutions, and the two-way dialogic relationship between the punisher and the punished. Now it is true that Brudner might want to reserve the notion of critique for the Kantian inheritance in his own position, but I endorse the idea of a modern critical theory tradition that starts with Kant and Hegel, moves on to Marx, proceeds to 20th century dialectical thought, most prominently in the work of the early Frankfurt School, and onward still to others, including the dialectical theory of Roy Bhaskar (1993, 1994; Norrie 2010).

Brudner does say that a negative critical approach has 'enduring worth' and that he himself deploys it in passing to a positive reconstruction of the penal law, but he claims its fatal flaw, citing my work, is that it reveals 'laziness of thought' (Brudner, 2009: 7). It does not move beyond the negative critical moment to the sense of positive reconstruction that a totalising approach to objective rationality would bring. Well. Amongst Hegel's quite amusing, but ultimately less endearing, features was the lofty, impersonal insult that still manages to sting (there is no thinking without a thinker), but perhaps these should be left to the master. In any case, I do not accept that critical thinking only goes so far and not far enough: that is a criticism I would direct at more conventional forms of Hegelianism.

Brudner is quite correct to say that Hegelian philosophy has both a negative critical and a positive reconstructive moment, but the problem for critical and dialectical thinking after Hegel has been not to acknowledge the positive critical moment in his thought, but to be able to make sense of it as it pertains under

3 Hegel for example wrote of the role of the police in quelling conflict in periods of tension to ease 'the working of a necessity of which [those involved] know nothing' (Hegel 1952: 148).

4 And, indeed, Kantian liberalism (Adorno 1973: 232); for critical discussion, see Norrie (2005a: ch 9).

5 See e.g. Kelman (1981).

6 As long ago as 1993, I complained that critical legal studies work 'does not move significantly beyond the activity of 'trashing', *simple negation*, of the rationalist premises of orthodox criminal law theory' (emphasis added), and argued for an approach that was synthetic of 'internal' and 'external' approaches to criminal law and that took criminal doctrine seriously. See Norrie (2001: ix).

modern social conditions. Adorno's (1973) negative dialectic, for example, is not negative because he is 'lazy' and has not thought to include the positive resolution, but because, having thought long and hard about Hegel, he cannot find it under modern social conditions.

In my *Law, Ideology and Punishment* (1991), I discuss Hegel's philosophy of punishment and its problems, making the point that Hegel's account of rightful punishment in the sphere of Abstract Right is not maintained through to his account of the administration of justice in the further totalising sphere of Ethical Life; that is, the further positive, englobing move breaks down. I also show how the problems of modern social life under late-19th century capitalism (the problem of the poor and a social underclass) pressed British Hegelianism (Green, Bradley and Bosanquet) to shift its balance away from individual right and toward an authoritarian social totality, thereby opening the door to 20th century utilitarian preoccupations.

Historically, the further positive–resolutive move in Hegelian dialectic had become transformed into a contradictory move against individual right. In *Punishment, Responsibility and Justice*, I consider (Norrie 2000: ch 4) dialectical method in both its negative and positive moments, the problems to be found with Hegel's account of objective reason and the consequential development to a more critical dialectical philosophy this requires. In accusing the critical approach of one-sidedness, Brudner does not see any of this argument. Indeed, he makes no reference, in footnote or bibliography, to my critical reading of Hegel and Kant's philosophy of punishment in *Law, Ideology and Punishment*; nor does he respond to my detailed criticism of his Hegelianism as in its own way one-sided, by too simply reconciling negative critique and reason (Norrie 2000: 74–75). It is surprising in such circumstances to be accused of not having thought about positive totality and, dare I say, of 'laziness of thought'.

The forms of freedom and the nature of law

From the above we obtain two questions that I now want to explore in more depth. The first, addressing the moral standpoint, is: what is the place of substantive moral information and moral judgment in light of Brudner's political account? The second, addressing the critical standpoint, is: what role does and can totality, the sense of the whole, play in synthesising the plural levels of formal and substantive moral information indicated by the political theory of justice? As I will hope to show, these two questions can ultimately be brought together in an appropriately dialectical view of the three approaches before us: the political, the moral and the critical.

Let us begin by spelling out in more depth the nature of Brudner's political theory of penal justice. At its core is an account of freedom that gives rise to three different and overlapping spheres of freedom and justice. The first of these involves formal freedom or agency and is 'the bare capacity to have chosen otherwise than one did'. This is the freedom analytic to agency itself, independent of whatever material determinations may lead to it. It is purely formal in the sense that it is not linked to any particular determinations or substantive goals that an agent might have. It has nothing to do with the substantive values that may inform action: all that is required is the capacity to, for example, raise one's hand when one chooses, as opposed to having it raised by another person who grips it. Its formalism is radical in that it is compatible with slavery (Brudner 2009: 297–300), provided that the person enters into slavery voluntarily rather than by force, and it is compatible with duress provided that the agent chooses to follow the duressor's threats.

This radically formalist account of freedom lies at the core of the liberal theory of criminal punishment, according to Brudner. It is the one true universal starting point for human life that one achieves by abstracting from all particularity to find a stable ground for authority (ibid: 23). Formal agency grounds both freedom and coercion for its negation, so that punishment becomes the hinderance of a hinderance (Kant),[7] or a negation of a negation (Hegel), of freedom.

Now this account of abstract formal freedom lies at the core of the criminal law, where it is a necessary but not a sufficient ground for criminal punishment. Why necessary but not sufficient? Precisely because of the degree of abstraction that the theory involves. Formal freedom will tell you that a punishment is required but not what the punishment should be. It will link an actor to an act, but it will not specify the quality of the link and whether there is responsibility for it. For that you need a second kind of freedom that is immanent in formal freedom but needs to be brought out. That second form of freedom is what Brudner calls 'real autonomy', and it is not 'simply the capacity for undetermined choice, but . . . the actuality of self-determined choice'. This permits the possibility of rejecting ends given by material impulses in favour of acting from ends deliberately set by the actor.

This enriched conception of freedom has a number of consequences. One is that it emphasises that human beings act in a world and have impact for good or ill upon it. This is a world in which actors can cause harm to others, and they do so by acting in ways over which they have control. Because they can produce harms, actors provide the law with a measure of harm in what they have done to which a measure of harm in punishment can be returned to them. Hence if the right to punish comes from formal freedom, the measure of punishment comes from real autonomy; that is, a world in which agency goods and harms exist and represent the material from which self-determined choices are fashioned.

Further, because the important link between acting and outcomes is through the idea of control by an autonomous agent, the various ways in which an actor takes

7 That this involves a metaphysical account of justice is something I discuss in Law, Ideology and Punishment (1991: ch 3), but it is very clear from Kant's own words. See Kant, 1965: 35–36; 1996: 25. Brudner (2011) disputes this link between Kant and Hegel, arguing that Hegel's negation of a negation is 'conceptual', while Kant's is 'physical'. I think any fair reading of the Kant passage in question can only see it as metaphysical (what I think Brudner roughly means by 'conceptual'), and certainly not 'physical'. Kant (1996: 25) writes that the 'hindering of a hinderance to freedom' is 'consistent with freedom in accordance with universal laws, that is, it is right'.

control of an event are relevant – whether for example she intends or only foresees a harm as likely to happen. These different mental states, which are of course central to the criminal law, shape a person's responsibility and its level. They take us further than formal freedom, which provides a basic link between agent and act yet offers insufficient information to establish a just measure of punishment by a court. For that we need to know what harm was actually done and with what mental state a person did it, so we need an account of real autonomy alongside formal agency.

But real autonomy does not stop there. Thus far we have seen how formal agency and real autonomy ground just punishment, but this is only for that group of crimes known as 'real crimes'. Alongside these are the so-called regulatory or welfare offences, which have their ground in the specific nature of real autonomy. Real autonomy posits a context or conditions in which formal agency can be exercised. For a person to be able to author her own ends, she needs to have access to sufficient agency goods to make her freedom real. As Brudner says, liberal legal thought cannot stop at a right against interference because freedom may be short-circuited by conditions that leave the individual only to act from basic biological ends, rather than ends that are self-chosen. Examples would include poverty, illness and accident (ibid: 136), and these establish a duty on the liberal state to promote a range of forms of regulation and, where need be, regulatory criminal offences whose aim it is to police harm and protect real autonomy.

This is an argument that unfolds with elegance, but Brudner is not finished yet, for he still has to come to the third form of freedom: communal belonging. This is the freedom of the citizen who belongs to a community and in so doing 'is free in willingly conforming his or her conduct to the moral expectations the community has of someone occupying various social roles, such as spouse, parent, job-holder, and citizen' (ibid: 6). These give rise to roles with corresponding virtuous expectations that are voluntarily assumed by citizens. Such a freedom of the citizen also plays a crucial role in the criminal law, for the law 'communicates shared norms of conduct all can reflectively endorse, while calling citizens to answer to their fellows collectively for alleged wrongdoing – through exculpatory explanation if innocent and through re-integrative penance if guilty' (ibid).

The three forms of freedom thus developed now have to be analysed as they are instantiated in the structure of the law. Here the relationship is complex, but Brudner distinguishes the traditional distinctions between offence and defence and justification and excuse as they relate to the three accounts of freedom (ibid: 81–85). Thus, formal freedom not only grounds the basic conditions of mens rea and actus reus but also allows for certain exculpatory defences where a defendant did not make a culpable choice. These include involuntariness of action, infancy, mistake of fact and insanity. In these there is no decision or choice to break the law. Also included here are justificatory defences where the defendant in effect argues that he acted rightly despite seeming to break the law; thus, justifications such as self-defence are included because they do not deny formal right in their implication, and linked to this is the rationale for mistaken self-defence, which although it does involve a breach of right, comes under the exculpation provided by the theory of formal right on account of the existence of a mistake.

As regards matters of justification and excuse, there is huge controversy in law and legal theory about how best to classify different defences, and I will not try to go much further here (but see Norrie 2000: chs 7, 8; 2014: especially chs 8, 10). Brudner distinguishes different kinds of the necessity defence for example, some of which fall under justification, some under excuse. His opening line in his chapter on justification is: 'Almost no general statements about legal justifications are true', and I will respect this judgement for now – indeed, I may invoke it at a later date as evidence of the need for critique!

Matters are a little clearer about excuse. Here are grouped certain kinds of necessity and the defence of duress, as well as partial defences including provocation and diminished responsibility. Here the rationale is that the defendant has transgressed the boundaries of public right but is excused because, in so doing, he has not essentially acted against the norms of good citizenship. Thus, excuses operate on the basis of applying the third form of freedom – communal belonging – where the first form – breach of formal freedom – has occurred. (It should also be noted that there is another kind of necessity where real autonomy is called into question, although I am unable to explore that here.)

Criminal justice as a complex totality: two cases

With this in mind, perhaps some examples will help us to think through the implications of this argument for the complex unity of the criminal law. What will be important will be the extent to which Brudner's trichotomy is able to rationalise or redesign core distinctions in the law itself.

Exculpation: DPP v Morgan[8]

In *Morgan*, the defendants claimed that they had made an honest mistake in believing that the woman they had raped had consented, on the basis of assurances from her husband that she liked to have sex in a rough and apparently non-consensual way. Their defence of lack of mens rea was accepted by the House of Lords on the basis that rape was an offence involving knowledge that sex was non-consensual. Against this, it was argued at the time that any mistake had to be reasonable before it could exculpate, but why should this be the case? One argument is that a bare factual account of the defendants' mental state does not take into account the moral seriousness of the harm that lies in rape. So serious is this that the defendant is under an obligation to find out whether the victim consents and, if he does not do so, his ignorance is in itself culpable.

8 [1976] AC 182.

Another argument might be that his ignorance reveals a morally bad character, one that displays a callous indifference to the effects of pursuing one's own desires without consideration of the harm done to others in the process. Against this line of argument, it might then be said that there are some men who are genuinely callous, and some who are simply culturally unsophisticated or naïve in their understanding of what sex is about. A line would have to be drawn between the callous and the ignorant. The change in English law under the Sexual Offences Act 2003, with its reference to a reasonable belief requirement as to consent, is in part a response to a case like *Morgan*.[9]

How would Brudner deal with *Morgan*? If believed, the defendants are exculpated on his account. Their mistake of fact means that, under the paradigm of formal agency, they have not consciously disdained another's capacity for freedom; their belief means that they have shown a respect for her freedom, albeit mistakenly so. Accordingly, as I understand Brudner, the defendants in *Morgan* are rightly acquitted. The suggestions that others have made to take into account the moral colour of the mistake in light of the context in which it is made are irrelevant: the formal account of freedom holds sway. But this seems counter-intuitive, and not necessarily derived from Brudner's account. If we recall that on a complex account of freedom, we have to consider formal freedom, real autonomy and communal belonging, then it might be said that Brudner's account of formal freedom respects freedom at one level but only by ignoring it at the two others.

Thus, the defendant's formal freedom according to public reason is respected, and note, the victim's formal freedom, despite the fact that she has been forcibly held down and raped, is also so respected. This is because formal freedom is the basis for universal justice. If the defendant does not deny formal freedom in his agency, then formal freedom is not denied universally. This is in itself surprising news for the victim, but also denied here is the additional relevance of her real autonomy, for she has not had sex under conditions that give her the chance to choose her own ends. Furthermore, the norms of the community to which the defendant belongs must also be ignored here, for surely according to its roles and manners, in which the defendant participates, the defendant has come up very short in the way he has conducted himself.

Now against this argument, Brudner will say that the kinds of considerations I have introduced here are irrelevant precisely because they are generated by a moral view of responsibility, one that does not see the importance of the true political principle of formal agency at the core of the criminal law. My concern is that in placing so limited a conception of freedom at the core of the criminal law, Brudner's account in a case like *Morgan* is stuck with a form of freedom that he himself concedes is radically incomplete. This might be said to work sufficiently well where formal freedom inculpates a defendant, who then can use an excuse in

9 Sexual Offences Act 2003, s 1(1) and (2).

response to formal inculpation, because then formal inculpation is not required to do all the work. It is supplemented by questions of real autonomy or community expectations. But where formal agency operates to exculpate, then other considerations of freedom, which are required to think through the situation of the defendant and the victim, are not available.

Furthermore, it is surely the case on Brudner's own account of a sinuous and dialectically connected set of accounts of freedom that they ought to be available – especially when the basal mode of freedom is so thin that it can be turned against any substantive conception of freedom at all. Formal agency is so lacking in those things that Brudner recognises to be central at their different levels to freedom that it is hard to see why he could found lack of mens rea on so impoverished a conception. The wrong *of rape*, in short, is not avoided *in all cases* by virtue of a simple factual mistake on consent, but in Brudner's account it is.

In a sense, however, Brudner is following the logic of the law of mens rea, which does tend itself to rely on a formalistic account of intention, that is, one that is factual, psychologistic and technical: that is why the defendants had an 'out' in *Morgan*. But then it is small wonder that a moral approach to responsibility should find a foothold in the law through its critique of the formalism of legal judgment, and it is precisely moral attitudes that, it has been argued, should be judged in the law of mistaken belief concerning consent for rape. Brudner criticises me in this matter for talking of the poverty of criminal responsibility, but I think his account fortifies my point: he himself has to recognise its formal abstraction. If I do so, I am not ignoring 'the moral stature in a body of principles securing the distinction between punishment and violence' (ibid: 167). Rather, I am pointing to the incapacity of this formal body of principles *properly to reflect* the distinction between punishment and violence. To do so would involve introducing proper, substantive moral understandings into the doctrine of mistake. Such an introduction is consistent with Brudner's synthesis of the three paradigms of freedom, but not with his emphasis on the independent role formal freedom is allowed to play with regard to mens rea.

Does this argument seek to overload formal freedom at the expense of its other form, real autonomy? Brudner can propose that there be a separate welfare-style offence for the ignorant rapist pertaining to his negligent inadvertence to non-consent. The problem with this is that inadvertence comes in different forms and levels of culpability: simple ones in which there is ignorance caused by stupidity, naivety or 'cultural ignorance'; and egregious ones that fall short of turning a blind eye, but include callousness, indifference or a 'couldn't care less' attitude[10] to the position of the victim.

10 *R v Satnam and Kewal* [1983] 78 Cr App Rep 149 (CA). Brudner (2011) reiterates his argument about the possibility of a public welfare offence distinct from the criminal wrong. My point, drawing on the moral approach, is that the *crime of rape* can be committed with practical indifference, which Brudner's approach must rule out *ex hypothesi*. The grand synthesis ordains that this must be so.

Although a welfare offence could catch the former, the latter cases are most properly placed in the more serious 'real crime' category. In Brudner's terms, the culpability inherent in the callousness of the egregious ignoramus is caught neither by his cognitive attitude to the crime (by formal freedom) nor by a simple, negligent inadvertence (in real autonomy). It is an attitudinal culpability that is person centred but not cognitively so and, as such, it escapes Brudner's categories.

For Brudner, the problem is that such an attitudinal approach cannot be made susceptible to legal rule. Once one moves away from formal freedom's cognitivism to inadvertence-based approaches, lines become blurred between culpable and non-culpable forms of inadvertence, ultimately in law between crime and tort, and this is an unacceptably slippery slope (ibid: 94–95). That may be true, but Brudner seems here to be switching the direction of his line of argument. According to his philosophical approach, it is the first principles enshrined in the three forms of freedom that shape and give form to the divisions of law. The former vindicate the latter. In arguing that it would be dangerous for law if his philosophical model were not deployed, he is using *post hoc propter hoc* a legal problem to buttress his philosophy. An alternative view might be that there is a problem both in law and in philosophy in deploying a cognitive-based formalist philosophical stance at the core of thought and in expecting it to do the work of normative judgment that the criminal law requires, either by itself or in conjunction with other ethical forms. An uncomfortable conclusion, perhaps, but when the rational philosophy runs out, sometimes the philosopher has to accept she lacks an answer, and that complexity, tension and contradiction win.[11]

Inculpation and exoneration: R v Steane[12]

If mistake of fact shows formal freedom in exculpatory mode, the law in *Steane* shows how it normally works to inculpate, although it did not do so in *Steane*. Steane was found not guilty of an offence of intending to assist the enemy by broadcasting for the Germans in the Second World War, despite the fact that there was a logical connection between broadcasting for them and assisting them, or at least a virtual certainty in this regard, to put it in the terms of today's English law of criminal intention. Under the usual application of the law, he should be said to have intended to assist the enemy, but the law was narrowed to hold open the possibility that his sole intention had been to save his family from being sent to a concentration camp, despite the fact that assisting the enemy was the only way to save them. Here an account of formal freedom coupled with one of real

11 For a view along these lines on the problems of advertence and inadvertence, see Norrie, 2014: 89–100. Brudner (2011, 207) misunderstands my argument by reading it in terms of his own when he writes that I think a blurring of boundaries is 'consistent with synthesis'. As I say here, 'complexity, tension and contradiction win'. The overall synthesis of a grand design in which everything fits in its place is Brudner's preoccupation, not mine.

12 [1947] 1 All ER 813.

autonomy seems to convict the defendant so that his only recourse is to an excusatory defence of duress.

That is argued to be the case by many, and Brudner would agree (ibid: 152–53). In his terms, the existence of a valid intention to do something that is one's purpose or that one knows will almost certainly come about as a result of one's intentional choice means that the person both has acted in a bare and formally free sense and has exercised the autonomy that is hers to follow self-selected goals. Accordingly, on the first and second forms of freedom, the person is inculpated and her wrongdoing properly described. The person then has recourse to an excusatory defence, the principles of right having been negated by a formally free and autonomous choice. In the process the typical doctrinal division between offence and defence is respected.

This seems fine until one remembers that freedom as real autonomy has two sides to it. One side is the fashioning of our self-selected ends according to a variety of mental states as we come into contact with the possibility of actions resulting in substantive harms. The other side, however, is the establishment of a social domain for action in which the possibility of formulating free choices for action requires a layer of protection from those things that push us back into a reliance on simple biological imperatives, such as the will to survive. Real autonomy stipulates that humans should be protected from poverty, illness and accident, and the ground for this is that people are not free if thrown back on their bare natural choices.

But what is duress if not a matter of being thrown back on just such choices? It follows that the person who experiences duress is a person who not only acts as any citizen would be expected to act in a community of which he was a member (the third form of freedom), but a person who does not enjoy real autonomy under the gunman's threat. Thus, on Brudner's own account, I think it is the case that the person under duress suffers a lack of freedom as both real autonomy and communally appropriate belonging. Since the law of intention couples together formal freedom and real autonomy – the just punishment requires both for a proper inculpation – then these two forms of freedom cut against each other. Brudner does not discuss the matter in these terms; he sees formal freedom and real autonomy as happily combining, and then (quite elegantly) synthesising with communal belonging to provide the offence–defence structure of intention and duress.

But if I am right in saying that real autonomy cuts as much against as runs with formal freedom, then the only way to maintain the intention–duress distinction is to say that real autonomy is not relevant here to liability, and it is the balance between formal freedom and communal belonging alone that matters. That, however, would be to defeat his own claim to synthesise the three forms and to fall back again on absolutely impoverished formal freedom. He needs an account of real autonomy to furnish him with an account of intention to apply in a case such as *Steane*, but then must abandon it halfway. Steane intended to assist the enemy 'because he chose it' (ibid: 153), but he also, I think, chose it because he intended it, and it is analytic to intention that it works where the ability to act is not reduced to motives that are simply heteronomous because they are biologically reduced.[13]

Penal justice and social injustice

A third area for discussion is the overall relationship between penal justice and social justice. Brudner is prepared to accept that social injustice causes crime, so he must confront the old claim that you cannot have just punishment in an unjust society. Poverty, he says, can inspire unjust deeds brought about by 'noble feelings' (ibid: 324), but what would make poverty-inspired deeds 'unjust'? The answer is that social injustice cannot make 'private violence or takings permissible'. It can neither justify nor excuse 'an individual's violating rights that the perfectly just society would itself protect', and these would include any possessory right, which belongs to all, even to a thief. What kind of right is a possessory right? The perfectly just society includes the universal right to possess things and, since it is universal, it seems to rest on formal agency.

In a passage on formal freedom and slavery, Brudner is very clear about just how limited formal freedom is. At its root, formal freedom is a condition that is antithetical to human dignity because it involves the ability to abstract from everything that we are in the world, in our materiality and in our particularity. It is merely a bare freedom to abstract, 'simply a capacity to renounce every end, with the result that all specific ends actually chosen, including self-preservation, are subjective values one may either have chosen to further or not' (ibid: 299). It is identical to arbitrariness, and this means that we have a 'dichotomy between a contentless capacity for non-determination generic to agents and the subjective ends of the individual'. Now, if this is the case, then it seems to me that this is indeed so bare a freedom that it would not include anything so worldly as possession of a thing, so that 'possessory right' is not properly of the domain of abstract, formal freedom. At this point, Brudner pushes out to argue that one can build from this to worldly 'agency' goods such as life and bodily integrity – and even property because ownership 'is also essential to self-determination' (ibid: 300), even if this or that piece of property is an object of preference.

13 At this point, there is still the possibility of a 'floodgates' argument. Admit that an offence might be denied on the basis of a lack of real autonomy, and you open the law up to all sorts of claims based thereon. Anyone who is hungry could deny the offence of theft. I am not sure this is right where, for example, alternative means of fending off hunger are available. In any case, I am not sure that it is a valid argument because, once again, it uses a problem in law to vindicate a philosophical first principle, and we are entitled to ask why the argument should be inverted. To Brudner's (2011) claim that the principles of autonomy and formal freedom must be clearly partitioned so that they 'mind their own business', my point is that a properly dialectical argument would have to confront the terrain where the two principles are in competition with each other. To fail to do so is to hypostatise the principles. Lacking an achievable grand design, law must do this all the time.

I am not sure from this where the bounds of formal freedom actually lie. On the one hand, Brudner seems to want to take a rigorous Kantian line on the abstraction of freedom from all determinations as the only autonomy; on the other, his approach seems here, at the end of the text, to be going towards Hegel, who argued that it was the nature of the self-determining will to move from total abstraction into things in the world as part of a process of self-determination that at once, dialectically, both abstracts and engages the will.

The problem with the former is that it gives us nothing to link to concrete determinations. The problem with the latter is that it establishes too much in the way of determination. If we say that, for example, possession is necessary for a will in any possible world, do we then have to argue that private property is a necessary universal good? And if we argue that, do we have to say that any distribution of property is equally valid, so that a right of private property entails the right to be a billionaire whilst others starve? Brudner might say that within the billionaire's property there is nested the right to property, which is in turn nested in the right to possession, which is in turn nested in a basic freedom to be in the world. But against that, one might argue for lines to be drawn between the universally necessary and the contingent, so that the billionaire's property rights extend a bare possessory right far beyond what it entails. Possessory right is immanent in plutocratic wealth, but hardly vice versa.

Further, if we take private property to be a matter of agency goods, related to the production of real autonomy, not formal freedom, then do we not get a different basis for judging the matter? That is, what would the world have to look like for everyone to be able to select their own ends and not to be thrown back on bare nature? In a world inhabited by extremes of wealth, where the poor are poor because the rich are rich (let us just suppose that is the case), would that not be a world in which the claim of real autonomy might stand against a claim for universal possessory rights? Of course, if you say that universal possessory rights are sacrosanct because they are the only true universals, then you will hold onto those against arguments based on the achievement of real autonomy. But recall that formal autonomy is a simple bare universal and one that does not *ex hypothesi* produce justice in terms of real autonomy or communal well-being. It would also be a bare universal in the face of a theory of structural inequality and structural economic violence that explains how so many in the world are thrown back on an intransigent 'bare life'. Start with Kant under modern social and economic conditions, and you might end up with Agamben.

It seems to me that Brudner's basic position in defence of the possibility of legal justice is based upon a notion of bare freedom rooted in formal universality, but his argument, it must be recalled, is for a synthesis in which the demands of formal freedom are synthesisable with the demands of real autonomy and communal being. It will not do, therefore, to pin the argument back on formal freedom alone. To do so is to present a theory in which the demands of one kind of freedom are at war with the demands of another, and not comfortably synthesised with each other. In this regard, it is worth ending with a quote from Hegel, who thought more deeply and aporetically about these things than he is sometimes given credit for. In his account of the third sphere of Ethical Life, sitting uncomfortably with the right to punish theft in the sphere of Abstract Right, he writes:

> . . . against nature man can claim no right, but once society is established, poverty immediately takes the form of a wrong done to one class by another. The important question of how poverty is to be abolished is one of the most disturbing problems which agitate modern society (ibid: 277–78).

Of course, the 'immediately' is relevant here, for Hegel still thinks modernity holds the key to a rational ordering of society, but he could see the other side and the dangers that his objectively rational order might not prove so rational and objective under modern conditions, in which case the different sides of his theory would also be brought into conflict with each other.[14] This, of course, brings us back to our beginning and the question of being 'humble' before an 'objective rationality', although I hope by now the fear of 'laziness of thought' has abated.

Conclusion

I have argued for the importance of Brudner's work in affirming the centrality of a politically-based formal morality as lying at the core of the modern criminal law. One can argue this as a matter of first philosophical principles (Brudner's political approach) or as a matter of historical and sociological structure (my critical approach), but one should not be reductive. Ultimately, it is the conjunction of the philosophical and the historical that grounds the particularity of the normative forms that make up the account of responsibility in modern criminal law, although from the standpoint of sociology, it is the latter that drives, whilst being reflexively informed by, the former.

If these are the political and critical approaches, what of the moral approach? From Brudner's perspective, those aspects of the moral approach that are excluded by the political approach in its initial manifestation as formal freedom are rationally reallocated through the theory as elements of real autonomy or communal belonging. In the critical approach, they also have their salience as identifying those aporia where the formal approach to freedom at the core of the

14 See Norrie (1991: 83–85). It might be said this is only a problem in a society where no genuine and thorough set of welfare arrangements exists to mediate the effects of wealth on poverty. But that was not the kind of society we are talking about. Poverty was a problem that modern civil society could not resolve, threatening the dialectical inversion of justice and injustice. See Hegel (1952: 241–45). How much better placed are we today? Brudner (2011) clarifies his position here on what is a central question: how are the dictates of formal freedom reconciled with the material consequences of their structural elaboration in the social world. This passage from Hegel shows *his* awareness of the problem, one that continues to undermine any modern system of abstract formal right.

criminal law does not deliver an appropriate justice in different kinds of cases. The prospect of a satisfactory synthesis of the more 'formal' and more 'substantive' forms of justice promised by Brudner is undermined by critical investigation, as in the discussions of *Morgan* and *Steane* above, and that leaves a situation in which criminal law is structured around unsynthesised oppositions between formal freedom and more substantive moral concerns. Critical thinking then is in the position of identifying the problematic and necessarily tense, structural and historical, relationship between 'political' and 'moral' standpoints on criminal law.

I welcome Brudner's work as a reassertion of the political side of criminal responsibility, and especially his account of the salience of formal freedom to the law. I resist, however, his view that the political account in its Kantian–Hegelian form can resolve the law's problems through a reallocation of forms. Those problems in my view remain unresolvable by either a more formalistically centred, political approach or a more substantively oriented, moral approach. The criminal law should be seen as entailing a dialectical tension between 'political' (in Brudner's sense) and 'moral' considerations. In viewing the relation between the moral and political approaches from a deeper historical and dialectical standpoint, critical thinking is located as the diagnostic master. It is the place of *Aufhebung*-without-resolution of the antinomy of form and substance embedded at the heart of modern criminal law. It provides a modern, critical phenomenology of the broken character of modern legal form.

Part II

Law's constellation

Chapter 7

Justice on the slaughter bench: the problem of war guilt in Arendt and Jaspers

> 'There is only one rational way in which states co-existing with other states can emerge from the lawless condition of pure warfare . . . [T]hey must renounce their savage and lawless freedom, adapt themselves to public coercive laws, and thus form an international state (civitas gentium).'
>
> (Kant 1991: 105)

> 'Passions . . . respect none of the limitations which justice and morality would impose on them . . . When we look at . . . the consequences of their violence . . . when we see the evil, the vice, the ruin that has befallen the most flourishing kingdoms . . . we can scarce avoid being filled with sorrow at this universal taint of corruption . . . regarding History as the slaughter bench at which the happiness of peoples, the wisdom of States, and the virtue of individuals have been victimized . . .'
>
> (Hegel 1956: 20–21)

Justice on the slaughter bench

If Hegel is right about the 'slaughter bench' of history, what does this mean for our understanding of justice for acts of wrongdoing, even of the worst kind? On his description, humankind's destiny is to reproduce time after time, by both the judge and the judged, the most terrible excesses. In such a situation, what can the ethical status of justice be? Can endless, systemic, acts of egregious violence be requited morally where nothing is learned and nothing in essence changes? In such a light, does justice not appear as vain repetition and false consolation, as the illusion practised by the barbaric victor over the vanquished? Writing in the 1820s, Hegel retained a redemptive optimism, suggesting that even if we regard history as the slaughter bench, 'the question involuntarily arises – to what principle, to what final aim these enormous sacrifices have been offered' (ibid: 21). For him a path of progress, a reason beyond the unreason, could be discerned. Two hundred years later, having experienced horrors that might have given even him pause for thought, is there any consolation through principled justice for history's slaughter bench?

Such a question will find lawyers reaching for the international statute book. They will point to the establishment of an International Criminal Court, and the creation of individual tribunals with regard to the former Yugoslavia and the genocide in Rwanda. Things surely have changed for the better, in line with another Enlightenment account, that outlined by Kant in his essay on 'Perpetual Peace' (Kant 1991).[1] For him, savagery and lawlessness could be avoided by an international state and laws, and it will be argued that these new institutions represent a step in the right direction. They produce the hope, and something of the reality, of a new international justice that can stand against history's slaughter bench. But, ethically, what kind of justice do these new institutions deliver? If new outrages continue after their establishment, do they become convenient ways of assuaging guilty consciences, whilst operating as part of a world order in which genocidal actions continue, in part because of the alibi that 'something is being done'? In such a light, to what extent do they themselves become complicit, delivering a 'victor's justice' for successful warmongers, prosecuting those who find themselves on the wrong end of global power relations?

The bite of such questions depends on how we understand the justice that international institutions are able to deliver and, in this essay, I consider two works, written in dialogue with each other, which can claim to have first addressed the problem of justice 'on the slaughter bench' in modern times: Hannah Arendt's *Eichmann in Jerusalem* (1964) and Karl Jaspers's *The Question of German Guilt* (2000). Both Arendt and Jaspers saw serious problems in delivering a morally valid international justice. For both, the moral categories that would vindicate such a justice were found wanting in the face of the Nazi slaughter bench. In Arendt, this is seen especially at the end of the epilogue and in the postscript to *Eichmann in Jerusalem*, where her support for international penal law runs up against the problem of doing justice to one so egregiously wicked, yet so unexceptional, as Eichmann. In *The Question of German Guilt*, it is seen in Jaspers's troubled reflections over the effect of his own guilt typology in allowing Germans to evade a proper sense of their guilt for Nazi crimes, and in particular in his deep ambivalence to a conception of collective guilt.

However, I will argue that there is more to be said ethically for international justice than their arguments allow. There is much to be said for the slaughter bench view of history,[2] but for still accepting something of the sense of moral justice delivered by international tribunals. Arendt and Jaspers in different ways confront the same problem, but I argue that there are resources in the latter's philosophy, in

1 Kant did not think it possible to go so far as this, but he provided a blueprint for subsequent thinking and practice.

2 There is an alignment between the slaughter bench view and Arendt's depiction of the violence associated with modern imperialism and totalitarianism, and her understanding of the problem of dealing with the Nazis as 'civilized barbarians'. Similarly, Jaspers's guilt categories are implicitly cut in the light of the need to reconstruct a society that had previously given itself up to the slaughter bench.

his metaphysical conception of justice, that can be pressed into service against his own argument. These can also help resolve Arendt's difficulties. It is not an easy moral conception of justice that emerges, rather one that is troubled and troubling, but it gives sense to the feeling that a wholly reductionist account of international justice can be avoided.

This chapter has five sections. In the next, I clarify the issue that lies at the heart of my argument, and of Arendt and Jaspers's positions in their early epistolary exchange on Nuremberg. This was triggered by Jaspers's book on German war guilt published at the end of the Second World War, and the issue was later pursued by Arendt in her discussion of the Eichmann trial. I will consider Arendt's contradictory position in *Eichmann in Jerusalem* and the problem with Jaspers's position in *The Question of German Guilt* in the two ensuing sections. In the final sections, I draw the threads of the argument together by picking up the tension in Jaspers's account concerning collective guilt and showing how it might be exploited in a way that holds out something for the ethical promise of international justice. I focus on the nature and implications of his idea of 'metaphysical guilt' in its relationship to collective guilt and counterpose it to the idea of history as the slaughter bench.

In considering Arendt and Jaspers, I draw to an extent upon themes that I have developed in other work on the relationship between the historical and structural forces shaping modern society and the nature of its ethical forms. In particular, I have argued that modern thinking about justice discloses a strongly antinomial structure, and this is seen for example in the relationship posited between 'individual' and 'social' justice, or between (what has become constructed as) 'legal' and 'moral' forms of guilt.[3] Here, I prefer to move by way of immanent critique from the problems I find in Arendt's and Jaspers's work. I will, however, in the final sections sketch a 'difficult' relationship between legal and ethical justice in the area of international justice, which draws on my previous work on the relationship between 'the conditional' and 'the unconditioned' in modern ethics. This links up with my interest in the relation between an ideal, displaced ethics and the nature of law in modernity, showing some affinity with Jacques Derrida's view of justice as deconstruction, whilst drawing on Roy Bhaskar's critical realist account of dialectic (Bhaskar,1993; 2002; Norrie 2010).[4] The result is a conception of guilt or responsibility that delivers a sense of justice, albeit in a difficult form.

3 The latter distinction lies at the core of Jaspers's philosophy. For accounts of the antinomial structure of the philosophy of criminal justice and legal doctrine, see Norrie (1991; 2000; 2014). For antinomialism in legal theory more generally, see Norrie (2005a: pts 1–2).

4 On deconstruction, law and judgment, see Derrida (1990: 919; 2001). On deconstruction and dialectics, see Norrie (2005a: pt 3); on Derrida and Bhaskar's dialectical critical realism, see Norrie (2005b: 96). On the ideal and the actual in criminal justice, see Norrie (1998: 101).

Judgment and justice: the problem of moral community

'still, there is a difference . . .'

(Kohler and Saner 1992: 54)

An initial question concerns what we mean by justice in a penal context. In the classical theory of the nation-state, institutions of criminal justice stand against violence in two ways. First, they seek to prevent it (re)occurring by conviction and punishment which deters further such acts. As in the national context, the deterrent effect of international criminal justice is unproven, and perhaps will remain unprovable, but there is a second goal of justice which is more important. That is the delivery of a sense of retributive justice by the capture, prosecution and conviction of those who have done wrong and who are held to account for their acts before a justice that condemns and, in condemning, declares the moral negation of the criminal act. How capable are international criminal justice institutions of delivering this most central understanding of what justice is? To what extent, in terms of our initial quote from Hegel, can they deliver a moral condemnation of wrongdoing, which stands as a human achievement, over against the vision of human history as a 'slaughter bench'?

Before proceeding to Arendt and Jaspers on this question, I briefly explore a problem in the theory of punishment discussed in relation to national penal justice contexts. This links, I will suggest, with Arendt and Jaspers's early epistolary exchange on justice at Nuremberg, setting up the ensuing positions. The problem hinges on the difficulty in creating a consensual community of judgment under modern social conditions.

The need for a community of judgment

The problem I have in mind has classical reference points in both Kant and Hegel (Norrie 1991: chs 3–4). With Kant, it is seen in the issue of doing justice to the mother who kills her illegitimate child, or the soldier who kills in a duel. In these cases, 'honour' killings, there is a problem in justly punishing the wrongdoer for murder. After some deliberation, Kant holds that the moral law remains in force in such cases but that legislation and the civil constitution represent a real underlying problem. So long as there is conflict between honour and the penal law, the civil constitution will remain 'barbarous and underdeveloped' and be 'to blame for the fact that the motives of honour obeyed by the people are subjectively incompatible' with the objective law, 'so that public justice as dispensed by the state is *injustice* in the eyes of the people' (Kant 1965: 107).

In Hegel's case, there is a similar problem concerning criminal justice and poverty. Private property is of course one of the foundations of his *Philosophy of Right*, and the built-in dynamic in modern society towards impoverishment of those at the bottom of society leads poverty to 'take the form of a wrong done to one class by another' (Hegel 1952: 277). There is a consequent 'loss of the sense of right and wrong' amongst the poor, who consequently become a 'penurious rabble' (ibid: 150).

These comments by Kant and Hegel point in the same direction, to the erosion or displacement of a sense of right and wrong in society, to a sense that society's condition leads to a loss of moral compass or consensus within a community, and to a resultant threat to moral judgment. The comments could be interpreted in two ways. One would be to see a loss of a *subjective* moral grip on the individuals concerned – the mother, the soldier (Kant), the poor (Hegel). These people are not really to blame for failing to obey the law because of their circumstances. The other would be to see a loss of *objective* moral purchase on the situation. It is not so much that individuals are to be excused by their subjective circumstances for failing to obey the law, but rather that the law has objectively lost its moral claim to validity. The civil constitution (Kant), or the dispensation of property (Hegel), are no longer justified by the overall circumstances in which they operate (ignorance, poverty). Social development has generated a moral position in which a common sense of right and wrong cannot exist, and such a common sense is just what would be needed for justice and judgment to occur. Justice requires, in short, a common framework within which the judge and the judged co-exist.

These two aspects of the problem – its subjective and objective dimensions – are, I would suggest, integral to any modern discussion of guilt and punishment, justice and judgment. In addition to the philosophy of punishment (cf Duff 1996),[5] they are seen, for example, in modern legal accounts of (subjective) excuse and (objective) justification (Greenawalt 1984). It is the objective dimension that I think is the more significant in its implications for the debate between Arendt and Jaspers, although both come out in Arendt's writings. Let us now turn, however, to examine the early exchange between the two over Jaspers's book on German war guilt in the light of this problem of judgment.

An epistolary exchange

As we will see in detail below, Jaspers's *The Question of German Guilt* (2000) established a fourfold typology of forms of guilt: he wrote of *criminal*, *political*, *moral* and *metaphysical* guilt, from which he distinguished a fifth form, *collective* guilt. We will have cause to consider the link between his typology and this fifth form later but, for the moment, we need only note that Jaspers's schema provided a means for distinguishing those who had led the Nazi war machine, who were *criminally* guilty, from the bulk of the population who suffered political sanctions (and therefore responsibility – *political* guilt – as members of the German polity). In this typology, *moral* and *metaphysical* guilt are deeper forms which affect the individual's ethical

5 Punishment is unjustified where offenders have not 'wronged members of a genuine community . . . that respects and cares for them, and that thus has the moral standing to criticise them' (Duff 1996: 85). See also nn 9 and 20 below.

rather than legal or political position, and work *in foro interno*, whilst *criminal* and *political* guilt work *in foro externo*. Jaspers erects a barrier between internal and external forms of guilt, although he acknowledges, without developing, the sense that these are ultimately connected. Whatever the implications of this typology, one thing is clear: Jaspers identified what was for him a valid form of criminal guilt, which vindicated the isolation and punishment of the most egregious Nazi war criminals.

Arendt's response in correspondence was to question this situation given the nature of national socialism:

> The Nazi crimes . . . explode the limits of the law; and that is precisely what constitutes their monstrousness. For these crimes, no punishment is severe enough . . . That is, their guilt, in contrast to all criminal guilt, oversteps and shatters any and all legal systems . . . We are simply not equipped to deal, on a human, political level, with a guilt that is beyond crime . . . The Germans are burdened now *with thousands or tens of thousands or hundreds of thousands of people* who cannot be adequately punished within the legal system.
>
> (Kohler and Saner 1992: 54, emphasis added)

Her letter prompted a warning from Jaspers that she was close to describing 'a guilt that goes beyond all criminal guilt [which] inevitably takes on a streak of "greatness" – of satanic greatness', whereas it was necessary 'to see these things in their total banality, in their prosaic triviality, because that's what truly characterises them' (ibid: 62). Replying, Arendt accepted that her words might have invited this understanding, but that she totally rejects such a view, and that she was in fact trying to make a different point:

> But still, there is a difference between a man who sets out to murder his old aunt and people who without considering the economic usefulness of their actions at all . . . built factories to produce corpses . . . [I]ndividual human beings did not kill other individual human beings for human reasons, but . . . an organised attempt was made to eradicate the concept of the human being.
>
> (ibid: 69)

Arendt's comments can be aligned with the problem we have identified in Kant and Hegel, both in its subjective and objective dimensions.[6] *Subjectively*, she is

6 I use the terms 'objective' and 'subjective' to denote the two dimensions in the liberal theory of punishment (i.e., the need for a judging community and a responsible subject) required for justice. In *Eichmann in Jerusalem*, Arendt uses the terms slightly differently, arguing that where the 'subjective' dimension of guilt is missing, only an 'objective' justification of punishment is possible, meaning a non-liberal 'Old Testament' form of justice (1964: 277–78). In order to avoid confusion and preserve the important point that a liberal account itself involves an 'objective' dimension, i.e., an emphasis on the need for a community of judgment which can engage with the individual

arguing that the Nazis had fallen below a level of normal human intercourse, had developed a wholly distorted sense of right and wrong, had carried out acts only attributable to persons who had lost essential elements of their humanity. There was something just lacking in their moral psychology, something psycho- or socio-pathological in their actions, which made them unpunishable according to modern moral–legal protocols. Later, she would follow up such a view in her account of Eichmann's limited, although normal, personal moral capacities,[7] and in her account of the modern 'mass man' (Arendt 1968: pt 3), but I do not think this is the most important aspect of her argument.

Abutting the subjective dimension is the problem that, *objectively*, Nazi Germany had established a system of government in which a common, modern, liberal understanding of right and wrong had disappeared. A whole people, or at least a huge chunk of it, had redirected their moral compass radically and abhorrently. Nuremberg was an attempt to restore the sense of a common moral framework, which could unite judge and judged in a system of justice, but it grappled with the fact that the Nazis did not share the same assumptions as those judging them. There was an absence of a sense of shared moral community or consensus, and this called into question the possibility of justice in Arendt's view.

Comparing Arendt's problem with the Nazis with those identified in national contexts by Kant and Hegel, there are of course important differences. In the latter cases, the problem is that the liberal understanding of law is exposed by the failure of liberal society to provide the social arrangements which would sustain it. In Arendt's case, liberal society has paved the way for a totalitarian polity which does not share its (proclaimed) values (ibid).[8] But in all cases, we have the idea that a common set of values that can unify a community of judgment has been subverted by underlying social developments. It would be injustice to punish the maternal infanticide or the duellist (Kant), or the criminal pauper (Hegel). Surely it could not also be injustice to punish the Nazi? Of course, Arendt has no sympathy for such people (as she might have had, let us say, for the mother or the pauper), but sympathy, or antipathy, are not at issue.

The question of justice is raised because Arendt senses the loss of a crucial element required for any modern system of justice. There is a radical disjuncture between the morality by which the person is judged and the beliefs on which she

subject(ivity), I have tried to avoid the terms 'subjective' and 'objective' in describing Arendt's position below, but see the text preceding n 13 below.

7 In *Eichmann in Jerusalem*, she writes that the nub of the problem was to understand that 'an average, 'normal' person, neither feeble-minded nor indoctrinated nor cynical, could be perfectly incapable of telling right from wrong' (1964: 26). David Cesarani has argued that Eichmann *was* indoctrinated in anti-Semitic ideas, which he embraced, and he attacks the theory of totalitarianism which underpins Arendt's assertion to the contrary (Cesarani 2004: 361–63). As I indicate below (n 18), I do not think that Cesarani's criticisms of Arendt affect the problem of judgment and justice with which I engage here.

8 This anticipates the position Arendt develops in her *Origins of Totalitarianism* (1968).

acted. Justice requires a common normative order so that if the judged do not, at some level, share the basic precepts by which they are judged, then they may be sanctioned, but they may not be justly punished. There can be no moral dialogue between the judge and the judged where the actions and views of the latter place them so far beyond the moral pale that they are also beyond the possibility of judgment, as expressed in the form of law.[9] That is Arendt's concern in these letters and, in her subsequent writing on the trial of Eichmann, she returned to it. In the next section, we consider the fuller development of this argument in *Eichmann in Jerusalem*.

The problem of judgment and justice for Eichmann

'There is a normative "melancholia" in Hannah Arendt's work.'
(Benhabib 2000: 65, 80)

In this section, I consider Arendt's reflections on the Eichmann trial, as developed in the epilogue and postscript to *Eichmann in Jerusalem*. Initial perusal of the epilogue may provoke doubt over my claim as to Arendt's position. For the most part, she seems to eschew the above concern about the possibility of justice. The epilogue indeed, for most of its length, takes the form of a *defence* of the Eichmann trial against claims that it lacked justice. The trial is placed in a line that includes Nuremberg and the post-war 'successor trials' in various countries. These, she proposes, disclose a trajectory precisely towards a more complete form of international criminal justice (Fine 2001: ch 9), not an ethical logic against its possibility.

Where she acknowledges criticisms of the Eichmann trial, these are generally presented as negative *faute de mieux* juridical consequences of the absence of an all-encompassing international justice. In their formalism, or the absence of alternatives, they are not to be taken too seriously. However, the possibility of achieving an ethical order of international justice is undermined in the closing pages of the epilogue, and also in the later postscript. In both places, it is the possibility of a community of judgment as the foundation for the moral and legal legitimacy of criminal justice that is called into question. I shall suggest that in *Eichmann in Jerusalem*, it is the failure of a community of judgment that contributes to the sense of 'normative melancholia' that Seyla Benhabib finds in Arendt's account, and I return to this point at the end of this section.

9 In a later essay on the German Auschwitz trials of the 1960s, Arendt (2003a: 227, 234) describes the practical outcome of this theoretical impasse: 'Only one of the defendants . . . does not show open contempt for the court, does not laugh, insult witnesses, demand that the prosecuting attorneys apologise, and try to have fun with the others'. Of course, many people are punished by law for crimes with which they morally disagree. Problems of moral community come to the fore where the disagreement is structural in a society, systematic, or maintained by a whole class of persons, and especially, as in the case of the Nazis, when the crime in question is egregious.

Towards an international criminal court

I begin, however, with Arendt's initial arguments, which support the internationalisation of criminal justice. Many complaints were levelled at both the trial of Eichmann and of the leading Nazis at Nuremberg, but Arendt's response to these is generally unsympathetic. The main argument she confronts is that, in both trials, the defendants were exposed to a retroactive law in the court of the victors. She responds that the charge of retroactivity applies meaningfully only to acts known in advance to the legislator, and not to new crimes such as genocide, which suddenly appear and require a judgment according to a new law (1964: 254). For lawyers, there is something instinctively problematic in this, but Arendt opposes arguments based simply on 'legalistic' premises: there are other, more substantive, issues to weigh in the balance against formalistic complaints based on the rule of law.[10] She also argues that of the three main heads of crime tried at Nuremberg, 'crimes against peace', 'war crimes' and 'crimes against humanity', only the last was really new and unprecedented, and it was the one the judges felt least comfortable to use.

This observation deserves further exploration. In Arendt's account, Nuremberg negotiated an uneasy path between conflicting problems. The first two categories of crime were vulnerable to criticism on the basis that the allies, who had set up the tribunal, were themselves guilty of such crimes. This is the *tu quoque* argument: that the Russians had themselves attacked Finland and divided Poland, that the Americans had dropped the atomic bomb on Hiroshima and Nagasaki, that more generally modern war conducted by any party does not separate soldier and civilian. Accordingly, there was an incentive to distinguish Nazi guilt by focusing on those crimes carried out during the war where 'gratuitous brutality' or 'a deliberate inhuman purpose could be demonstrated' (ibid: 256). However, this led to the most radical and novel criminal charge at Nuremberg, the 'crime against humanity', which in principle had nothing to do with existing war crimes. Such a crime was 'in fact independent of the war', involving 'a policy of systematic murder to be continued in time of peace'. It took as its focus 'the blotting out of whole peoples, the "clearance" of whole regions of their native population'. It involved, most importantly, a 'crime against the human status' (ibid: 257).

This presented the authorities with a dilemma. On one hand, the 'crime against humanity' was the one crime to which the *tu quoque* argument did not apply (ibid: 255–57),[11] and this made it ostensibly an attractive basis for prosecuting the Nazis.

10 For example, with regard to the kidnapping of Eichmann in Argentina, 'the realm of legality offered no alternative' (Arendt 1964: 264).

11 This is questionable if one thinks, for example, of the genocides carried out on the American Indians and on indigenous peoples in Africa, Australia, and South America. Lawrence Douglas (2001: 48–53) has shown that the circumscription of crimes against humanity by crimes of war or against the peace in the Nuremberg Charter and at the Tribunal was designed to protect the general sovereignty of states and to avoid the *tu quoque* argument from spreading into the area of crimes against humanity.

On the other, this was the charge with which the court was least comfortable on account of its novelty, and the judges preferred to convict on the more traditional war crimes. Yet, when it came to sentence, the hardest punishments were meted out to those defendants who were in fact most guilty of those atrocities best described as 'crimes against humanity'. The court resolved its legal dilemma in terms of the criminal categories at the sentencing stage where more discretion was available to it.

The Nuremberg Tribunal was, in short, caught between a legalistic desire to confine guilt to the more orthodox forms of war crime and a need to recognise the specific suffering of the Jewish people. Without a crime to reflect the latter, it would have been impossible to encompass the Germans' mass murder of their own Jewish nationals (Arendt 1964: 258). Nuremberg was a hesitant first effort at a trial of a new type. As such it raised issues of a formal, legalistic kind, but its real ethical and juridical significance was that it introduced the idea of a 'crime against humanity'. It recognised a prototype of a new form of crime, one that was worse than any single atrocity:

> It was when the Nazi regime declared that the German people not only were unwilling to have any Jews in Germany but wished to make the entire Jewish people disappear from the face of the earth that the new crime, the crime against humanity . . . appeared . . . [G]enocide . . . is an attack upon human diversity as such, that is, upon a characteristic of the 'human status' without which the very words 'mankind' or 'humanity' would be devoid of meaning.
> (ibid: 268–69)

Turning from Nuremberg to Eichmann, this observation casts light on certain problems associated with the latter. From one point of view, trying Eichmann in Jerusalem presents no problem. It is rather like trying Nazi war criminals in Poland or Czechoslovakia for crimes committed in those countries. It 'was in actual fact no more . . . than the last of the numerous Successor trials which followed the Nuremberg trials' (ibid: 263). But the identification of a new kind of crime against humanity suggests the need for a new kind of tribunal. Whilst a Jewish state could in Arendt's view try crimes against Jewish people (ibid: 259–60),[12] the idea of a crime against humanity makes it clear that this is a universal crime, one against the status of being human, that is perpetrated on a particular group, 'the body of the Jewish people'. Insofar as we have a crime against Jews, there is no reason why a Jewish state should not try it, but insofar as we have a crime against humanity perpetrated on Jews, there is the need for 'an international tribunal to do justice to it' (Arendt 1964: 269).

Building on Nuremberg, which established the 'crime against humanity', Eichmann points to the need for an institutional progression in international penal

12 But see Benhabib's argument that this collapses questions of national identity and political citizenship (2000: 77–88).

law. In the absence of such a progression, it lacked the form adequately to reflect the wrongdoing of the Nazis:

> These modern, state-employed mass murderers must be prosecuted because they violated the order of mankind, and not because they killed millions of people. Nothing is more pernicious to an understanding of these new crimes, or stands in the way of *the emergence of an international penal code that could take care of them*, than the common illusion that the crime of murder and the crime of genocide are essentially the same, and that the latter therefore is 'no new crime properly speaking.' The point of the latter is that *an altogether different order is broken and an altogether different community is violated.*
>
> (ibid: 272, emphasis added)

In sum, Arendt points here to the logic immanent from Nuremberg to Eichmann in favour of a new kind of crime, to reflect a new kind of wrongdoing, and to be tried under a new kind of tribunal. The thrust of these arguments is for an international legal order which includes an international criminal court, and Arendt seems to anticipate no ethical obstruction to this progression. However, we now come to the final part of her epilogue, in which she does raise such a problem.

The problem of justice

In the last four pages of the epilogue, Arendt picks up the theme that had animated her earlier correspondence with Jaspers. She begins by referring to the 'conspicuous helplessness the judges experienced when they were confronted with the task they could least escape . . . of understanding the criminal whom they had come to judge' (ibid: 276). The problem was that there were so many like him, who were 'neither perverted nor sadistic', but were rather 'terribly and terrifyingly normal', and this was more terrifying 'than all the atrocities put together'. It implied that 'this new type of criminal . . . commits his crimes under circumstances that make it well-nigh impossible for him to know or to feel that he is doing wrong' (ibid). This fact undermines the assumption on which modern criminal justice occurs, that there must be a subjective element of recognising wrongdoing before any criminal can be convicted:

> Foremost among the larger issues at stake in the Eichmann trial was the assumption current in all modern legal systems that intent to do wrong is necessary for the commission of a crime . . . Where this intent is absent, where . . . the ability to distinguish between right and wrong is impaired, we feel no crime has been committed.[13]
>
> (ibid: 277)

13 In strictly legal terms, at least Anglo-American ones, Arendt is wrong, for there is a strong tendency to seek to separate legal from moral issues, to seek to distinguish questions of 'cognitive' or 'factual'

Arendt points here to the need for a sense of wrongdoing in the accused, and she asks what is to be done when an Eichmann, together with a substantial section of an entire people, lacks it. It is true that the Nazis tried to cover up what they had done, but this was an admission of defeat rather than wrongdoing: 'Would any one of them have suffered from a guilty conscience if they had won' (ibid)? When Eichmann aligned his conduct with a Kantian sense of duty (ibid: 135–36), that is, claimed he had acted as a moral person according to his own lights, he placed himself beyond the comprehension of his judges, who could not believe that an 'average, "normal" person . . . could be perfectly incapable of telling right from wrong' (ibid: 26, 146). It is for this reason that Arendt suggests that any justification for executing Eichmann must fall short of modern ethical expectations for justice. Whilst a modern moral sensibility refuses what we might call an 'Old Testament' sense of vengeance as a sufficient basis for punishment and indeed considers it 'barbaric', just such a rationale has to underlie his execution.[14]

Justice at Jerusalem meant addressing the defendant in terms of a 'premodern', biblical understanding that 'guilt and innocence before the law are of an objective nature, and even if eighty million Germans had done as you did, this would not have been an excuse for you'. The court was only concerned with 'what you did, and not with the possible noncriminal nature of your inner life and of your motives or with the criminal potential of those around you' (ibid). Even if it was only misfortune which made a person a part of mass murder, that person was still a part of it, and had to be punished for this fact. Whatever his individual state of mind, Eichmann had participated in actions which set him beyond the human pale, and it was this fact, which made moral judgment impossible, that permitted his execution:

> Just as you supported and carried out a policy of not wanting to share the earth with the Jewish people and the people of a number of other nations . . . we find that no one, that is, no member of the human race, can be expected to want to share the earth with you. This is the reason, and the only reason, you must hang.
>
> (ibid: 279)

It is important to grasp what Arendt is saying here. It is not as a member of the human community that Eichmann must die, but as one whose actions, whatever their subjective moral quality, has made him an outcast, a general enemy of humanity (*hostis generis humani*) (ibid: 276). This rationale draws upon and reflects

from 'moral' intent or guilt. Arendt is nonetheless right to point to the underlying moral relation that modern legal systems generally assume between criminal and moral wrongdoing, at least for the more serious offences. Since her general point is not about law, but about the need for criminal punishment to be morally appropriate, her argument stands.

14 Arendt (1964: 278) cites the biblical story of Sodom and Gomorrah, 'which were destroyed by fire from Heaven because all the people in them had become equally guilty'.

how the Nazis had treated the Jews, and throws it back on Eichmann himself. They had labelled their victims as unworthy of normal human consideration, and Eichmann's punishment returns the compliment. Like the crime, the punishment must step outside the terms of a common humanity, grounded in the possibility of common moral values and responses, judgments and responsibilities, in order to hang Eichmann. These normal conditions of morality and law are lost where a person reveals that he cannot be reached on a common ground of right and wrong, and this was the position of Nazis like Eichmann.[15]

Postscript: justice revisited

These concerns in the last four pages of the epilogue anticipate earlier passages in the work (Arendt 1964: 26 and ch 8), yet are rather strange to encounter in the light of its main argument concerning an international penal code. They plainly stayed with her, because it was to just these concerns that she returned in the postscript to *Eichmann* two years later, at greater length but with no less ambivalence. She addresses the problem here in terms of what I have called its subjective and objective dimensions, beginning with the former and drawing upon her analysis of totalitarianism and its effect on human subjectivity. This then leads her into consideration of the impossibility of valid legal judgment in a morally bad polity, where a community breaks away from a common sense of right and wrong. She wrestles with and against these problems without resolving them.

As regards Eichmann's *subjective* position, Arendt says that he was not an intrinsically 'bad man': no Iago, Macbeth or Richard III (ibid: 287). Other than personal ambition, he had no real motives at all. It was 'sheer thoughtlessness . . . that predisposed him to become one of the greatest criminals of that period' (ibid: 288),[16] but this is precisely what is troubling about him, and leads to the question of 'what kind of crime is actually involved here'. Whereas previously, Arendt had portrayed the Holocaust as involving a new kind of crime, now she indicates that 'massacres of whole peoples are not unprecedented' either in antiquity or the present world of 'administrative massacres' and the 'automated economy'. What she points to, introducing ideas from her *Origins of Totalitarianism* (Arendt 1968: pt 3), is a systemic genocidal tendency (her version, I would suggest, of Hegel's 'slaughter bench') in modern human affairs of which Nazism is one stark example. It is such propensities that challenge our modern moral and legal concepts, and that are 'very difficult to grasp juridically'.

Take the idea, put forward by the defence in Eichmann, that he was just a cog in a machine. Arendt confesses that she attached no importance to this idea at the time of the trial, because 'the whole cog theory is legally pointless'.[17] In a trial, 'all

15 This state of mind was commonly observed at trials of former Nazis. See Arendt (2003).

16 Others such as David Cesarani have contested this view of Eichmann. But see n 7 above and n 18 below.

17 Arendt (2003: 17) returned to this issue.

the cogs in the machinery, no matter how insignificant, are in court forthwith transformed back into perpetrators, that is to say, into human beings'. For a criminal to claim to have been a cog is as if he 'pointed to the statistics on crime . . . and declared that he only did what was statistically expected of him' (Arendt 1964: 289). However, the cog theory remains essential to political scientists for whom it is the essence of totalitarian government, and of bureaucracy, 'to make functionaries and mere cogs . . . out of men, and thus to dehumanise them' (ibid).

Thus, there is a gap between the understanding of lawyers and that of social scientists. Here, Arendt displays an ambivalence about the workings of social theory and its relation to law. On one hand, she is in her own work committed to understanding the effects of bureaucracy, totalitarianism and history on human actions, and therefore sees law as outmoded under modern conditions. On the other hand, she draws back from the conclusions to which her own understanding takes her. In the following passage, she hedges her bets:

> True, we have become very much accustomed by modern psychology and sociology, not to speak of modern bureaucracy, to explaining away the responsibility of the doer for his deed in terms of this or that kind of determinism. Whether such deeper explanations of human actions are right or wrong is debatable. But what is not debatable is that no judicial procedure would be possible . . . and that the administration of justice, measured by such theories, is an extremely unmodern, not to say outmoded, institution. When Hitler said that a day would come in Germany when it would be considered a 'disgrace' to be a jurist, he was speaking with utter consistency of his dream of a perfect bureaucracy.
>
> (ibid: 290)

Plainly, Arendt is no supporter of the effects of bureaucracy on conceptions of responsibility, but her defence of legal responsibility is cast in functionalist rather than normative terms: 'this is how law in fact works', and the question of law's historical possibility under modern conditions is left hanging. The implication is that, whilst she might have initially dismissed the cog theory promoted by the defence, her own thinking on modern totalitarianism and its effects on ethics have made it more compelling than she might now care to think when considering Eichmann.[18]

18 Cesarani (2004: 351–56) criticises the cog theory and its relationship to an underlying theory of totalitarianism as overly abstract and general, and as failing to see the specifically anti-Semitic, fanatical, engaged quality of Eichmann's actions. Whilst I agree with his comments, I think that the two linked theories nonetheless have something to say about the systemic nature of modern genocidal violence, and the challenge it poses to justice and judgment. He himself concludes his work with reference to the idea of 'Everyman as *génocidaire*'. He writes that: 'The key to understand Adolf Eichmann lies not in the man, but in the ideas that possessed him, the society in which they flowed freely, the political system that purveyed them, and the circumstances that made them

As regards the *objective* moral dimension of a community of judgment, Arendt considers two ways in which criminal law fails to deal morally with problems in a polity that has abandoned a common sense of right and wrong. These concern 'acts of state' and 'superior orders'. Both examples point to the problem of legal–moral justice in a state based upon the systematic acceptance of morally wrong acts. 'Acts of state' are discussed by Arendt as those emergency measures which suspend normal law in order to protect the overall conditions for law. They are regarded as necessary but abnormal exceptions to the rule of law in a normal political system, and are therefore not subject to legal penalty. They represent potentially criminal acts that are not punished, and the liberal state can comprehend such acts as wrong, but permissible exceptions in the circumstances. For a criminal state, whose normal acts are essentially wrong, this kind of thinking does not work. Here, the exceptional act in concession to an overriding necessity becomes the *non-criminal* act: not the bad act rendered permissible, but the good act which needs no doctrine of permissible exception to excuse it.[19]

Things are morally turned upside down also in relation to 'superior orders'. In a normal country, a soldier should not obey a manifestly wrong command. Where unlawfulness flies 'like a black flag above [an order], as a warning reading, "Prohibited"' (ibid: 292), any soldier ought to know he was asked to do something wrong. Here the law hinges on the exceptionality of the manifestly wrong command, and the soldier may reject such an order. In the case of Nazi Germany, however, the manifestly wrong commands Eichmann followed were entirely unexceptional, so no clause of manifest exceptionality could be triggered.

Both illustrations show how a situation of overall wrongfulness interrupts the normal assumption in a liberal polity that the criminal is a wrongdoer who has strayed from the right. Where lawful actions are in themselves wrong, it makes no sense to seek to establish individual exceptions or excuses in favour of rightful actions. The bigger problem is that where the accepted moral compass has been abandoned so radically, it makes little sense to think in terms of what makes 'this individual' guilty, another innocent. Where all are systematically implicated in guilt from the start, there is no basis for distinction, and this 'demonstrate[s] the inadequacy of the prevailing legal system and of current juridical concepts to deal with the facts of administrative massacre organised by the state apparatus . . .' (ibid: 294).

acceptable' (ibid: 367). Against Arendt, he contends that this is not to say that 'we are all potential Eichmanns', but that under the right circumstances, 'normal people can and do commit mass murder'. Is this not really Arendt's point, even if we do not accept her specific theory of totalitarianism, and her rather 'affectless' account of the bureaucrat as cog?

19 Arendt gives the example of Himmler's order in late summer 1944 to halt deportations in the light of the necessities imposed by impending defeat (1964: 291). Under the Nazi regime, this was a criminal act requiring a defence. From a liberal point of view, it was a non-criminal one, requiring no specific exception to be made.

The underlying problem is the loss of an appropriate sense of right and wrong, which leaves the legal concepts stranded:

> What we have demanded in these trials, where the defendants had committed 'legal' crimes, is that human beings be capable of telling right from wrong even when all they have to guide them is their own judgment, which, moreover, happens to be completely at odds with what they must regard as the unanimous opinion of all those around them . . . *Since the whole of respectable society had . . . succumbed to Hitler, the moral maxims which determine social behaviour and the religious commandments – 'Thou shalt not kill' – which guide conscience had virtually vanished.*
>
> (ibid: 295, emphasis added)[20]

The radical and systemic evacuation of the morally right removes the possibility of justice. Where right and wrong have been turned upside down, where lies the commonality between judge and judged that makes a finding of guilt possible? Arendt's final comments reveal her resisting her own conclusion. Having shown the failure of moral and legal judgment in the light of Nazism, she writes, disingenuously, against 'the reluctance evident everywhere to make judgments in terms of individual moral responsibility' (ibid: 297), and against the view that one can 'judge and even . . . condemn . . . trends, or whole groups of people – the larger the better', but in a way that 'distinctions can no longer be made, names no longer named' (ibid: 296). It is as if, she says, an instinct in matters of judgment should be the last thing to be consulted in such matters, in favour of the view that individuals are not to be held responsible. But her own argument has taken her to just this position.

20 To this one reviewer has suggested that the failure of community depicted by Arendt is not completely convincing. Conscience had not vanished, for the Nazis were not insane and knew the difference between right and wrong in general. They were simply unable to include Jews in the category of those to whom moral obligations applied. There was a commonality between judge and judged, even if the latter did not share the same moral standpoint with regard to Jews. But this is just Arendt's point: the Nazis *were* in many respects quite normal, yet on a crucial, central, issue, they lived in a different moral world. What was perturbing was just the lack of moral commonality on such an issue, given commonality on others (e.g., being kind to pets and small (non-Jewish) children). A second objection would be to say that such a moral deficit does not remove the moral right of the judge. Many crimes are committed by people who do not agree with the moral values of a community, and sophisticated accounts of the morality of punishment accommodate a dialogical relation in which wrongness is communicated to the morally aberrant. See e.g. Duff (1996). In such work, there is no need for an ultimate acknowledgment of wrongdoing by individuals for punishment to remain valid. However, a systemic or structural refusal to accept major wrongdoing by a whole class of people renders moral communication redundant because it destroys the idea of moral community, and this is what makes the penal communication possible in the first place. That the refusal is in relation to acts that are utterly egregious in their wrongfulness serves only to point up the issue.

Her complaint against the law, and the moral concepts that track and validate it, is that they are outmoded and can no longer explain how people should be judged. Having argued herself for the difficulty of legal judgment, in both its subjective and objective dimensions, it is hard to know what to make of her argument that, if individual judgment were not possible, 'the administration of justice . . . would [never] be possible' (ibid: 296). Her concluding comment reflects the ambiguity in her position:

> [T]he question of individual guilt or innocence, the act of meting out justice to both the defendant and the victim, are the only things at stake in a criminal court. The Eichmann trial was no exception, even though the court here was confronted with a crime it could not find in the lawbooks and with a criminal whose like was unknown in any court, at least prior to the Nuremberg Trials. The present report deals with nothing but the extent to which the court in Jerusalem succeeded in fulfilling the demands of justice.
>
> (ibid: 298)

As if her own argument had not made the 'nothing but' in this last sentence deeply problematic. In the light of her own critique of the possibility of legal justice, one can read an ironic inflection here. To what 'extent' *could* the court fulfil such demands; what *did* the 'demands of justice' on her own account entail?

To conclude this section, Benhabib (2000) has written of the normative melancholia that informed Arendt's reflections on justificatory political discourse and its ability to restrain or control politics in the 20th century. Whether it is the validity of human rights, principles of equality or the obligation to treat with respect, she resists efforts to think foundationally or to offer modern institutions easy legitimacy. To this list should be added the question of valid punishment. Of *Eichmann in Jerusalem*, Benhabib writes that it is 'volatile and difficult to decipher' because Eichmann's treatment became 'the prism through which some of the most touching and difficult issues of Arendt's life and work were refracted' (ibid: 82).

If my reading is right, then the last four pages of the epilogue with the postscript reveal just such a volatility. On one side, Arendt displays a real support for an international penal justice system, whilst on the other, she pulls the rug from under it. In terms of my two prefatory quotations, she wants to run with Kant and hunt with Hegel. My own view is that so antinomial a view cannot be correct, and that her conclusions, even if reflecting a real problem, cannot be the whole story. In what follows, we will consider Jaspers's work in the light of the same problems, and see whether it affords any resolution to Arendt's volatility and melancholia.

Jasper's typology and the question of collective guilt

> '. . . damned and Hegelised Christian-pietist-sanctimonious bilge'
>
> (quoting Heinrich Blücher in Rabinbach 2001: 300)

I now turn to Jaspers and his fourfold account of guilt in light of the problem of justice and judgment elicited by Arendt. Jaspers, as stated above, identified conceptions of criminal, political, moral and metaphysical guilt, and I will probe his account for what it says and, as importantly, does not say about a *fifth* form, collective guilt. Whilst Jaspers radically limits this in his 'official' typology,[21] it has a greater, highly disruptive, role to play in his analysis than he initially allows. This is seen at a pivotal, and 'symptomatic', point in the text where Jaspers, after speaking of an extended role for collective guilt, pulls himself up short: 'As a philosopher I now seem to have strayed completely into the realm of feeling and to have abandoned conception' (2000: 75). What was it about collective guilt that could have driven this austere philosopher to such a pass?

Of this work, Heinrich Blücher wrote to Hannah Arendt that: 'despite all beauty and nobility, the guilt-brochure of Jaspers is . . . damned and Hegelised Christian-pietist-sanctimonious bilge' (Rabinbach 2001: 300). Purged of vitriol, the criticism is that Jaspers's analysis evades the true sense of guilt that should fall on the German people. In viewing the effects of his guilt typology and the tension around the idea of collective guilt, I will consider to what extent this was a fair comment. In opening up the issue of collective, and through it metaphysical guilt, I will also lay a foundation for returning to the problem of justice and judgment in Arendt.

Jaspers's typology of guilt

In considering the four types of guilt, it is important to bear in mind that Jaspers divides them into pairs as they reflect either an 'internal' or 'external' sense, that is, whether they relate to the 'external' legal or political world, or the 'inward' demands of conscience and ethics (2000: 75). *Criminal guilt* is expressed by Jaspers in positivistic terms. It relates to the violation of unequivocal laws established by objective proof. Jurisdiction rests with the criminal court, which in formal proceedings finds the facts and applies the law. Such guilt meets with punishment in which a determination of will is acknowledged, but as a formally free act, and there is no need for the guilty to acknowledge their wrongdoing or the justice of punishment (ibid: 33).

Criminal guilt is then a matter resolved *in foro externo*, and the same is true with regard to the second form, *political guilt*. This is the result of a state's misdeeds, and every citizen must accept such consequences as flow from them. If one lives under the order of a state, one bears responsibility even where one did not support it. Every German suffers a political liability for what was done in their name by their leaders. Jurisdiction lies with the power and will of the victor, and liability takes the form of reparation (ibid: 30). Since we are here in the realm of the political, as Jaspers envisions it, guilt is marked by issues of what it is prudential to demand,

21 He limits it to the 'external' form of political guilt.

and the victor may choose to moderate its requirements in the interests of its governing strategy. Political guilt is 'external', de facto guilt, imposed and suffered through this-worldly processes in accordance with consequential calculation.

Neither of these forms of guilt affects the internal ethical dispositions of the accused. In the third form of *moral guilt*, however, the individual is morally responsible for all his deeds, and even if these were the result of superior orders, they remain subject to moral judgment. However, jurisdiction is inward, resting with one's own conscience, or in communion with one's closest associates: those that know one best and are 'lovingly concerned about my soul' (ibid: 26). Such guilt consequently leads neither to punishment nor to reparation, which are external sanctions, but to insight involving penance and renewal. Such an inner development may have its own effects upon the world, but that is not its point, which is to curate the individual soul.

Similarly, *metaphysical guilt*, the deepest form, represents an intrinsic solidarity amongst people that is felt as an inward responsibility for all the wrongs that occur in the world, regardless of one's role in promoting them. The consequence of metaphysical guilt is the transformation of human self-consciousness before God, for it constitutes an 'indelible sense of guilt'. This leads to 'that humility which grows modest before God' and, in this form of guilt, jurisdiction rests with the 'supreme being' (ibid).[22]

Metaphysical guilt

Since it will become the focus of this essay, two initial points on metaphysical guilt should be addressed here, the first concerning Jaspers's reference to God. It was with this fourth form in mind, that, one imagines, Blücher described Jaspers's 'guilt brochure' as no more than 'Christian-pietist-sanctimonious bilge', but Jaspers's position can be discussed to a significant extent without reference to Christianity or God. Jaspers is pointing to a sense of universal solidarity that is both transcendent and experienced, and that makes all human beings in some way responsible for every injustice in the world. If one fails to do anything one can to prevent a wrong, one is guilty, and even where one could do nothing, the sense of

22 From Jaspers's account, one can identify a number of different but connected meanings of the 'metaphysical' as it connects with guilt. They include (1) to live in history and politics; (2) to live in relations of power given to one; (3) to identify but not live by the unconditioned in human relations; (4) to live after a crime, to survive it; (5) the lack of absolute solidarity with the human being as such. These link with (6) the collective guilt of a people; and (7) the common guilt of mankind (original sin). These are addressed by (8) living in relation with God; and (9) reflecting on the way to humble self-purification. The last two clearly reflect the pietism to which Blücher objected. Whilst Jaspers often describes the subjective feeling of metaphysical guilt, for example in survivor guilt, it seems clear that subjectivism is not necessary for such guilt to exist. It is the relationship to 'the unconditional' that is crucial, and this exists by virtue of being human. An *ontological* relation is posited, and therefore one that cannot be defeated by *epistemological* criteria.

guilt remains. This is the guilt, for example, of the survivor understood as something more than a psychological foible: 'That I live after such a thing has happened weighs upon me as indelible guilt' (ibid: 26). This is humankind's 'original sin', a sense of guilt that accompanies every de facto or 'conditional' political order, and consists in the knowledge that a basic relationship of 'the unconditional' underlies every such order.

In the following passage, Jaspers contrasts moral responsibility, which bridges the conditional and the unconditional, with metaphysical guilt:

> Morality is always influenced by mundane purposes . . . Metaphysical guilt is the lack of absolute solidarity with the human being as such—an indelible claim beyond morally meaningful duty. This solidarity is violated by my presence at a wrong or a crime. It is not enough that I cautiously risk my life to prevent it; if it happens, and if I was there, and if I survive where the other is killed, I know from a voice within myself: I am guilty of being still alive.
>
> (ibid: 65)

There is no doubt a Christian pietist inflection here, but the idea of a universal solidarity per se is not simply a Christian, or even a theistic doctrine (see chapter 10 below for further discussion). Such a sense of guilt exists even though it is not fully brought out, or brought out at all, in a given order. Indeed, it is of the nature of such guilt that it cannot be brought out beyond people's immediate human ties, this is part of what makes it what it is:

> Somewhere among men the unconditional prevails – the capacity to live only together or not at all . . . Therein consists the substance of their being. But that this does not extend to the solidarity of all men, . . . but remains confined to the closest of human ties – therein lies this guilt of us all.
>
> (ibid: 26)

The second initial point concerns the very idea of metaphysical guilt, which is the hardest to accept in Jaspers's typology, particularly if we are urged to think 'post metaphysically' (Habermas 1992). It is not possible to develop a full account of what is intrinsically a complexly used and contested term here and, as I have made clear above, Jaspers is himself rather vague as to its meaning and implications (Jaspers 2000).[23] A full settling of terms must await another occasion. For present purposes, I would note three things.

The first is that metaphysical conceptions of justice have always proved attractive in terms of understanding guilt, and this is seen in the continuing attraction of guilt theorists to Kant, even if he is sometimes represented in non-metaphysical terms.[24] Therefore it may be helpful to explore the work of one frank proponent

23 See n 22.

24 For a representation of Kant as a neo-contractarian philosopher, see Murphy (1979); see also Norrie (1991: 41–45).

of a metaphysical conception of guilt here. Second, an emphasis on the metaphysical is observed in much modern critical thought, even where one might not expect to find it. I have in mind here in particular Jacques Derrida's conception of deconstruction as a justice that is itself undeconstructable (Derrida 1990), and his posing of the question of forgiveness as a relation between the unconditional and the conditioned (Derrida 2001).

It will indeed be such a conception of the metaphysical that I will draw from Jaspers and align with Derrida, and Roy Bhaskar, in the final section of this essay. Third, I would note, in anticipation of my conclusion, that Jaspers's account of metaphysical guilt does offer one way of dealing with the problem of guilt observed by Arendt. Since her position on the impossibility of judgment in Eichmann's case is in my view, and also I think in her own, deeply problematic, some benefit of the doubt might be given to a way of addressing it.

Metaphysical and collective guilt

With these initial points made, Jaspers's typology can be explored with regard to two further questions. First, how do his categories fit together? Jaspers has in mind a system of structured differentiation, but one which at the same time involves clear distinction. Thus, the concepts of guilt are closely connected and manifest elements 'the consequences of which appear in the spheres of the other concepts of guilt' (Jaspers 2000: 27). Metaphysical guilt represents the most basic form, then moral, and then criminal and political. If people could free themselves from metaphysical guilt, then 'they would be angels, and all the other three concepts of guilt would become immaterial' (ibid). However, despite these structured connections, Jaspers wants to draw a clear line between the internal and external forms of guilt. The accused is either 'charged from without, by the world, or from within, by his own soul' (ibid: 33).

When charged from without, 'the charges are meaningful only in regard to crimes and political guilt' (ibid) leading to punishment and other forms of worldly liability. From within, 'the guilty hears himself charged with moral failures and metaphysical weakness' (ibid). If these led to crimes or political wrongs, he also hears himself charged with these, but this is his moral and metaphysical sensibility reflecting on what he has done. The criminal and political effects carry no internal ethical charge. Morally, a man 'can condemn only himself, not another', for 'No one can morally judge another', and to refer to another's guilt is to refer 'only to certain acts and modes of behaviour' (ibid).

The second question concerns the nature of collective guilt, an issue of major significance at the time Jaspers wrote. What we might call his 'official' position is very clear. It is that such guilt can only be relevant to the issue of political liability. All citizens are collectively liable for what their state does, 'but the liability is definite and limited, involving neither moral nor metaphysical charges against the individuals' (ibid: 34). Individuals alone can be guilty of crimes, and the same is true for moral and metaphysical guilt. Collective guilt exists only in the very limited, external, form of political liability, and Jaspers disparages bluntly anyone who would suggest otherwise:

> There is no such thing as a people as a whole . . . One cannot make an individual out of a people . . . The categorical judgment of a people is always unjust. It presupposes a false substantialization and results in the debasement of the human being as an individual . . . To pronounce a group criminally, morally or metaphysically guilty is an error akin to the laziness and arrogance of average, uncritical thinking.
>
> (ibid: 35–36)

We shall see that this was not Jaspers's last word on collective guilt, and that he effected a significant return to it. Nonetheless, this is his typology, and how he relates the categories. It will be noted that, unlike Arendt, Jaspers clearly identifies a form of guilt that can constitute the basis for a valid criminal charge. But its casting in legal positivist terms involves a very different approach. For Arendt, law was of course distinguished from morality, but that did not mean they should be appraised separately: her account of justice depended on law's ethical connection. Despite Jaspers's claim that the metaphysical underlies everything, his splitting of guilt into internal and external forms posits a clear line where Arendt saw a critical relation.

We will return to this difference below, once we have probed further Jaspers's account of collective guilt. My argument will be that his further discussion of this topic is the key to understanding what is problematic in his typology, but ultimately also of finding a way to deal with the problem of justice and judgment identified by Arendt. For, as we will now see, Jaspers found his own position on collective guilt to be problematic.

Collective guilt: A fifth form?

Having considered German guilt in the light of his typology, there is a point in the text where Jaspers stops and considers whether his categories permit the substance of guilt to fall through his fingers. Can his distinctions not in fact 'be speciously used to get rid of the whole guilt question', to 'hide the source and unity' of guilt, 'to spirit away what does not suit us' (ibid: 68)? Take political guilt: it could be said that this only 'curtails . . . my material possibilities' (ibid) and does not affect my inner self. Criminal guilt similarly affects only a few, and not 'me'. On these 'external' scores, the individual German need not worry too much. What of the 'internal' forms of guilt? Moral guilt involves only the jurisdiction of one's own conscience, and some might say 'my conscience is not going to be too hard on me' (ibid).

Similarly, metaphysical guilt cannot be charged to another and involves a 'transmutation' of the soul. This could be seen as the 'crazy idea of some philosopher' (ibid) and dismissed. What worries Jaspers is that, in separating out the different forms of guilt, most people are let off the hook so that the categories are 'turned into a trick' (ibid) for evading the overall moral issue. Somehow, the externalisation of political and criminal guilt and the internalisation of moral and metaphysical guilt lead to a loss of the overall quality of guilt that the categories should reflect. Such distinctions 'hide the source and the unity [and] enable us to spirit away what does not suit us' (ibid). In responding to his own concern about where the categories lead, Jaspers finds himself, having radically limited the concept, returning 'in the end to the question of collective guilt'. Although his distinctions are, he insists, 'correct and meaningful', something 'has been lost in the process', which 'in collective guilt is always audible in spite of everything' (ibid: 69).

In the end, Jaspers adds a fifth 'unofficial' (my term) form of guilt to his typology, giving it a validity he had previously denied. What had previously been the province of 'the laziness and arrogance of average, uncritical thinking' (ibid: 36)[25] is now shown to be central to Jaspers's own thought about guilt. People live under evolving conditions which determine the moral aspects of a nation's life and which 'help to determine individual morality'. The individual lives 'as a link in [a] chain' and there 'is a sort of collective moral guilt in a people's way of life which I share as an individual' (ibid: 70). The world of which the Germans were a part could produce a regime such as the Nazis, and this is a moral fact for which all Germans are responsible.

> We . . . feel that we not only share in what is done at present—thus being co-responsible for the deeds of our contemporaries – but in the links of a tradition. We have to bear the guilt of our fathers. That the spiritual conditions of German life provided an opportunity for such a regime is a fact for which all of us are co-responsible . . .
>
> (ibid: 73)

Reflecting on this collective sense, however, erodes the distinctions between other forms of guilt, so that political liability and moral responsibility entail 'no radical separation' (ibid: 71). This brings out the ultimate, much expanded, significance of metaphysical guilt, which now embraces the whole German people:

> By our feelings of collective guilt we feel the entire task of renewing human existence from its origin – the task which is given to all men on earth but which appears more urgently, more perceptibly . . . when its own guilt brings a people face to face with nothingness.
>
> (ibid: 75)

25 In highlighting the role of collective guilt, I do not want to suggest that it is an easy conception to work with. Further thought would need to be given to its meaning and implications than Jaspers provides. Like metaphysical guilt, it is likely to provide a difficult conceptualisation. My main aim is to indicate how such a sense, related to metaphysical guilt, is invoked by Jaspers's own typology. On collective responsibility, see Kutz (2000). See further, below, ch 10.

This late efflorescence of metaphysical guilt in his text propels Jaspers into wider speculation, taking him beyond the Germans: 'Everywhere people have similar qualities. Everywhere there are violent, criminal, vitally capable minorities apt to seize the reins if occasion offers, and to proceed with brutality' (ibid: 93). For this reason, 'German guilt is sometimes called the guilt of all: the hidden evil everywhere is jointly guilty of the outbreak of evil in this German place' (ibid: 94). He insists that consideration of such 'original sin must not become a way to dodge German guilt' (ibid), yet it points beyond it. Finally, Jaspers ends by retrenching the role of metaphysical guilt in the relation between an individual and his God. After Nazism,

> our life remains permitted only to be consumed by a task. The result is modest resignation. In inner action before the transcendent we become aware of being humanly finite and incapable of perfection. Humility comes to be our nature . . . Purification is the way of man as such.
>
> (ibid: 113–114)

At the beginning of this discussion of Jaspers, I mentioned a point of perplexity in Jaspers's text, where he wrote of the sense that 'as a philosopher', he now seemed 'to have strayed completely into the realm of feeling and to have abandoned conception' (ibid: 75). This perplexity comes immediately after he has admitted the further significance of the metaphysical-collective form of guilt for his account. Analytical-philosophical concept formation versus a metaphysical conception of guilt which exceeds all conceptualisations: it is this conflict that leaves him aerated. Jaspers finishes his chapter with a flourish in the direction of the limits of the analytical:

> Language fails at this point, and only negatively we may recall that all our distinctions – notwithstanding the fact that we hold them to be true . . . must not become resting places. We must not use them to let matters drop and free ourselves from the pressure under which we continue our path, and which is to ripen what we hold most precious, the eternal essence of our soul.
>
> (ibid)

In the light of this account of the four forms of guilt and the odd role played by collective-metaphysical guilt within it, I now turn to assess the validity of Jaspers's argument in the light of the criticism it attracted from Heinrich Blücher. Was this really a self-serving piece of argument on behalf of the German people? In answering this question, we will identify the point at which we can address Arendt's concern about justice and judgment from the previous sections.

Assessing Jaspers

At first sight, Blücher's judgment on Jaspers may seem grossly unfair. It smacked for him of apologia, yet one of Jaspers's central concerns is to confront the many contemporary forms of evasion he observed around him, and he spends much time so doing.[26] However, there is an important question as to whether his typology does not provide its own forms of evasion, and the interesting thing, as we have seen, is that Jaspers himself was aware that this could be the case. To begin with, however, we should consider the four forms of guilt within the 'official' typology.

The key to understanding Jaspers's position is to see him both in relation to the rebuilding of Germany after the Second World War, in which he was keen to participate, and as an individual who had lived with a Jewish wife in Germany through the war, in a condition of 'internal exile'. He wished both to condemn the past and to help find a path of political and moral reconstruction for Germany after the war. His division of guilt into two spheres, the external and the internal, contributed to this. External forms involved prosecuting a small group of war criminals separated from the mass of people, and accepting the (temporary) fact of war reparations that fell on the Germans whether they liked it or not. They recognise the facts of post-war life and build them into an overall view that will permit Germany to move forward after an initial period of recrimination.

The internal forms of guilt could be said to pursue the same aim by different means. Moral and metaphysical guilt become a matter of private individual reflection, not something imposed by legal or political processes. The internal therefore becomes the only place in which general ethical wrongdoing may be contemplated, and at the same time the place where it may be evaded by all who want to 'go easy on themselves'. Private forms of guilt depend on individuals possessing a built-in conscience, so that there is no public form of moral debate with which to engage. The overall effect of this split is to permit post-war reconstruction by sidelining a few criminals and permitting the rest to resume their lives without thinking too deeply about what they had done.

It is this effect of the split between internal and external forms of guilt that gives Blücher's criticism its bite. The 'hallowed' quality of the representations of moral and metaphysical guilt do have a sanctimonious and falsely pious feel. What rescues Jaspers from the cutting edge of Blücher's criticism is his final resolve not to let distinctions become 'resting places', and his struggle against the apologetic implications of his own argument. It is true that the earlier condemnation of a conception of collective guilt still stands, despite his recourse to it later in the text, so it is his overall ambivalence that blunts Blücher's charge. Jaspers could not accept the moral soft-pedalling enabled by his own typology. The underlying philosophical problem, however, is that the ambivalence generated by the late acceptance of collective-metaphysical guilt tends not to the perfection of his categories but to their destabilisation and reconfiguration.

An extended application of metaphysical guilt comes not just to underlie an otherwise differentiated typology in which it plays a limited role, but to suffuse and

26 Jaspers (2000: chs 4, 5) does so in various places in the two chapters 'Differentiation of German Guilt' and 'Possible Excuses'.

undermine it. Metaphysical guilt becomes the guilt of all, emergent 'in this German place' (ibid: 94),[27] and therefore not something to be sequestered and controlled in 'external' legal and political processes, or in self-chosen 'internal' dialogues between a person and his or her God or close friends. It is 'out there' in the world, and all are obliged to acknowledge their complicity in it. The categories provide no hiding place, so that a notion of collective-metaphysical guilt threatens to destroy the distinctions that lay at the core of Jaspers's official position, and therefore to undermine its tendency to support a general turn away from the guilt of the past.

On first sight, Arendt and Jaspers appear very different in their thinking. Arendt's reflections on Eichmann have a reactive, 'phenomenological' quality to them, and are far from the systematic philosophy of Jaspers. However, Jaspers's problem with his four forms of guilt can be seen to result from the same issue as concerns Arendt. How is it possible to attribute guilt where a whole people have given themselves over to wrongdoing? Only the concept of collective guilt, informed by an underlying idea of metaphysical guilt, can capture the sense that war guilt lay with the vast majority of Germans. In taking this position, however, the neat typology of forms of guilt, with everything in its appropriate box, disintegrates. It is for this reason that Arendt's initial epistolary exchange with Jaspers, before she had elaborated her own view, really hit home. Her questioning touched the raw nerve that his own discussion of collective guilt exposed.

Are we then left with Arendt's own unhappy dilemma: that a valid justice cannot be done to the Nazis, and that all we are left with is the slaughter bench and victor's justice? The answer, I will suggest in the next section, is that there may be moral truth in the broad metaphysical conception of justice that Jaspers's own contradictory positioning forced out of him, against his own logic. It may indicate a way of thinking about our ethical experience (a meta-ethics) of judging egregious wrongdoing, which can at least begin to indicate how, even if history is a slaughter bench and justice is that of the victor, there still remains an ethically valid charge in processes of international justice.

The value and difficulty of metaphysical guilt

'Dialectic . . . the art of thinking the coincidence of distinctions and connections.'
(Bhaskar 1993: 180)

27 Chris Thornhill has argued that Jaspers's emphasis on guilt in 'this German place' carries with it a politically unpleasant, nationalistic sentiment, making possible an ultimate evasion of fundamental wrongdoing by reference to the idea of 'another Germany' that was somehow present and not implicated in what had happened (Thornhill 2002: 175–77). Whilst I accept this point, I do not think that Jaspers's resort to a broader sense of metaphysical wrongdoing can be entirely repudiated because of its 'German' connotation. It has to be remembered that Jaspers was also keen to point out the universal quality of the metaphysical conception: a sense of wrongdoing that transcends his reference to 'this German place'. Besides, what had happened *did* occur in 'this German place': different inflections operate here.

If Jaspers's typology is brought under threat by extending metaphysical justice, I begin this section by considering its significance for our understanding of Arendt's problem of justice and judgment over Eichmann. I then move on to think about the implications of thinking in this way for issues of responsibility in international criminal justice contexts. The argument is necessarily sketched and provisional, but I want to note the need to think dialectically about both distinctions and connections in relating an overall metaphysical sense of guilt to the conduct of individuals and groups in particular contexts. The main thrust of this section is, however, general and meta-ethical rather than particular and concretised. It is about a way of seeing, rather than a detailed application of an ethical method, and is, therefore, in the best, or worst, tradition of the philosophy of punishment, 'prolegomenal' (Hart 1968: ch 1).

The value of metaphysical guilt

If we think about Jaspers's initial typology, we could treat it as an anticipatory defence to Arendt's critical questions. A positivistic account of criminal guilt finesses the problem of achieving a community between judge and judged. All that is required is a formally free act contravening an established prohibitory norm (law). But Arendt's underlying problem remains in place, for the resort to positivism cannot answer the moral questions she raises. We come back to the initial concern in her correspondence with Jaspers that the Nazi crimes 'explode the limits of law'. No punishment 'is severe enough' and we 'are simply not equipped to deal, on a human, political level, with a guilt that is beyond crime'. 'But still, there is a difference' between killing your old aunt and building 'factories to produce corpses'. The Germans are burdened with 'hundreds of thousands of people who cannot be adequately punished'. Criminal justice is never, as legal positivists would like, a matter of simple rule infraction for formally free acts and Nazi crimes make this abundantly clear. They break down the positivistically constructed limits of law. As between Jaspers's initial typology and Arendt's criticism, I think Arendt is right.

My suggestion, however, is that what undoes Jaspers in his late revisionism is precisely that which saves Arendt from her rightness and the discomfiting conclusions, the moral melancholia, of her epilogue and postscript. It is the extended form of metaphysical guilt which offers a way of addressing Arendt's problem. For her, the problem with Eichmann was that he was in so many ways a normal member of a community, yet one with whom no process of judgment could have moral connection. He was both a normal human being and morally beyond the pale, a moral outcast. Punishment should involve a moral communication, but how could you communicate with someone who held his views? In this regard, he was like an animal who had mauled a child, or a sexual psychopath who had committed a terrible crime, although these analogies only take one so far. Precisely what was so chilling about him was that Eichmann was neither of these and remained throughout a competent human being. Worse, nor was his problem an individual one but that of a whole community, of which he was a normal member.

Arendt's answer was, as we have seen, to treat Eichmann as a 'general enemy of humanity' (*hostis generis humani*), but because of his alienation from humanity's general norms, he could not be punished according to the accepted moral rationale. Punishment could not be based on individual guilt, but rather on a valid social expunging on other grounds, a more simple and atavistic refusal to share the earth. Arendt's solution to the problem of how one punishes an Eichmann is to treat him as one who lacks the full moral capacities of the human being, but this acknowledges the lack of moral community that otherwise makes justice possible. The moral communication between more or less equally placed human beings that lies at the core of modern justice is discarded in favour of a condescension *faute de mieux*. Eichmann and his kind appear to extract a bitter revenge against their judges: they seem to bring them down to their level.

How does Jaspers help us here? His conception of metaphysical guilt operates not at the level of an actual human community or in the abilities of particular persons to engage in moral dialogue. It may do, but it does not have to: the metaphysical element in being human operates through people but also beyond them. Jaspers describes it as a solidarity that makes each person 'co-responsible for every wrong and every injustice in the world' (Jaspers 2000: 26), and he says that this is especially so for crimes committed in our presence or knowledge. The 'especially' indicates that the responsibility operates also despite our presence or knowledge. It operates, for example, in our sharing in the 'links of tradition' so that we 'have to bear the guilt of our fathers' for the 'spiritual conditions of German life' (ibid: 73).[28] The essence of metaphysical responsibility does not lie in what we do or know, but in the relation between what we do and know and what lies beyond our acts and knowledge, in the broader world of which we are a part. It relates to the existence of an unconditional relation between all human beings: that 'somewhere among men the unconditioned prevails – the capacity to live only together or not at all' (ibid: 26).

The need for such a transcendent ethical quality, I suggest, lies at the back of Arendt's dilemma as regards Eichmann. On one hand, she cannot reconcile punishment with a modern sense of justice; on the other, she is morally convinced of the need for punishment. The problem is that her analysis of community and judgment is too 'empirical', too linked to the actual views of the judge and (especially) the judged. It lacks a sense of the metaphysical and transcendent that lies, albeit uncomfortably, at the core of Jaspers's work. Eichmann and those like him, regardless of their own views on the matter, owed a responsibility to the idea of the human, so that their punishment does not cease to be ethical because they cannot or will not acknowledge the wrong they have done. Their punishment

28 An interesting analysis of Jaspers's idea of collective responsibility in relation to restorative justice and reconciliation is provided by Andrew Schaap. See Schaap (2001).

rather operates as an invocation of how much their conduct failed to relate to a sense of the unconditional relation between human beings, what they owe to each other, regardless of their own sentiments in the matter. It maintains its validity even if they cannot see it, for the conditional possibility of dialogue within an actual community is a manifestation of an underlying unconditional metaphysical relation, rather than a necessary condition of judgment per se.[29]

A difficult solution: distinctions and connections

The above argument is limited in what it achieves, indicating no more than that a way of dealing with Arendt's 'actual' or 'empirical' problem may be to have resort to Jaspers's 'ideal' metaphysical ethics, to press on the ideal in the relation between the ideal and the actual in modern punishment theory (See Norrie 1998; 2005a: ch 10). Another way of putting this is to speak of the relation between the conditional and the unconditioned, a relation which, as I have said, is reflected in modern critical thinking associated with Derrida, and also with the dialectical tradition. In effect, the relationship between the unconditional and the conditioned involves thinking immanently, critically or deconstructively about justice, and what justice relations disclose.[30]

29 At the end of her life, Arendt was moving in a direction similar to the one I have drawn from Jaspers. Compare his argument with the position Arendt draws from Kant in the posthumously published *Lectures on Kant's Political Philosophy*, where she writes that: 'One judges always as a member of a community, guided by one's community sense, one's *sensus communis*. But in the last analysis, one is a member of a world community *by the sheer fact of being human* . . . When one judges and when one acts in political matters, one is supposed to take one's bearings from *the idea, not the actuality*, of being a world citizen and, therefore, also a *Weltbetrachter*, a world spectator' (Beiner 1992: 75–76, emphasis added). This development helps answer a question raised by a reviewer of this article: can *Jaspers* provide a solution to *Arendt's* problem? She pays attention after all to the *historical* fact of German moral blindness in *Eichmann*, and would therefore not be persuaded by the idea of an unconditional relation between human beings operating 'behind the back' of their subjectivities. In what sense could my argument therefore claim to involve an *immanent* critique of Arendt, one that is authentic to her own questions, rather than an 'external' one? There are two reasons why this is an immanent critique. The first comes from the dilemma that she finds herself in as between her support for an international penal court and her denial of the possibility of such a court doing justice to the likes of Eichmann. This requires of her a move beyond the historical or 'empirical' description of the moral position of someone like Eichmann. The second reason is that she herself senses the need to think in more unconditional terms, for example in her rejection, without good ground, of the 'cog theory' in favour of legal judgment in the postscript, or in her suggestion that Eichmann's failure is in terms of not 'think[ing] from the standpoint of someone else', or that people who opposed the Nazis had to 'judge freely' (Arendt 1964: 295). These comments reveal her working away from the impasse in her analysis engendered by her reliance on the actual subjectivities of people like Eichmann under modern historical conditions towards broader ethical premises. She experiences the need, indeed, immanent in her own work, to move in a direction that turns out to be not dissimilar to Jaspers, so that he is not an 'alien' imposition on her thought from outside. The late *Lectures* bear this out.

30 I have argued elsewhere that the distance between dialectics and deconstruction is not so great as is sometimes thought, Derrida himself having a much more ambivalent attitude to Hegel than is

Although such ways of thinking are in many ways distinguishable, they also have much in common, giving rise to a common problematic in which it becomes necessary and possible to think the relationship between the ideal and the actual in a particular way. In particular, it becomes possible to think of the limits of any particular concept, and necessary to think about how *distinctions* between connected phenomena and *connections* between disparate phenomena are conceived.

These are two sides of the same coin. As regards *distinctions*, a metaphysical sense of responsibility that lies everywhere may be a necessary, but cannot be a sufficient, condition of guilt, for it is over-inclusive. In Jaspers's account it makes sense to speak of the responsibility of a whole people and of future generations, but this cannot be at the cost of not also differentiating varieties of guilt within the whole. Otherwise, it hardly permits us to distinguish degrees of responsibility, so that by itself, it would not, for example, make any particular distinction between an Eichmann and a boy foot soldier at the end of the war. Both would be members of the Nazi war machine, both would share a sense of responsibility for the whole, yet they would stand differently in relation to it. To identify a general metaphysical sense of responsibility does not lead to a lesser need to distinguish cases, but it does sensitise us to the limits of the distinctions we make, and the underlying connections of which we should not lose sight. It requires us to examine distinctions in terms of their limits, and to think beyond, and critically about them: what do they exclude, and how validly do they do it (see also below chapter 10)?

The criticism of Jaspers's typology, including his own, is a kind of auto-critique or self-deconstruction in the face of an historical position. From that point on, there is a need to re-interrogate the results of his own categories, and to consider their validity. How could or should criminal responsibility for the Nazi war machine be recalibrated in the light of the broader underpinning established by metaphysical concerns? In return, how should the metaphysical be shaped to deal with the conditional world it informs? At present, all that the above argument establishes is that a metaphysical grounding asserts that there may be an ethical ground for responsibility where actors would deny it, but it does not in itself disclose what this might mean in practice.

If the general effect of such an approach is to problematise our distinctions in the light of the connections they disclose, it generates a 'difficult' conception of ethical judgment, one which has parallels with Jacques Derrida's ethics of forgiveness. Derrida considers the philosophy of deconstruction as involving unconditional standing in relation to a conditioned world. As he notes, such a bipolarity of standpoint inevitably leaves a gap which individual acts of judgment must fill. Here is Derrida speaking about a matter close to that discussed by Arendt

often allowed. More boldly, there is a good argument for locating deconstruction within a broad conceptualisation of dialectic that is not limited to Hegelian thinking. See Norrie (2005a: ch 8; 2010); see also Barnett (1998). This argument draws upon the work of Roy Bhaskar. See Bhaskar (1993; 2002).

and Jaspers, the issue of forgiveness for historic wrongs, in terms of a double order of an unconditional justice and a need to decide here and now:

> Here is the most difficult moment, the law of the responsible transaction. According to the situations and according to the moments, the responsibilities to be taken are different . . . One is never sure of making the just choice; one never knows, one will never know with what is called knowledge. The future will give us no more knowledge, because it itself will have been determined by that choice. It is here that responsibilities are to be re-evaluated at each moment, according to concrete situations, that is to say, those that do not wait, those that do not give us time for infinite deliberation. The response . . . is more than difficult; it is infinitely distressing. It is night.
>
> (Derrida 2001: 56)

Derrida points here to a sense of the intrinsic difficulty of any differentiation of categories, yet a process of differentiation must occur. It must be said, however, that we do not start with a blank canvas. Justice operates between the conditioned and the unconditional, so it always starts in relation to those categories of judgment already in existence, in this case those categories of liberal criminal jurisprudence with which we are already familiar. Categories such as those of complicity, or of principal and accessory, for example, or of the degrees of responsibility based upon positions in a hierarchy of command remain relevant to a process of differentiation. Specific acts carried out by individuals are also relevant to marking guilt. Just decisions, however, involve a relating of legal categories, which close off decisions about responsibility, to broader moral reflections.

Western law and its philosophy is generally marked by the individualisation of responsibilities within social relations (Norrie 2000), and that is why, when Jaspers came to question the negative consequences of his typology, which starts with law, it was in terms of a collective-metaphysical conception of guilt. Such a conception cannot, I argue, ride roughshod over existing categories, but must remain a necessary, troubling supplement to them.

As regards *connections*, in the German situation, the process of attributing guilt would not rest content with the criminal identification of the leading few, to the benefit of those many who willingly assumed executive duties in their footsteps, or even to those who were active supporters of Nazism but not the actual agents of atrocities. It would suggest an extended sense of critical engagement with the responsibilities of all those involved at different levels in Nazi Germany. It would, in other words, pursue the implications of Jaspers's extended notion of metaphysical-collective guilt for the German people, not in the abstract, but in terms of their various activities under the regime. In particular, many ex-Nazis came to hold positions of power, wealth and influence after the war and were supported by the former allied countries for real-political and economic reasons (Bower 1997).

If such cases resulted from a failure to apply existing or established law, then the fault is clear. If they resulted from the limits of actually existing legal categories, then a deeper ethical reckoning was in part thwarted by the limits of the law. To argue that such a reckoning became in any case counter-productive after a certain time in terms of the need to rebuild German society may involve a certain kind of political or strategic truth, but the underlying ethical issue is not thereby cancelled. The connection between what was and was not achieved in terms of justice then becomes the ghost at the feast of political and economic recovery in the post-war world.

Finally, emphasising connections has a significance beyond the German context. Generally, it encourages thought about how individual criminal acts are often systematically organised. It takes us beyond those who are most obviously perpetrators, and into the webs of power that sustain them. It encourages the problematisation of boundaries between different kinds of wrongdoing, and this includes wrongdoing by a judging community itself. It makes us think about how the commission of egregious acts relates to the process of history that produces them, and it confronts the issues with which we started this investigation: the nature of justice as something that is brought about by victors, and of history as, in Hegel's term, a slaughter bench.

Imagine a world in which country A, an international hegemon, sets up a dictator in country B in order to act as a bulwark against developments occurring in country C. All goes well until the dictator starts to get ideas above his station and attacks other countries, at which point A invades B, deposes the dictator and has him put on trial for crimes committed when A supported and armed B. In such a situation, an underlying metaphysical sense of guilt would indicate that it does not stop with the dictator, his henchmen and any other leading perpetrators. The metaphysical conception of guilt would rightly open these kinds of issues to scrutiny, and for that reason, its justice is no 'easy' form. Nonetheless, if our aim is to consider ethically the quality of the justice that processes of judgment produce, then these are surely issues relevant to the matter at hand.

Justice *and* the slaughter bench

If we now return to my introductory comments about justice and the slaughter bench, it will be recalled that Hegel's philosophy, against the spirit of my prefatory quote, nonetheless held out hope that the deployment of reason could provide comfort, in the sense of ethical progress operating behind the back of history's manifest forms. International justice, coming out of the Nuremberg trials, pushing towards an international penal process which now has come into being, could be evidence of just such a progress, and we saw how Arendt, on one side of her thinking, interprets the Eichmann trial as a part of that development. The future ultimately belonged, on this view, to Kant and his hopes for cosmopolitan justice. There is, however, a great temptation in the light of the history of the 20th and the incipient 21st centuries to want to reject Kant and the reassurance of Hegelian *Nachdenken*, and to look askance at international justice.

History really has proved itself to be the slaughter bench, and everything else is window dressing for those who would wish to be fooled by the justice of victors. Arendt's views towards the very end of *Eichmann in Jerusalem* can be cited in support of such an alternative view. In the age of death factories, of imperialism and totalitarianism, of the mass man without a conscience, whole communities giving themselves up to violent depravity, the slaughter bench has only become the bloodier. Only a sense of biblical judgment can make any sense of the cruelty of human being.

To draw on a phrase used by Robert Fine, what Arendt saw as the defining feature of the 20th century was the growth of a nihilistic, dehumanized, 'spiritless radicalism' (Fine 2001: 113–119). In human affairs, this could produce precisely an Eichmann and millions like him, rendering principles of morality, reason and responsibility, judgment and justice redundant. Given the existence of such a mindset, which lies at the core of Arendt's thought about modernity, it might be suggested that her endorsement of international criminal justice could only be at loggerheads with this deeper trend. The last pages of the epilogue, and the resumed discussion in the postscript, mark the conflict between tectonic plates in her thinking: a renewed belief in liberal modes of law and reason hitting hard up against her account of spiritless radicalism and its effects.

From my point of view, Arendt's account of spiritless radicalism is a modern way of describing the evolution of history's slaughter bench. Arendt was clear that ways of thinking about ideas must involve an understanding of how they are historically shaped and evolved. Spiritless radicalism is the specific form that racist, totalitarian and genocidal ideas took in the 20th century, but it is important to be clear about the nature of history, and to recognise that its development is not all one way. To describe modern history as a 'slaughter bench' is to recognise only one aspect, and to ignore those other developments that are equally embedded in our understanding of modernity.

For Arendt, new concepts emerge from and evolve out of the world as it itself develops, so that the spatio-temporally emergent fact of wrongs done against humanity at the same time generates the conceptualisation of the crime against humanity. The structure of events gives rise to the concept, and this suggests a more complex historical vision than that represented either by the ideas of totalitarianism and spiritless radicalism, or more generally that history represents only the slaughter bench. Things are not all one way. If one side of modernity is its violence, another side is its assertion of principles of human dignity, of the need for public justice, of a potential for international justice and a cosmopolitan purpose arising within it. Modernity is at once the violence of history *and* the consciousness of what human beings owe to each other, the coming into being of a metaphysical sense of the universality of human experience in a world of war.[31]

31 Such a counter-position does not deny that ideas of the universal can themselves be invoked to legitimate the violence of history, but it argues that such uses do not exhaust them.

In the struggle between Kant, Hegel and the slaughter bench, this formulation might seem to place me on the side of Kant or Hegelian redemption, but my aim is not to defend a Kantian standpoint from which to observe and to judge. Such a standpoint is too one-sided, too obviously prey to the problem of repetition: that we continue to observe and to judge, but the world continues to be barbaric. An act of judgment becomes only the latest in a sequence, whilst the need to judge conduct and communities never changes, so that judgment is always flawed, becoming at best otiose and at worst historically complicit. Its 'regulative ideals' never regulate anything. Such a position is not what I aim for. Rather, I am interested in the sense of an historically real world in which splits, antinomies, 'broken' forms of justice are the order of the day. Modernity's reality is that it is a world in which systematic violence and acts and institutions of judgment and justice are *both* constitutive elements. It is one in which the contradictions between the two elements are 'out there', lived and experienced, in the world. Thus it is that antinomialism is our given historical experience of justice and judgment (Norrie 2005a: ch 1).

When Arendt spoke of the Eichmann trial as a step towards an international justice, and at the same time reminded herself of the fundamental problems for law to which such justice gave rise, she did no more than reflect the realities of the world. When Jaspers wrote of the limited forms of guilt that he wished to portray as appropriate for the post-war world, he depicted them in a way that he thought appropriate for a particular historical time and place, one that should not, in his view, bear too much responsibility. But a part of him at the same time rebelled against his own categories, giving his work its most interesting – because contradictory – aspect.

What appears as a contradiction in both Arendt and Jaspers in fact reflects a process of historical development and emergence in which contradictory elements are brought into play in history itself. Underlying this process, giving a sense of a utopian ethical promise to the world – despite everything – is something like Jaspers's conception of metaphysical responsibility. Between the ideal and the actual, the unconditional and the conditioned, we are therefore able to hold onto something of the promise and the value of an international criminal justice, but in a way that recognises its ambiguous, aporetic, broken quality. History may be described as the slaughter bench, and justice may therefore be viewed as the privilege of the victors, but this is not the whole story. In light of this, I would like to revise the title of this essay. Justice 'on' the slaughter bench is better conceived as a two-way relationship, in which the better copula is 'and'.

Chapter 8

Ethics and history: can critical lawyers talk of good and evil?

This chapter explores what we might mean by good and evil, and argues that these terms remain salient for a critical, socio-historical, understanding of criminal law. It draws upon a meta-ethics of freedom and solidarity to explain what good means in recent mercy killing cases in England and Wales, and what evil means in Arendt's phrase, the 'banality of evil' (Arendt 1964). My original title was 'the Scene and the Crime', and the basic argument was that if we are to understand 'the crime', we need to understand its 'scene', which includes substantive ethical terms like good and evil. What might be surprising in this is the link between this argument for ethics and the general thrust of a critical understanding of criminal law.

If we were to identify in short order what forms the core of a critical understanding of criminal law, it might involve seven points:

1. that concepts of legal responsibility are shaped by their role in historically configured political-institutional arrangements which they help operationalise;
2. that, across an historical field in which different political-juridical forms are required, a key figure in criminal law, as in other areas of law such as contract, is that of the formal, abstract and general legal subject;
3. that this formal legal subject, because it abstracts the individual from the social and political context in which he or she operates, acts to neutralise or finesse social, moral and political conflicts brought about by structural inequalities and violence; whilst
4. providing an individualist 'morality of form' grounded in a conception of negative liberty that is not without its own (limited) ethical value; that this
5. generates a range of effects in the criminal law that are centred on a core architectonic of offence (mens rea and actus reus) and defence; which in turn
6. leads to a range of oppositions, form-substance dichotomies and the antinomial 'doubling' of concepts in the law (offence and defence, motive and intention, direct and indirect intention, subjective and objective recklessness). At the core of this antinomial doubling is an engagement between legal forms and the social contexts in which they operate ('crimes' and their 'scenes'). This engagement ramifies within legal forms (hence the doubling of concepts), but

also leads to complex relationships between those forms and the practices, processes and institutions in which they are embedded.[1]

To this conception of a critical project, there might then be added:

7. an understanding of late or post-modernity, which sees modern Western societies as ones where normativity has been thinned out, formalised, or reduced to a vanishing point, where legal formalism reduces law to an instrumentalising agent solely operating in favour of political-institutional arrangements.

In this essay, I start from propositions (1) to (6), and whilst not wishing to deny a place for (7), the formalising and instrumentalising nature of social and economic institutions (including law), especially under present social and economic conditions, I want to explore a more nuanced understanding of the relationship between law, its ethics and context as part of the broad picture of how criminal law relates to its environment. Whilst arguing for (1) to (6), I do not deny the relationship between formal legal concepts of responsibility and substantive ethical issues, but I see the relationship between law and ethics as complicated, oblique and inherently difficult.

When we look at morality through law, we look 'through a glass darkly' (Norrie 2005a: 196). Thus, I argue, first, that the 'morality of form' at the core of the criminal law itself is normative (especially in its formal support for negative liberty), but, second, that it operates to block substantive normative issues and then to articulate such issues obliquely and contradictorily through its concepts (as in for example contestation around the meaning of intention or recklessness), and then, third, that this blocking/negotiating strategy is particularly seen in how it deals with 'thick' moral concepts of good and evil.

It is in this context of a complicated relationship between law and ethics that I want to explore, as the specific argument of the essay, how a critical understanding of 'the scene' in which criminal law operates should resist (7) to the extent that we still need to talk about substantive ethical issues such as good and evil. Thinning to the point of vanishing is different from obliquity, contradictoriness, complexity, confusion and self-undoing. I argue, therefore, in the light of the 'banality of evil', and recent English cases on mercy killing, that it is necessary to talk in such terms vis-à-vis the criminal law. Such conceptions can be derived from a meta-ethics of freedom and solidarity that I will elaborate, and these represent an important part

1 An example given below concerns the interaction between the formalism in core legal concepts and jury discretion in mercy killing cases. Both formal law and the discretion it invokes are constitutive parts of the legal whole. I think it important to draw attention to the structuring of that whole by core legal concepts, without in any way asserting that they represent the whole story. It is important to take a socio-legal understanding into the territory that is often seen as purely legal, but there should be no intention to substitute an understanding of the legal core for the broad contextual operation of the law that socio-legal studies have always involved.

of the terrain in which a formalistic conception of the criminal law and the legal subject operates.

Unsurprisingly, given its formalistic quality, such conceptions tend to give criminal law problems, and they may be counter-intuitive to critical or historical thinkers too, but I still want to argue for their importance. This involves going beyond the idea of a 'morality of form' to think about how substantive ethical issues link constellationally to the broader picture of how the criminal law operates. In short, if criminal law is historically, structurally and politically shaped in morally formalistic terms, can it involve morally substantive terms such as good and evil, and if so, how?

Why talk of good and evil?

Why, it might be asked, should we want to talk from a critical perspective of good and evil in relation to the criminal law? The previous chapter on war guilt in Germany after the Second World War concerns how we hold onto a notion of moral value in a world which systematically denies it. In part, it focused on Hannah Arendt's account of the Eichmann trial in Jerusalem, and her idea that his bureaucratic approach to murder represented the 'banality of evil'. At that point, I focused, as many do, on the idea that evil was *banal*, but that of course left open the bigger question as to what Arendt meant by *evil*. What did the word signify? Should we, who live in secular times, especially when we see the word 'evil' itself banalised and turned to bad purpose – think of the 'axis of evil' to which we in the Anglo-American world were all signed up recently – avoid this idea? Did Arendt mean it rhetorically? I do not think so, and I therefore think we should ask what she meant by using this term.

As well as thinking about the banality of evil, I had been working on the way criminal law deals with mercy killing and assisted suicide, and I was drawn to two cases in England in 2010 involving mothers who had killed their adult, badly damaged, children: Frances Inglis and Kay Gilderdale (see Chapter 5 above). My focus had been on the difference between legal and moral notions of guilt, but I began to wonder what was morally so compelling about the case of Kay Gilderdale in particular, that a jury had refused to convict her of attempted murder despite clear evidence that she should in law be guilty. What was it about the moral quality of her action? Looking at the case, I concluded that it was because her actions could be described as in some relevant sense essentially good.

So without really meaning to, I found myself thinking about questions of good and evil in relation to criminal law, and wondering what these terms, which previously I would have avoided, meant. Perhaps, I would have left it there but for a third piece of work I was completing in this period: a book on Roy Bhaskar's dialectical reworking of the philosophy of critical realism (Bhaskar 1993; Norrie 2010). This work has many important ideas in it, but one that seemed to link in with my interest in good and evil is its argument for a *meta-ethics* grounded in the nature of human being. Now that probably seems a forbidding term, and one in which no lawyer should be interested. Nonetheless, it is the idea that there are things about the way that human beings as a species or a natural kind are that enables us to reflect upon the ways we think about ethical questions. A meta-ethics is about the *grounds* of ethics, morality or normativity, and it seemed to me that one could deploy such an understanding to what it means to act in terms of good and evil. Let me explain that a little bit now before we move on.

A meta-ethics of legal freedom

At the core of Bhaskar's meta-ethics is the idea of human beings as both individuated, self-acting individuals and as beings who need the solidarity of others if they are to survive and act in the world (Norrie 2010: ch 5; and see chapter 9 below, pp 174–9). Infants need and demand food, but only others can provide it for them. They need shelter and protection, they are capable of learning and language, but these will only be achieved by way of others acting with and on them, and in that way being in solidarity with them. What is true of children is just as true of adults: we cannot survive or thrive except in cooperation and with the help of others. It is sometimes said that we come into and leave the world alone, but if this is a statement about the existential quality of being human, it is one-sided. We are born of others, and we die as social animals after a lifetime of being in relation to others. When we are old, we require others to care for us.

This idea of human beings as social animals, as actors in relation with others, is the basis for an understanding of what it means to be free, but in that freedom also to be connected. The core possibility of acting for ourselves lies in each of us, but cannot be realised save through the work, example and care of others. To be free is first to have the ability to act rather than to be acted on, a certain basic spontaneity within human beings. This basic idea of freedom as spontaneity leads to the further idea that we would need space in which to exercise our choosing agency. This is the negative requirement that our active freedom be not interfered with, and it leads to the positive conception that we would need support for our agency to be enabled. Further, we are capable of grasping who we are and the context in which we act, and of acting either to maintain or to change it. So we are capable of a measure of autonomy with regard to our context. When we identify barriers to, or blocks upon, our action, we can seek to overcome (to free or emancipate ourselves from) these. Generally, note, we must do this in solidarity with others, and we can only do so if we act in accordance with principles that reflect their needs and desires as well as our own. Freedom in its various forms requires a complex, dialectical, dynamic, relation of solidarity with others, and freedom within that solidarity with others, to be ourselves.

This is a way of thinking about our core human nature, and how we can understand certain ethical possibilities in it. What I have been describing is a set of freedoms that are, at a meta-ethical level, co-related. In this way we move from basic ideas of freedom such as simple human agency (the spontaneous ability to act) and negative liberty (the freedom to act without interference) to more complex kinds of freedom including positive liberty (support for action), autonomy (rational independence of our action) and emancipation (freedom from institutions and structures that block our free action).

But even these more complex forms of freedom are only half the story, because we can also think of more enriched forms of freedom in which we are able to live well and to flourish according to what is unique in and best for us – according to what we may call our concrete universality.[2] In the end, we can think of the meta-ethical possibility that the final step for humankind would be a world in which each of us flourished, and a condition of each of us flourishing would be that we all flourished. Bhaskar calls this the 'eudaimonistic society', a term drawn from Aristotle, but one that also borrows from Marx, for whom the freedom of each was a condition of the freedom of all. It is, he argues, a real possibility immanent in human beings, albeit one that remains sadly unactualised or under-actualised at this point in our species development.

That is a basic flavour of the idea of a critical realist meta-ethics. It raises many questions that I cannot answer here and now – how these forms of freedom are linked, or in tension, in modern society being one (see Chapter 9 below) – but what I want to bring out is this. At the core of human being, our core human nature, lies the possibility and necessity of acting freely, and in solidarity with others, as a means of promoting the possibility that we should all flourish.[3] My suggestion will be that people who act in something like this way act in ways that are good; and people who act fundamentally to deny these possibilities act in ways that are evil. But that is to take us ahead of ourselves: let us go back to our examples of good and evil.

Speak of the devil: the banality of evil

What does it mean to talk of evil? Is this just a misplaced word, so that we would be better to think in terms of acts that are bad, really bad, egregiously so? The question is implicit in Arendt's writing on the Holocaust, where she coined the phrase 'the banality of evil'. Most discussion of this phrase turns on the claim of 'banality', but what of the term 'evil'? Her thinking has its seeming genesis in correspondence with Karl Jaspers after the Second World War (see also above, pp 121–4). To him, she wrote that:

> The Nazi crimes . . . explode the limits of the law; and that is precisely what constitutes their monstrousness. For these crimes, no punishment is severe

2 A conception of the concrete universal/singular draws upon Hegel, but needs to be developed to include an understanding of the effect of real spatio-temporality on individual human being: see Norrie (2010: 113–117).

3 From the references to Aristotle and Marx, as well as from discussion of negative and positive liberty, it will be understood that what is being argued for is not new in terms of its discrete elements. Rather, it is the syncretic and dialectical progression to the most enriched forms of freedom from the

> enough . . . That is, their guilt, in contrast to all criminal guilt, oversteps and shatters any and all legal systems . . . We are simply not equipped to deal, on a human, political level, with a guilt that is beyond crime . . . The Germans are burdened now *with thousands or tens of thousands or hundreds of thousands of people* who cannot be adequately punished within the legal system.
>
> (Kohler and Saner 1992: 54)

Her letter prompted a warning from Jaspers that she was close to describing 'a guilt that goes beyond all criminal guilt [which] inevitably takes on a streak of "greatness" – of satanic greatness', whereas it was necessary 'to see these things in their total banality, in their prosaic triviality, because that's what truly characterises them'. This may have been where the idea of the banality of evil came from, although initially in her published writing, Arendt spoke of 'radical evil', a term she drew from Kant, before shifting to the idea of banality. Replying, she accepted that her words might have invited this misunderstanding, but she still wanted to make a point:

> But still, there is a difference between a man who sets out to murder his old aunt and people who without considering the economic usefulness of their actions at all . . . built factories to produce corpses . . . [I]ndividual human beings did not kill other individual human beings for human reasons, but . . . an organised attempt was made to eradicate the concept of the human being.
>
> (ibid: 69)

Note two things here: first, that what would become 'the banality of evil' is here represented in the first place as a guilt that goes beyond all *criminal guilt*; and, second, that at the core of her conception of evil is the idea of 'an organised attempt . . . to eradicate the concept of the human being'. On the first, in what sense does the guilt go beyond 'all criminal guilt'? Clearly, it was possible at Nuremberg, as it is now, to prosecute and convict the Nazis for crimes against humanity, although various questions could be asked about the legal validity of Nuremberg and its 'successor' trials. The nub of her point, however, does not lie in that kind of problem. Her concern is rather that what had been done surpassed what could be registered by standard criminal law categories.

The Holocaust indicated a moral failure that could not be caught by legal concepts of the guilty mind or act. Why? An inhuman system with inhuman ends had been operated by people who had fallen so far below the level of humanity that no courtroom dialogue of guilt or innocence could engage them. Certainly, the Nazis, or some – but not all – of them, could be tried, convicted and punished, but no legal process involving judgment and dialogue between citizens or human individuals could address the enormity of what had happened. It could punish, but

lesser ones that is important. The further link in the chain of thought here is Hegel, with his dialectical universalism.

not find guilt, because guilt involved a human relation that here was absent. The law was rendered in a deep moral sense void by its context, the crime by its scene. Perhaps, we might say, the perpetrators had proved themselves 'human, all too human' (Nietzsche 1967), but this show of humanity, where anything goes, was beyond our limits to judge. When everyman becomes a *génocidaire* (Cesarani 2004), the legal field lacks traction to find guilt, to condemn, to punish.

The second point to note is this: that the core problem was that 'an organised attempt [had been] made to eradicate the concept of the human being'. This is in part a meta-ethical statement, and it is relevant to my argument about good and evil. I will return to it below; for now, I will pick up the other moral quality we need to talk about, the nature of good.

Speaking of good: towards a meta-ethics

If we have to think of evil in connection with criminal law, do we also have to think of its seeming contrary, good? My thoughts here are prompted by two cases that came before the English criminal courts in January 2010. Both involved 'mercy killings', but they had different outcomes (see above, pp 93–4). In the first, Frances Inglis injected her badly brain damaged son Thomas with street heroin and killed him. It was a tragic case. Thomas had been assaulted on the street and been persuaded against his will to go to hospital in an ambulance. Whilst in the ambulance, the door opened three times and, on the third occasion, Thomas fell out and suffered serious head injuries whence came the brain damage. Whilst the doctors were of the view that there was some prospect of recovery, Mrs Inglis became convinced that Thomas was in an inexpressible agony. She eventually killed him, by design, and, she said, 'with love in her heart'.

There is no defence, nor lesser offence, of 'mercy killing' in England and Wales, and Mrs Inglis was convicted of murder. She had the mens rea (guilty mind) exhibited by her intention to kill Thomas, and her good motive was irrelevant to law. She was given a mandatory life sentence with a recommendation that she serve a (lower than average) minimum of nine years for what the judge called her 'calculated and consistent course of criminal conduct' (*Guardian*, 21 January 2010). On appeal, this was reduced to five (*Guardian*, 12 November 2010).[4]

The Court of Appeal was very clear that there was no defence of mercy killing, and that she did not fall within the provocation defence (there was no loss of control). She might have had a defence of diminished responsibility, but she had declined to plead this, it seems, because she wanted to have a trial and to highlight the fault of the medical services. To have claimed diminished responsibility would also have focused the case on her own vulnerability. Nonetheless, the eventual *reduction of sentence* was based on the possibility of *mitigation of sentence* on account of her mental condition, and the fact that this was a 'mercy killing' – both

4 *R v Inglis* [2010] All ER (D) 140, [2010] EWCA Crim 2637.

factors that can be taken into account in sentencing (Criminal Justice Act 2003), although not in the formal adjudication of the trial.

The second case is that of Kay Gilderdale (*Guardian*, 26 January 2010, unreported), who killed her daughter Lynn with an injection of morphine and air into the blood stream. Lynn had suffered from myalgic encephalomyelitis (ME), or chronic fatigue syndrome, for 17 years and was at the time of her death 31 years of age. She had attempted to kill herself and had clearly expressed the wish to die. At her trial, Mrs Gilderdale pleaded guilty to aiding and abetting a suicide, but not guilty to attempted murder (the charge of 'attempted' presumably to avoid proving questions of causation). The Crown Prosecution Service (CPS) was convinced that what she had done had gone beyond assisting another to take her own life, and that there was an intention to kill. As with the *Inglis* case, they prosecuted for the more serious offence, but the jury refused to convict on attempted murder. The judge, handing down a conditional discharge for assisting suicide, openly questioned the CPS decision to prosecute on attempted murder. The CPS response was that they were satisfied that the evidence was there to provide a realistic prospect of conviction, and that it was therefore in the public interest to prosecute.

Why did the jury in the one case convict, but not in the other? In Mrs Inglis's case, the Court of Appeal judgment provides a sense of how the judges saw the defendant. Whilst they had some sympathy for her, seen in the reduction of the sentence, it was also clear that they felt that she had acted out of her own concerns and interests rather than her son's. She had declined to acknowledge that part of her son's condition stemmed from her own previous botched attempt to kill him. She had suffered from stress disorder and depression for a number of years prior to the accident, so the court's judgment was that she had in part acted for herself, albeit in conditions where her responsibility should be mitigated.

In Mrs Gilderdale's case, it was different. She declined to give evidence, but the sense one gleans from the press was of a woman who acted as a 'caring and loving mother', as the judge put it, who having resisted her daughter's requests for help to die, had only acted when her daughter had herself failed in a suicide attempt, and had exposed herself to the criminal law only for her daughter's sake. We can only guess at what the jury thought, but the impression of Mrs Gilderdale was of a parent who had cared for her daughter for 17 years, whose marriage had broken up in consequence, who had acted only with great reluctance and against her own feelings. She had acted, I would suggest, in what one might call loving identification with her daughter's pain, unhappiness and expressed wish to die, and against her own wishes and commitments in the matter. Her act was both self-sacrificing and other-oriented, to the daughter's wishes, needs and, hard as it is to say, well-being. It was, in its solidarity with another's self-expressed sense of what was truly best for her, regardless of the consequences to Mrs Gilderdale, a fundamentally good act.

Note here, as with our discussion of Arendt and the Holocaust, that two issues come out of this discussion. The first is law's problem in dealing with this case.

By legal rights, the defendant was guilty of either murder or its attempt. She possessed an intention to kill or cause serious harm, the mens rea for the crime. There was a guilty act. The CPS was in law perfectly entitled to prosecute. It could have declined to do so 'in the public interest', but that is a problematic route to follow because it would override the settled view of the law that mercy killing is a crime, and it would have involved deploying a discretion that would have looked quite anomalous with regard to other cases. If Mrs Inglis is to be prosecuted, so too should Mrs Gilderdale be, and let the cards fall as they will. Accordingly, the only route available was a jury acquittal in the face of the conviction they should in law have delivered. This is known as either a perverse verdict or jury equity depending on your standpoint, but it runs against the letter of the law.

Is the problem here simply that the law has not evolved properly to deal with a hard case such as mercy killing? It could be seen in this way, but that would avoid noting a structural quality of the law, which is its systematic bias towards formalism in its concepts and therefore its tendency to marginalise or finesse substantive moral issues in favour of seemingly neutral, technical or factual, fault categories. I cannot pursue this line of argument here, but it is one that lies at the heart of the way I have analysed criminal law previously (see the introduction to this essay, and Norrie 2000; 2014 more generally). Intention, for example, a core legal concept, is understood in factual and psychological terms. What did the accused mean to do or foresee as virtually certain to happen is the key question. Did a purposeful thought go through her head, regardless of the moral badness or goodness in the thought? Thus, as every criminal law student learns, there is no difference in law between the contract and the mercy killer. They are both in formal legal terms guilty of murder. They both mean to kill, and the moral substance or context of their action is irrelevant to the law's core concepts of act and intention.

Thus, the problem posed by the morally good act is a deeper problem than one of plain law reform, although that might cure it in the instant case, if we could agree as a society about the value of mercy killing – which, by the way, we cannot. In my work, I have argued that this problem goes to the heart of modern law because, historically, Western societies set up law in a formalistic way in order to finesse and avoid moral, political and social contention about good and bad motives. A formalistic approach to law can be universal, i.e. it can apply to everyone, but only because it is abstractive of the substantive moral and political issues modern societies would otherwise argue about, and which abstractive formalism removes from the picture. More broadly, the formalism at the core of the law shadows the formalism at the core of modern ethics. It is for that reason that formalistic, Kantian-style accounts of ethics are so persuasive in legal thought today. It would be an exaggeration, but not a wildly inaccurate one,[5] to say that

5 See Norrie (1991) and the development of the argument about philosophy in Norrie (2000) and about law in Norrie (2014). My point is that a formalistic law as described sets the general terms in which the legal system operates, but it inevitably entrains counter-movements to compensate for this

modernity gave birth to two great movements: Kantianism in ethics and the modern individualist, responsible subject in law, and that they complement each other because both have an essential formalism at their core.

The second issue is what we mean by a good act, and here, I have already indicated what I think lies at its core in the case of Mrs Gilderdale. It is an act of loving identification that was both self-sacrificing and other-oriented (to the daughter). To that, I would add that the 'other-orientation' was to what was concretely best for the daughter, in her situation and according to her wishes. Now, at the core of the idea of what is best for any person, according to our discussion of meta-ethics, lies a sense of how things can best go well for people in their lives, how ultimately they flourish. It might be said that this is a strange idea in relation to someone wishing to die. How can dying be a way of things going well, of human flourishing?

But it is not so strange really, if one thinks that what we are speaking of here is euthanasia, the good death. Death is a part of every life and, whilst from the point of view of wishing to live we may find it hard to think of a good death, we clearly have to accept that death will happen and that, however reluctant we may be, our deaths can go well or badly. A key element in this is the concern that we should be in control of our passage from life, and assisting a death can be part of this too. Part of a life that had gone well and had flourished would be the ability to leave it when one chooses. The other element here is to act in self-sacrificing solidarity with the possibility of a good death and it is that combination that made Kay Gilderdale's act a fundamentally good one. Elements of freedom, flourishing, solidarity – the three elements at the core of the meta-ethics of human nature – are all present in her acts.[6]

The meta-ethics of evil

If we can link the good to our meta-ethics in this way, what of Arendt's case of evil? Here I need to say a little more, for there has been much said in this area. Perhaps two routes in particular stand out as predominating in Western thought.

within its own system. For example, it works through formal rules but also through counter-applications of discretion which are required to mediate the formal rules. These counter-applications are themselves part of law too. Legal systems are as much constituted by institutional operationalisations as by formal rules so that when we look at law as a whole, we must look at its central forms but also its practices, processes, institutions, and how all these interact within legal wholes. My aim is to show how central forms of legal abstraction at the core of the formal rules structure legal systems in practice and as a whole.

6 It is important to understand that the interaction between meta-ethical principles and any actual moral situation is not one that can be mapped through clear analytical propositions. It is more a question as to whether the former is ingredient in the latter and so can be read into and out of it. Different cases have their own particularity, implications and gradations. Whilst elements of freedom, well-being and flourishing can be seen in the case of Mrs Gilderdale and her daughter, this does not stop it being tragic and full of loss.

One predates the Enlightenment and is based upon the Christian thought of St Augustine and Thomas Aquinas. Whilst religious in its inspiration, it is capable of non-religious interpretation, and it is in that way that I will take it. The other is firmly located in the Enlightenment, in the philosophy of Kant, and his account of 'radical evil'. Let us begin with him.

Rather promisingly, Kant spoke of what he called the possibility of 'radical evil' in the world. A key part of Kant's commitment was to rethink religious themes that relied upon God in terms of human reason, and the universal for Kant was based upon the idea of the categorical imperative, the claim that one should act on maxims that could be universally applied. To act for the good was to act in terms of universal demands of reason, and to act in a manner that was radically evil was to act in ways that were inconsistent with the categorical imperative: 'Whoever incorporates the moral law into his maxim and gives it priority is morally good; and whoever fails to do this, but gives priority to other non-moral incentives (including sympathy) is morally evil' (Bernstein 2002: 18).

The problem with this approach is that its account of what is 'radical' in evil refers to the failure to choose *to think* in a particular way, rather than the content of what is thought or done. It is epistemic rather than ontological. Choosing not to act according to the categorical imperative is 'radically evil' even where one acts out of sympathy with another. It is the failure to choose rationally that is significant and this is the 'radical' element in the wrongdoing because it goes to the root of human being as rational. Someone who consciously acts from the heart against the law of reason is said to be acting in an evil manner: paradoxically, Kay Gilderdale, on this view, would have committed an evil act. It is true that this focuses our attention on the question of human thought and choice, which is an important element in our understanding of evil, but it gives us no real sense of what an evil act is, or at least gives us so broad a notion as to be unhelpful.

In focusing the discussion of radical evil on the element of free thinking and choice, Kant is in line with Christian thought in the tradition of St Augustine, but there is an important element in that thought that is not brought out. That is the ontological idea that, substantively, being is good, and that evil is to be understood as a negation or privation of being. For Augustine, all being is good, there is a hierarchy of beings, and evil is not being but its privation or lack: 'an evil is eradicated not by the removal of some natural substance which had accrued to the original, or by the removal of any part of it, but by the healing and restoration of the original which had been corrupted and debased' (Augustine *City of God* XIV: ch 11, quoted in Collier 1999: 63). This can be compared with the later thought of Aquinas: 'No being is said to be evil, considered as being, but only insofar as it lacks being' (*Summa Theologica* I: 5.3, quoted in Collier 1999: 64).

This provides a sense of evil related to being, that is an evil that is in the thing itself, an absence of the good. Such an approach has its problems, but it seems more fruitful than Kant's epistemological take (choosing to think wrongly). Recently Terry Eagleton has used this tradition in a modern, non-religious way to think of evil as a fundamental absence in the way in which a person might treat others, and how she might be in herself. As for others, evil is in love with the annihilation of the possibility of life: 'there is a diabolical delight to be reaped from the notion of absolute destruction. Flaws, loose ends, and rough approximations are what evil cannot endure. . . . Goodness, by contrast, is in love with the dappled, unfinished nature of things' (Eagleton 2010: 101).

Such evil, Eagleton goes on to write, has a correlative lack in the evil-doer: to wreak havoc on being is to express the inner lack that psychoanalysis describes as the death drive. In the evil act, this is 'turned outward so as to wreak its insatiable spitefulness on a fellow human being. Yet this furious violence involves a kind of lack – an unbearable sense of non-being, which must, so to speak be taken out on the other' (ibid: 127).

This nihilism with regard to being is important, and Eagleton is right to press us to think about the motivation of the evil-doer. The overall perspective is right, that there are two issues that we need to look at: the evil in the act and the evil in the motivation of the actor. However, his account of good and evil is very broad. I would like to bring in our discussion of the meta-ethics of freedom, flourishing and solidarity. Here, I turn again to Hannah Arendt for further guidance. Arendt is often thought of as following in the line of Kant, for she adopted the notion of 'radical evil' in her discussion of the Nazis and the Holocaust, and she linked it to the thought process and motivation of the evil-doers: 'And if it is true that in the final stages of totalitarianism an absolute evil appears (absolute because it can no longer be deduced from humanly comprehensible motives), it is also true that without it we might never have known the truly radical nature of Evil' (Arendt 1968: viii–ix).

Later, without seeming to wish to change her analysis, Arendt (1964) dubbed this absence of 'humanly comprehensible motives' the 'banality of evil' because the Holocaust, in her view, was carried out by ordinary people in a mundane, unthinking, way. It has been pointed out, however, that there was in fact a significant difference in Arendt's thought from Kant's, even if they shared a term. Arendt was too much of a moral psychologist and ontologist to remain satisfied with Kant's account. In her work, issues of what was done to victims as human beings, and what the perpetrators thinking lacked *both* came to the fore. Here, we can find specific, and profound, lack in the ways human beings were treated that can help fill out Eagleton's terms.

For the victims, the evil of the Holocaust was seen in the denial of their humanity: both their freedom and their solidarity with others. Of their (legal) freedom, Arendt wrote: 'The aim of an arbitrary system is to destroy the civil rights of the whole population, who ultimately become just as outlawed in their own country as the stateless and homeless. The destruction of man's rights, the killing of the juridical person in him, is a prerequisite for dominating him entirely' (ibid: 451).

But what happened when a totalitarian system denied legal freedom was a prelude to the denial of what at the most basic level it meant to be human: 'After the . . . annihilation of the juridical person, the destruction of individuality is almost always successful . . . For to destroy individuality is to destroy spontaneity, man's power to begin something new out of his own resources. . .' (ibid: 455).

Spontaneity is the most basic form of human freedom, the freedom to start anew: a beginning and new agency with each new birth (and here Arendt cited Augustine, on whom she had written her doctoral thesis). The concentration camps were 'meant not only to exterminate people and degrade human beings, but also to serve the ghastly experiment of eliminating, under scientifically controlled conditions, spontaneity itself as an expression of human behaviour and transforming the human personality into a mere thing . . .' (ibid: 438).

In terms of our understanding of good as involving freedom to act in solidarity with others in the direction of human flourishing, the Holocaust's radical evil was that it attacked the root possibility of there being human freedom as spontaneity at all. The truly good act furthers the highest forms of human freedom; the evil act attacks its most basic forms. At the same time, it removed the possibility of any sense of moral solidarity between people: 'Who could solve the moral dilemma of the Greek mother, who was allowed by the Nazis to choose which of her three children should be killed?' (ibid: 452).

Faced with such a choice, what possible action of human solidarity was available to the mother? Not only, however, was there an annihilation of the moral bond on the side of the victims, the issue of motivelessness or the banality of evil meant that there was no human bond, no solidarity between the perpetrators and their victims. There is a difference, Arendt claims, between the person who murders for humanly recognisable motives and the person who does so for no apparent human motives at all. We have already seen how Arendt wrote of the 'difference between a man who sets out to murder his old aunt and people who without considering the economic usefulness of their actions at all . . . built factories to produce corpses . . .'. One can talk of a form of wickedness of the person who acts for bad motives, and Arendt saw that many Nazis acted out of a 'deep hatred and resentment against all those who were better off than themselves, and who now . . . were in their power'. But such resentment, she adds, 'which never died out entirely in the camps, strikes us as a last remnant of humanly understandable feeling' (ibid: 454).

Even if you hate someone, that is at least a humanly recognisable emotion, which indicates a moral connection, albeit a bad one, with the hated person. That person is at least worthy of hatred, and there is a kind of *negative* solidarity within it. The problem of the death camps was that even this was ultimately lacking, and this was at the nub of the idea of the banality of evil. Adolf Eichmann's motives were so mundane as to be no real motives at all when compared with the enormity of what he was doing. They revealed in their banality a complete failure to recognise any sense of the human in his victims, to be able to think of his victims as being human. Eichmann possessed 'an inability to think, namely to think from the standpoint of someone else' (Arendt 1964: 49). That is the core of moral solidarity, and it was entirely lacking. Some argue (e.g. Cesarani, 2004) that Eichmann really did hate Jews, that Arendt's argument misses this, and therefore lets him off the hook. But her argument is that, in not hating them, he was worse than that. What made his actions truly evil on their subjective side was that they were entirely void of human solidarity. On their objective side, they were aimed at crushing the very possibility of the most basic kinds of freedom for the victims.

Formal law: between history and ethics

At this point, I wish to move into some concluding thoughts. I do not have a neat finish to apply to what I have said thus far, to bring the loose ends together in a unified whole. What I did in the above was to follow a line of thought that was in some sense instinctual. I had been interested in Arendt, I had been struck by the moral problems of euthanasia for law, but I had not imagined I would end up thinking about good and evil, and putting these together with Bhaskar's meta-ethics around conceptions of freedom and solidarity. These ideas, when put together with some general thoughts about how critical enquiry approaches the criminal law, led to a sense of the need to think more fully about how ethical issues operate with regard to criminal justice thinking.

What are the consequences of this chapter? First, it has been to push forward an understanding of criminal law as a would be technical and formalistic discourse of mens rea, actus reus and the defences an architectonic in the light of the problems that morally substantive categories such as good and evil throw up. There is a kind of silence of the law before issues such as euthanasia or crimes against humanity, in part because these are the extremes of human conduct, and in part because law is not well equipped to deal with actions that wear their moral heart, for good or for ill, on their sleeves. In terms of my dialectic of freedom and solidarity, law is most comfortable, I think, with the lesser forms of freedom, which, important in themselves, are nonetheless limited in their scope. I have in mind in particular the kind of juridical freedom Arendt spoke of around simple notions of the ability to act (spontaneity) or of negative liberty – the freedom to act unhindered.

When it comes to the broadest notions of freedom, of human flourishing in solidarity and the eudaimonistic society, this is not ground on which law is comfortable. Nor is it comfortable with forms of action which obliterate the basic assumptions of freedom – the assumptions that spontaneity and solidarity are part of the human condition. When it comes to systematic attempts to deny the very possibility of legal subjectivity or solidarity, law again struggles. These are the terrains of good and evil, and I think it helps to stretch out the canvas of human freedom in order to see where on it we paint the colours and forms of the law.

At the same time, I concede my hesitancy to pursue such solid categories as good and evil if there is a risk that they themselves become a means of hijacking rather than doing rational work. Nonetheless, perhaps the best way of avoiding that happening is to be clear on the meaning, the nature and the limits of such concepts. In that way we can be clear when they are being pushed further than they should be.

I am consoled that I am not alone in pursuing this kind of thinking – it is notable that thinkers of the left such as Peter Dews (2008) and Terry Eagleton have also taken the issue up in recent times. Besides, if the genocides of the past and present have lessons for us, one is surely that we should name moral phenomena accurately. I have never felt that Arendt was wrong to designate the Holocaust as 'evil'.

To return to law: it is, as I say, most happy with formal notions of agency and negative liberty, but if we can identify such notions as a small part of the broader canvas which includes notions like autonomy, emancipation and flourishing, we can vindicate the need to provide a radical critique of the legal space at the same time as we identify the value that is in legal form. Of course, freedom as agency and negative liberty is compatible with, indeed it licenses, the kind of *laissez-faire* liberalism that has done so much damage to our social institutions and internationally over the years. So to note the moral significance of such ideas is to note also the impossibility of treating them by themselves. Negative liberty left to couple with the market can produce a range of terrible effects in the name of freedom. But that to me does not mean that we should dismiss ideas of negative liberty: they have real value when the police come knocking at 5 am.

More generally, what we need to do is always think of such liberty alongside the deeper, more substantive forms of freedom of which it is a part, so that we can ask how the simpler forms can be married with the more complex forms to produce societies in which well-being and flourishing can be achieved. Of course, that is by no means a simple matter – it requires contextual, socio-legal analyses of cause and effect and of the value of agency and intervention. But if we need to embed our understanding of moral agency in contextual analyses of society, we surely equally need to have a clear understanding as contextual lawyers of the moral values that are at stake in any given social situation. Overall, however, the aim should not be to discard our notions of freedom, but to pursue and deepen them alongside a critical understanding of how they may be used and abused.

The process of thinking in this essay has gone two ways. On the one hand, it has arisen from the problems generated by concrete legal problems to an underlying moral ground – the meta-ethics described above. It has sought to locate those problems on a broader theoretical canvas. On the other hand, it has anchored the meta-ethics in real life situations, and therefore revealed something of the necessity to think in such terms. The meta-ethics fill a space, and are validated in the process. When I have presented talks on meta-ethics previously, it has sometimes come across a bit like a list of forms of freedom; by linking these to a concrete analysis of legal problems, we can see, I think, their intrinsic importance. The canvas has been stretched – let us see where else it might take us.

At the same time, I am aware that this essay will probably satisfy few. It says too little about the law for lawyers, it says too little about the concepts of freedom for liberal philosophers, and it says too much about these same things for social contextualists. For me, however, it identifies the terrain where I want to work:

between legal problems, ethical forms and issues, and social contexts. I hope it provides one way of pushing forward an open contextual agenda for legal studies, and that it perhaps rings some bells with others trying to push forward a critical understanding of the criminal law that is adequate to its object. If criminal law is an historically produced, morally formalistic, architectonic of social control, it operates constellationally in a world where substantive moral categories and issues remain crucial to the human condition. It, and we, have to identify and come to terms with the resulting disjunction and conjunction.

Chapter 9

Law, ethics and socio-history: the case of freedom

> 'For not only the five senses but also the so-called mental senses, the practical senses (will, love, etc.), in a word, human sense, the human nature of the senses, comes to be by virtue of its object, by virtue of humanised nature. The forming of the five senses is a labour of the entire history of the world down to the present.'
>
> (Marx 1975: 353)

> 'The historical animal is one who is constantly able to go beyond itself.'
>
> (Eagleton 2010: 17)

What does the 'socio' in socio-legal studies mean, and what does it do? No doubt, it means different things to different people, and to some it is simply a *portmanteau* term. For many, it indicates a relationship between law and society, either narrowly in terms of empirical and pragmatic questions as to the impact of law and legal reform, or, more broadly, in theoretical terms as to how we understand both the nature of law and the relationship between legal forms and institutions and social relations. My work has been in the latter area, where one might expect the nature of the socio to have come under close scrutiny. I am not aware that it has, but it is an interesting and challenging question to think about what it denotes.

In this chapter, I am interested in the relationship between the socio and something else, the 'ethical', and for two reasons. The first is that I wish to argue that an ethical understanding lies at the core of the socio, and is not separable from it. This is despite the fact that the socio has generally been conceived as a problematic that, through its modernist commitments, is distinct from and superior to ethical enquiry. In my view, the socio has to be understood not as a master-perspective, but as an approach that participates in a deeper understanding of law and society, one that has often not been properly comprehended, as constellating socio-historical and ethical commitments.

The second reason is that it seems to me that the socio is nonetheless absolutely crucial to an understanding of the particular ethical commitments that animate our understanding of law. When we look at legal studies, we see a variety of such commitments on display. From an orthodox standpoint, the main position is generally Kantian in a broad sense. By this I mean that there is support for the forms of law as mechanisms for supporting a liberal society in which individual commitments to agency and responsibility lie at the core. The politically important idea of the rule of law essentially entails such commitments notwithstanding the plurality of variations on a theme – individualist, communitarian, perfectionist and non-perfectionist – it invokes.

From a critical standpoint, a variety of theorists have proposed that these ideas of individual liberty, agency, responsibility are barren, or worse that they are the means by which the master's work of enslavement is carried out. Here, one could include theorists such as Foucault, Agamben, Derrida, Adorno, as well as post-colonial and some branches of Marxist theory. On both sides, however, these arguments seem to me to be one-sided. Liberal theory does not appreciate the historical and socio-political commitments it masks, whilst critical theory too quickly denies the ethical validity in liberalism, and law.

We do not seem capable of grasping in a nuanced and complex way how juridical ideas of freedom both have a first order normative import and are complicit in hiding power. The key to a more subtle approach is to see how such ideas are historically shaped and 'thrown', yet retain something of their axiological (i.e. their ethically compelling) validity. So the second argument I wish to make here is that an understanding of the socio is crucial to an understanding of modern ethical approaches to law. The socio and the ethical thus have a relationship of mutual entailment, and cannot properly be separated. The ethical lies at the heart of the socio, and the socio informs and structures actually existing ethics.

This essay is tentative and exploratory. It seeks to identify a big picture and to travel in directions that modern-day legal, philosophical and, indeed, critical minds are unused to exploring. The direction of the argument is as follows. In the next section, I argue (briefly) that the ethical dimension that is immanent in socio-legal enquiry has been blocked since a 19th century 'pact' struck between Kantian philosophy and an emergent social science, and this needs to be unblocked. I argue that despite its emphasis on ethics, post structural philosophy is also implicated, by way of inversion, in this block. The third section argues, on the basis of modern legal issues, that the ethical dimension is intrinsic to understanding what is at stake in law, even from the point of view of a socio-legal approach. It has the form of an immanent critique of what the socio-legal lacks. The fourth section then considers what an ethical axiology of and for human being might look like, focusing on concepts of freedom and solidarity.

On this basis, the argument then goes in two opposing directions. In a fifth section, I go back to the socio-legal issues explored in the second section and show how an ethics of freedom and solidarity illuminates them. I show how an ethical dimension is crucial to a full understanding, including a socio-historical understanding, of legal phenomena. The socio-legal connotes the ethical, and is impoverished without it. This answers my first question above: what *is* the socio?

The second direction is then explored in a sixth and final section. This considers how an axiology of freedom and solidarity relates to actually existing legal ethics, and how socio-history shapes these. In this way, we see how a socio-historical interrogation of ethical forms is crucial to an understanding of modern day legal ethics. This answers my second initial question: what does the socio *do*? My answer is that it structures modern normative understanding of law. If the first question goes from law to ethics to socio-history, the second travels the opposite way, from socio-history to ethics to law. In both cases, the intimate connection between socio-historical and ethical considerations is made clear.

Starting points: ethics and the socio-legal block

My argument in this section is that the socio in socio-legal studies connotes a sense of the ethical in every socio-legal enquiry. I begin by noting that this claim may be regarded as contentious in itself, but also in historical terms. The sense of the ethical for which I want to argue has in fact been systematically lacking in socio-legal understanding since its inception in the 19th century. Post structural ways of thinking grasp this lack, but in a way that affirms the importance of ethics at the cost of a socio-historical understanding of law.

My starting point is the structural split in the way we normally think of the social and the historical on the one hand and the ethical on the other. Socio-legal studies is in a sense post-Kantian in that it takes its cue, as does the discipline of sociology as a whole, from the Kantian split between morality and materiality. I can only make this argument in broad brush-strokes, but it is important for what follows. For Kant, we achieve an ethical understanding by abstracting the ethical moment from all material determinations. The rational (noumenal) will is achieved by turning away from natural (phenomenal) impulses, drives, demands (Kant 1948).

Sociology in its founding thinkers essentially follows this line on, as it were, the other side of Kantian philosophy. An intellectual division of labour is established. From Comte through to the thinking of Durkheim and Weber, there is a sociological link to Kant by way of inversion. With Durkheim, the study of ethics, religion and law should be located within a social positivistic understanding of societal evolution, in which the normative dimension is explained in socio-historical, evolutionary terms. In Weber, we see the positivisation of law, with legitimation understood as involving forms of domination, in a modern world that has become ethically and spiritually 'disenchanted' – that has lost its first order normativity.

With Marx, the historical writer, both young and old, things are not so clear, but sociology in the way that it has taken Marx up has made it so. It is Marx, the theorist of class, or the writer whose work must be split into 'early' ethical thinking and 'mature' materialist analyses that is taken up within a sociological framework. Moves against the continuity of Marx's thought, most effectively pursued by Althusser (1969), are moves to divorce ethics as a primary or 'first order' field from the social, structural, historical and material, to produce a Marx available for a post-Kantian understanding of the relationship between the material and the moral. The result is an historical splitting of schools of legal theorists into natural lawyers, legal positivists and, following on the coat tails of the latter, sociologists of law. The different approaches are in relational tension with each other (Norrie 2005a: ch 2).

Since Marx, Weber and Durkheim are the founding figures for socio-legal studies, it is plain why the socio might have been interpreted in opposition to ethical standpoints, but we need to take into account a separate development in connection with the socio-legal discipline to understand why we should address this block in how we think. I refer here to the significance of post structural thinking as a critical edge to (or opponent of?) socio-legal studies, and the significance of writers such as Foucault, Derrida and Deleuze to modern socio-legal thinking. Foucault's ideas concerning discipline, governmentality and will to power place him fairly firmly in the camp of those who would deny the ethical significance of modern law. Yet, behind the insistence that modern law is turned to fundamentally non-ethical goals (power, control), there remained a deep-seated concern in Foucault for an ethics that could hardly be named (cf the 'late' Foucault, or a Derridean reading of his main themes: Fitzpatrick and Golder 2009). In that regard, he is rather like his philosophical forebear Nietzsche, for whom the unremitting nature of the will to power represented the backdrop against which a new morality in the form of the 'overman' struggled to define itself (Nietzsche 1967).

Similarly, the writing of Deleuze (1993) or Derrida (1992, 1994, 2001) is significant in terms of its insistence on an elusive, disruptive, ethical dimension in all action and being. This is notwithstanding the controlling power of reason or law. In Derrida, deconstruction has two moments, one of pulling things apart and observing their less-than-moral entrails, the other of insisting that within the thing constructed in discourse there exists an ethical moment. This lies both beyond and within – it is justice as a 'mad', 'messianic' moment both present and absent in every worldly act of judgment (Derrida 1992).

This, it strikes me, is important. If one thinks of the judgment of, say, an international court of justice, one must be aware that what it does is historically and politically inflected (cf Derrida, 2001). Why did *these* defendants rather than others come to be in the dock, even if the international criminal law claims a universality in its form? International justice finds it very hard to escape the label 'victors' justice'. Yet at the same time, is there not an element of the universal even within this partiality?

In her writings on the trials of Nazis after the Holocaust, Hannah Arendt was always critical of the legal processes themselves, but also on the possibility of a *judgment* against the perpetrators – notwithstanding the awfulness of their crimes (Arendt 1964; Kohler and Saner 1992: 47–48, 69–70). But a judgment, albeit one that was significantly flawed, needed still to be made. Derrida's (2001) account of the responsible judgment, one that must be made, but which one does not know if it is right, reflects something of Arendt's concerns (cf chapter 7 above).

Even in a world in which judgment has been extinguished, judgments still must be made.

All this is to say that there is a crucial ethical dimension to our thinking about social and historical justice, and the post structuralists, in a way that perhaps overstates the difficulty of ethical judgment, nonetheless see this clearly. My main concern with a thinker like Derrida concerns the relationship between his ethics and the nature of human being. For Derrida, in line with post structuralism's Nietzschean heritage, the ethical ground is provided by an infinite plurality, heterogeneity or flux that lies at the core of all being (Norrie 2010: ch 7). This provides the basis for a radical particularity in light of which all ethical judgments are challengeable.

Now, in one sense, such a radical particularity *is* present in all being, so is in that sense immanent in human being and social life. We *are* in our being all part of a process of becoming or change. Life never stays the same, and this is the core vitalist truth at the heart of Nietzscheanism. Yet, what is immanent in post-structuralist thought is *so* radically particularised as flow, flux or becoming that it tells us little about human beings per se, as opposed, for example, to dogs, plants or the planetary system (Norrie 2010: chs 6 and 7). In that sense, what is immanent is a flow of life, of becoming, that tells us little about what is specific to the natural kind that is human being.

In that regard, post structuralism's radical particularity is itself post-Kantian, by way of inversion. One has to think the ethical, but take no clue from the nature of human material being as it is, and therefore how the ethical is emergent in one species or genus rather than another. Here, it is important to stress the social and historical relationality of the human animal. We are emergent not just as a species, but as one that is self-evolving in history, and under particular social conditions. Post structuralism says little about this. Because that is so, the ethical 'beyond', adverted to by Derrida, lacks immanence, in the sense of an understanding of what specifically the human kind in itself and in its history is like. Its ethics are evolved in abstraction from human socio-materiality. Thus, if the sociological understanding starts from a rejection of ethical reference, post-structural thought affirms ethicality, but at the cost of socio-historical reference. We need to put the socio and the ethical back together – we need, finally, to mark our distance from Kant!

I can only indicate an alternative starting point here,[1] but I take my cue here from my two prefatory quotes. From the 'young' Marx, I derive a sense of the historical evolution and createdness of the human species. His reference to the five senses as the product of a humanised nature in both history and society provides us with an anthropological starting point for an axiology of human being. Note that Marx includes in his understanding what he calls the practical senses, will,

1 I have developed the argument in Norrie (2010) from Roy Bhaskar's work on critical realism and dialectics (Bhaskar 1993, 1994).

love, and so on. When Marx talks of human species being as a work of historical evolution, he does not mean to be reductive: love and will are not just the structural effects of historical, social or natural being. They are, it is true, emergent, historically and socially evolved qualities of human being, but as such, they are real qualities of the human species, particular to this social and historical animal. It then follows that the very possibility of valuing such things (the ethical starting point) would itself be one of the practical senses included within Marx's 'etc', as part of what it means to be human. An animal capable of love is one capable of ethical being. The possibility of moral value is accordingly inscribed in human anthropology. The historical animal, as Eagleton (2010) terms it (us), is inter alia an ethical being.

If such a human ontology and axiology gets us going, the brief quote from Eagleton indicates where the argument might go. The idea of an historical animal that is unfinished in its development indicates a possible utopian quality to human nature, the possibility of moving beyond the present. We could be morally better than we, under present conditions, are. This, I think, is important, and indicates, as I will say shortly, a link to other currents in critical thinking, such as Adorno's (1973) idea of negative dialectics or Derrida's idea of deconstruction. However, what is important here is to see that the ethical future has a ground in the present, in the socio-historical nature of what human beings already are, and latently could be. It is this basis in what human beings under particular, social and historical conditions are, and what they could be or become, that represents a starting point. From here, I wish to argue for the centrality of ethics or normativity to socio-legal studies, not just as an appendage to socio-legal thinking, but as something that should be at its core.

Ethical problems and the socio-legal

In thinking about the social and historical dimensions of legal issues, it is necessary to include an ethical dimension at their core. Let me explain by way of two examples. The first concerns the case of the two boys who killed James Bulger (Norrie 2005a: Ch 4).[2] James Bulger was a two-year-old who, in 1993, was abducted from a shopping centre in Merseyside by two 10-year-old boys and found murdered a few days later. From a contextual point of view, the most important thing to note in that case was the way in which the law, and the media taking their cue from law, focused on the individual guilt of the two boys as a means of decontextualising the crime. Whereas the account of wrongdoing might have focused on how it could be that two boys in a particular society could abduct a small child from a shopping centre in broad daylight, walk with him a considerable distance, and then kill him, the analysis focused on the two boys as wrongdoers

2 *R v Secretary of State for the Home Department, ex parte V and R v Secretary of State for the Home Department, ex parte T* [1998] AC 407 (HL).

pure and simple, as 'evil' or 'wicked' children. The focus could have been on the question: under what societal conditions is it possible for such a thing to happen? Instead, the dominant discourse focused on the notion of evil. This was a way of pre-empting a contextual discussion: if the boys were evil, why would there be any need to look beyond them and what they did? To call their actions evil abstracts and individualises their conduct, and renders it inexplicable.

In this case, it is important to recontextualise what happened by declining to go with the categories of individual guilt, and especially with a socially unrooted moral idea such as evil. And yet, there seems something wrong or at least one-sided in doing so. First, it seems important to think about the guilt of the two 10-year-olds. Perhaps this should not be in terms of standard legal-Kantian ideas of retributive justice, but is there not a sense in which those boys should be addressed in terms of what they did? Could any society simply decide to brush the entire event under the carpet without saying anything to the boys? Should they not in some way be brought to account for what they have done, in the same way as we would expect any 10-year-old to be addressed in terms of what she has done? There is here, alongside the contextual analysis, some more direct ethical accounting to be done.

Second, more controversially, there is the question of evil. I find it difficult to think that this is a useful ethical category to bring to bear on this case, at least insofar as we are attributing it to the two boys concerned. However, at the same time, what happened to James Bulger was hideous and, under a relevant moral description might be said to be wicked, or even evil. The problem might come from transferring what makes a wicked or evil act into what makes a person wicked or evil. Deducing the one from the other may be the problematic step but, at least, we see that there is a serious moral issue here. The word 'evil' is not obviously redundant.

To the socio-legal mind, progressive and modernist in its cast, this may still seem problematic and retrograde: there is just the question as to whether we should use words like evil at all, especially if we are thinking in a social constructivist, contextual, socio-legal way. Does evil have any purchase for such a way of thinking? The temptation might still be to banish the term entirely, but I want to resist it. Take as my second example Arendt's description of Adolf Eichmann's conduct as demonstrating the 'banality of evil' (Arendt 1964). For many, the focus in this phrase is on the seemingly scandalous first word, banality. What does it mean to refer to an administrator of the Holocaust as acting in a way that can be described as 'banal'? But in many ways the more interesting question is, what does it mean to refer to his conduct as *evil*?

Of course, at one level, this seems quite uncontroversial: if ever human actions deserved the label evil, surely it was ones that involved the Holocaust. When we speak of such actions, we do not mean actions that 'were socially constructed very negatively according to an historically evolved, normative cultural standard'. We *mean* evil, and we think that the actions of Nazis like Eichmann were indeed properly described as such. However, if that is the case, then ought we not to think about why we call some acts evil, and how a socio-legal investigation of the Holocaust (which is in effect what Arendt provides us with) could have the exploration of evil *at its core*? If we do so, do we not open the door to other questions for example, concerning evil's counterpart, a conception of the good?

These are difficult questions, but my initial point is that I do not think we socio-legal scholars can avoid them. Neither the boys in Liverpool nor Eichmann acted save in a social context, but that context does not exhaust the phenomenon we need to understand. Further, it is precisely that part of the phenomenon that is not exhausted which makes these two situations so important to understand. An ethical sense spearheads the enquiry, and I suggest it is crucial to an understanding of the socio in socio-legal enquiry. In order to take this further, however, I need to say something about the nature of ethics. Thereafter, I will return to the question of evil, and also say a little about its counterpoint: what is good?

Ethical grounds for human being

In this section I draw upon my own recent work on Roy Bhaskar's dialectical philosophy (Bhaskar 1993, 1994; Norrie 2010: ch 5) to provide an ethical grounding for the socio-legal enterprise. Bhaskar's approach to dialectics argues for a socio-historical understanding of the emergence and development of specifically human being; that is, it argues for a philosophical–anthropological understanding that underpins the quotes from Marx and Eagleton with which I began this essay.

Bhaskar writes of a 'natural necessity' which underpins human life as a social, material, historical and natural development. We are the kinds of creatures that our societies and our histories make us, but that is only a part of the story. The other part is that we are a specifically evolved type of being with characteristic capacities and qualities that represent our 'natural kind'. From the evolved species that we are, it is possible to glean a sense of our nature, of a natural necessity that underpins and grounds our ethical and other possibilities. That sense can be developed either from immanent reflection on the emergent ethical possibilities that humankind as species being possesses, or it can be deduced from the ethical possibilities that we have witnessed instantiated in history.

Most appropriately, it can be developed and deduced *both* from observing history's ethical possibilities and by reflecting on what we know human being necessarily to be like. This ethical ground within the natural necessity of human being as a socio-historical-and-natural species has as its key elements an account of freedom and solidarity. These are the bases for an ethical understanding of human being in modernity, in law and in society. They are therefore the basis for a socio-legal understanding of law as a social and ethical practice.

Freedom

Let me begin by analysing immanently the different elements that are present in any discussion of freedom as a natural quality of human being. At the core of what it means to be human is the possibility of acting, that is the power of agency or agentive freedom. Human beings have the power of action, that is the power to negate previously existing states of affairs. Arendt wrote powerfully of this as spontaneity, the power to start and act anew that comes with each new human being (Arendt 1968). This is human freedom at its most basic, represented, for example, in the distinction between me raising my arm and another taking a hold of it and raising it on my behalf. This power of acting to negate existing states of affairs never exists alone, however. The distinction between raising my arm and having it raised for me already implies an existential space, with moral, social, political or legal coordinates in which I can exercise that power. That space is understood classically in the English liberal tradition (Hobbes, Locke) – which is also an historical one, concerning the rise of bourgeois property and other social values – as a conception of negative freedom; that is, a freedom to do as one chooses in a space that is available to one.

At the same time, this implies a further conception of freedom that is positive: if one is free when one has the space to act as one chooses, then a reference to freedom also implies that one could be enabled or empowered to act in the ways one chooses. Freedom to act implies not just the space to act, but the conditions that make action possible. Again, such a view of freedom is instantiated, this time in its positive conception, in modern liberal philosophy, in the thought, for example, of Rousseau or Hegel, where an enabling, but potentially authoritarian, dimension to positive freedom is identifiable (cf Berlin 1969). Again, the historical backdrop to this is the rise of a liberal middle class, this time pushed in a more radical (Rousseau) or conservative (Hegel) direction by the social and political conditions of its time and place.

These three forms of freedom (agential, negative and positive) represent freedom at its most basic. They can be derived from the logic of human action and understood as the development in and of a particular historical period. Accordingly, they reflect both what it means to be human and what it means to be human under particular social, economic and historical circumstances: the choosing agent protected by negative freedoms is a liberal, bourgeois subject emerging in 17th and 18th century Europe. Both aspects of this development, the human and the historical, the human-in-the-historical, are necessary. It is crucial, however, to see that they are only a beginning of what we can say about human freedom.

If we move on, we come to richer notions of human freedom such as that entailed in the concept of emancipation. Emancipation can be understood as a process of transition from unwanted, unneeded or oppressive states of affairs to wanted, needed ones (Norrie 2010: 141). It may entail an agent freeing herself, or being freed, from legal, political or structural conditions, and as such the idea of emancipation refers to a variety of different practical historical situations. As 'legal', emancipation involves the abolition of chattel slavery; as 'political', it involves the rights of oppressed groups to an equal say in political processes; as 'structural', it involves consideration of exploitative or otherwise oppressive systematic conditions and their overthrow.

Emancipation is an agential form of freedom, which was in history aimed to bring about conditions of negative or positive freedom. As such it covers slaves revolting against ancient legal tyrannies, and the programme of Enlightenment democrats including Tom Paine, Mary Wollstonecraft and Jean-Jacques Rousseau. There is then a further edge: in thinking of social emancipation from exploitation, we are pushed to think about freedom at deeper levels, including those explored by Marx (on wage slavery) and those sensed by recent post structuralist writers such as Deleuze and Derrida, for whom circumstance so grips us that an idea such as emancipation becomes fundamentally elusive, and yet remains omnipresent.

Sometimes different approaches to emancipation are fused together, as in the case of Toussaint L'Ouverture, the Haitian slave leader who sought to overthrow French political rule and legal servitude on a wave of radical (utopian) enthusiasm inspired by the French revolution. In her recent book on Hegel and Haiti, Susan Buck-Morss recalls the moment when the French troops moored in their boats off the coast of St Domingue heard the former slaves singing the Marseillaise. A moment is glimpsed of 'universal history', that is a moment of radical emancipation which brings together the deepest impulse of the French revolution with the radicalisation of the slave revolt. However, Buck-Morss also notes the selective interest in emancipation shown by French democrats, who conveniently failed to see that it might extend to black slaves in their own colonies (Buck-Morss 2009).

This further edge leads us more deeply into freedom as a substantive concept. If emancipation represents a fourth form of freedom with an emphasis on overturning those legal, political and social conditions that obstruct it, it has something in common with a fifth form, autonomy, for in both emancipation and autonomy there is reflection not just upon the idea of freedom, but on the contexts in which freedom is possible, and the ways in which contexts may obstruct freedom. Autonomy might be both the condition for and the end of emancipation. It implies a degree of self-determination in the face of conditions that may obstruct it. The opposite of autonomy is heteronomy, being ruled by something extraneous and other, and, as with emancipation, this may be inflected in different ways. In Kant, for example, autonomy is achieved by abstracting from the conditions of heteronomous agency, so that the rational actor is autonomous because he has withdrawn from all non-rational forms of determination. Yet such rational autonomy can itself become a source of domination for an agent forced to repress her 'natural' inclinations (Adorno 1973). For Marx, autonomy is always more conditional in that it is exercised in history, so that to act autonomously is to act within history, but not in circumstances one has chosen for oneself (Marx 1968a). For him, the possibility of autonomy and emancipation are closely associated.

In moving from (1) spontaneity, and (2) negative and positive freedom to (3) emancipation and (4) autonomy, we develop a series of 'ratchets' in the language of freedom in which we move from more basic forms that focus on individual agency in an isolated way to thinking more about the contexts in which freedom occurs. There is, however, a third set of understandings of freedom which complete the picture by deepening our understanding. These involve conceptions of freedom as (5) well-being and (6) flourishing. Well-being involves the idea of living well as a form of freedom; that is, living free from ills that constrict us, and having our needs satisfied. To live well is to be placed in the condition in which we are able best to be what we have it within ourselves to be, and this leads to the ultimate state of freedom: human flourishing. For these conceptions, we invoke philosophers both ancient and modern: Aristotle, Hegel and Marx all play their part.

We can also observe examples of human flourishing in history: for example, in the form of the Athenian aristocrat or the Renaissance man, whilst noting the limited historical groupings within which individual well-being and flourishing could occur in the past. Beyond these deeper forms of freedom accordingly, we can identify a potential final state of being, which would be a completion of the state of full freedom for all, in what Bhaskar calls (7) the eudaimonic condition. This is a state of universal human flourishing, in which the full flourishing of each is a condition of the full flourishing of all. It is the logical completion of the six previous states of freedom. In this final state, we are in the realm in which each of us is most able to fulfil what we have it within ourselves to be. It is the realm of 'concrete universality', that is a universality based upon each flourishing according to what they singularly are. It is a condition which unites Aristotle (from whom the idea of full ethical flourishing is drawn (eudaimonia)), Hegel (from whom the idea of a universal ethical unity is drawn), and Marx (from whom comes the conditionality of each individual's freedom on the freedom of all (Marx 1968b)).

Such a final form of freedom is, of course, not historically observed: it is, however, a logical corollary of the first six forms, and arguably a possibility that is glimpsed in a utopian way in the present. Think again of the former slaves serenading the French troops in St Domingue, and where that might under different historical conditions have led.

Solidarity

I have focused on freedom here, but it should be made clear that equally significant in any account of the natural necessity that grounds human being and ethics is not just freedom but the need for solidarity among humans. Indeed, the possibility of freedom at the different levels just described is impossible without human solidarity in a broad sense. We can see this at various points in the way we live. At the very beginning of life, our ability to act is dependent upon the solidarity of others in supporting us to live. If the first act is the 'primal scream' of the newborn infant, it is plain that no infant will survive without feeding and care, that is, the solidarity of parenting figures. Similarly, to act as a human being is to bestow meaning, which takes us into the realm of language, and language is something we only achieve in the solidarising company of others.

Moving down the chain of freedoms, it is also the case, as we have noted, that negative liberty involves the forbearance, and positive liberty the support, of others, and the same is true of the possibility of well-being and flourishing, where, for example, neither education nor care for our physiological needs can be achieved just by ourselves. Or take a deep human need often ignored by ethicists and social scientists alike, love: this just is a form of flourishing through solidarity with another or others. Emancipation, with its emphasis on struggle and structural and group conditions, similarly implies joint action, in solidarity with others. And, finally, the eudaimonic condition is built upon solidarity: if my full flourishing is going to occur in a complete and unconditional way, it requires the solidarity of others to bring it about, but why should they do so unless their own flourishing is also possible? Full flourishing entails human solidarity, and has as its logical corollary the full flourishing of each as a condition of the free flourishing of all.

Two things should be said about this understanding of freedom and solidarity as the grounds of ethics and law. The first underlines what has already been said. It is that the seven forms of freedom are all borne out as real possibilities evidenced within history, with the exception of the last. I have tried to show that this is the case by referencing the writing of thinkers in history for whom the first six grounds of freedom were conditions they could write about just because they were historically available to them as experiences (the bourgeois marketeer, the Athenian gentleman, the Renaissance man, the enlightened man, woman or slave seeking different kinds of emancipation). What of the seventh, the eudaimonic condition? That, I have proposed, is a real possibility, immanent in history, even if it remains unachieved as an actualised reality. The grounds for so saying are based, first, on the logic of freedom and solidarity. Once we accept that the first six forms of freedom are possible human conditions, then the seventh is simply a development of what we have already accepted.

Second, the seventh condition may be glimpsed in history in the imminent utopian moments to which it gives rise. I have already noted Buck-Morss's moment of universal history when the St Dominguan slaves and the French troops almost made common cause against a mutual, if differentially experienced, oppression. To that, one could add those moments of revolutionary fervour and change in which societies can suddenly do without a police force because everyone suddenly gets along very well (see e.g. Sachs and Welch 1990). Of course, these moments are not sustained, because the conditions do not permit it. Nonetheless, such moments provide us with glimpses of how we might transcend our presents in favour of a eudaimonic future, even if that future remains only a promise.

Third, I want to anticipate the critical objection that the problem with freedom is that it always becomes a form of unfreedom. Once we start speaking of freedom, we end up using that concept as a means of exclusion or exploitation of others. This is a well known criticism, promoted, for example, by Adorno (1973), or by modern deconstructionists and post-colonialists (cf Fanon 1965), but I think it is important to see that it tends to be true where the argument in favour of freedom is not pushed to its logical conclusion (i.e. the eudaimonic condition), or the interconnection with solidarity is downplayed. Where, for example, negative or positive freedom is held to be *the* form of freedom, this is compatible with either the authoritarianism that accompanies *laissez-faire* individualism (based on negative liberty), or that which accompanies state intervention in favour of freedom (people are forced to be free). But where freedom is understood as a whole, where each form is seen in the context of the whole, it seems to me that this concern falls away.

Ethics in the socio-legal: good and evil

What then does this immanent, dialectical ratcheting up of the forms of freedom and solidarity have to do with law? They represent, I shall argue, the grounds that underpin our proper concerns with good and evil. As indicated in the third section of this chapter ('Ethical problems and the socio-legal', above), this is the area where a socio-legal approach is likely to baulk: why should the socio concern itself with such ethical categories, especially if they are often deployed so as to evade socio-legal discussion?

The James Bulger case[3] shows how our understanding of such an issue can be seriously deflected if it is sucked up into these capacious and socially problematic, abstract, ethical categories. We live in a modern, secular world and the socio-legal impulse is a child of that world, so good and evil are, and should, remain beyond its ken. Yet, there is something compelling, as I suggested, in the idea of evil, once one thinks seriously about the Bulger case, and even more so, about Arendt's account of the banality of evil. And if we are to think of evil seriously, then do we not need to think also of good? So the question might be how the socio can focus appropriately on such terms, in a way that does not leave them at large, ready to suck up all the explanatory material that is to be examined. In this section, drawing on the argument of the previous chapter, I consider how the analysis of freedom and solidarity relates to an understanding of good, drawing on a recent case of mercy-killing, and evil, considering Arendt's analysis of the Holocaust.

Let me start with Arendt's account of the banality of evil, and ask, what did evil mean for her? It entailed two main elements. One was a fundamental denial of the most basic form of human freedom, the freedom to act, or spontaneity, the other was a denial of people's solidarity with others. Of the denial of legal freedom, she said: 'The aim of an arbitrary system is to destroy the civil rights of the whole population, who ultimately become just as outlawed in their own country as the stateless and homeless. The destruction of man's rights, the killing of the juridical person in him, is a prerequisite for dominating him entirely' (Arendt 1968: 451).

What happened when a totalitarian system denied legal freedom was, moreover, a prelude to the denial of what at the most basic level it meant to be

3 ibid.

human: 'After the . . . annihilation of the juridical person, the destruction of individuality is almost always successful . . . For to destroy individuality is to destroy spontaneity, man's power to begin something new out of his own resources . . .' (Arendt 1968: 455).

Spontaneity is the most basic form of human freedom, the freedom to start anew: a beginning and new agency with each new birth. The concentration camps were 'meant not only to exterminate people and degrade human beings, but also to serve the ghastly experiment of eliminating, under scientifically controlled conditions, spontaneity itself as an expression of human behaviour and transforming the human personality into a mere thing . . .' (Arendt 1968: 438).

The Holocaust's evil was that it attacked the root possibility of there being *any* human freedom, at the most fundamental level. At the same time, all *solidarity* was willfully suppressed: solidarity between victims was rendered meaningless, for example, in the case of the mother invited to choose to save one of her two children. And the very possibility that the perpetrators could think from the point of view of someone else: that too was absent in the case of a man like Eichmann. (It is here that one can locate the claim that the evil was banal, in that it was completely unthinking – the victims were the sorts of entities that one just did not need to consider as human at all, just objects.) Thus, what is evil for Arendt is the systematic denial of the basic freedom and solidarity that lie at the core of what it means to be human – evil attacks the core moral ontology of freedom and solidarity outlined above.

What of good? To mention briefly again the argument developed previously, here I cite the case of Kay Gilderdale, a mother who was tried for the murder of her daughter in 2011 in England (see above, chapter 8). Whilst it was clear that there was sufficient evidence of an intention to kill the daughter for a murder charge, the jury refused to convict Mrs Gilderdale, and the judge at her trial criticised the Crown Prosecution Service for bringing the case against her. The daughter had suffered for 17 years from a highly debilitating form of ME, and had both expressed the wish to die and had attempted to take her own life. Kay Gilderdale eventually did for the daughter what she was unable to do for herself.

On my analysis what made this a good act was that it was one that was: first, carried out in loving solidarity with the daughter; second, was in line with the daughter's settled, considered view of what was in her best interests; and, third, was potentially sacrificial of the mother's own interests. In other words, the good act in this case is one that chimes both with the deepest understanding we have of what it means to be a free person (the well-being and flourishing of the daughter in her concrete situation – even where that freedom entails the will to die), and where the actor acts in solidarity with that understanding, even where it was against her own basic wishes in the matter. Kay Gilderdale sacrificed her interest in her own well-being as a loving parent as well as risked the loss of her liberty through criminal law in order to act in solidarity with her daughter's well-being.

It was that combination of circumstances concerning her and her daughter's freedom, and the solidarity between them, which made her act a good one.

In these cases, I argue that what lies at the core of socio-legal investigations is an understanding of what is ethically at stake within them. Indeed, I go further and suggest that what makes them important objects of socio-legal investigation is the fact that they are morally salient. At the core of the socio-legal there lies an ethical question. That is surely why we investigate issues such as mercy killing or genocide. What I have said here is quite limited, and only opens a bridgehead to further enquiry, but I have argued that an understanding of human being and the axiology of freedom and solidarity to which it gives rise can be related to a valid ethical account of good and evil at the core of socio-legal questions. In this section, I have argued that the socio has ethical concerns at its core. In the next, I go on to argue that our existing ethical understanding is shaped by socio-historical factors.

The socio-legal in ethics: an historical phenomenology

If ethics lie at the core of the socio-legal, my contention in this section is that, insofar as we view legal phenomena through existing moral lenses, the socio-historical radically shapes the way we carry out ethical analyses of law. I draw on the account of freedom and solidarity previously provided to think about the problematic and conflictual ways in which we 'do' ethics in relation to law. This is on the basis of the argument about freedom and solidarity in the previous section: an account of the nature of freedom for human being, an ontology of its different forms starting with the most basic and working up to the most complete. All the forms are instantiated as human possibilities in history, except for the last which extrapolates from what is available to an as yet unachieved future. This can be seen as an exercise in utopian thinking, yet one that posits the utopian possibility in the real condition of what it means to be human. The argument is then grounded in a sense of what is really possible for human beings, but it operates in a social and historical world which, as we know, does not actualise it.

The ideal, the actual and the real

What light can this exercise in 'real utopianism' cast on our actual legal and moral practices? Must it remain a distant illumination, disconnected from the present? My argument is that, if we start from actually existing ethical understandings of law, we will find that they share by implication in the possibility of an ethically utopian real beyond the present, but in a necessarily limited way.

Modern ethical life, especially insofar as it concerns law, generally starts out from Kantian premises, where the dominant ethical standpoint concerns a relationship between what is ethically 'ideal' and a related 'actuality' to which the ideal is applied. These are limited ethical conceptions, but my argument will be that the resulting relationships that are formed between the ideal and the actual have as their underlying substrate a relationship to a deeper, more complete, sense of the ethically real. This is based on the deep and complete sense of freedom, identified in the previous section. Accordingly, we can conceive of the relationship between the ethically real, the ethically ideal and the ethically actual as a dialectical one in which modern ethical formulae concerning the ideal and the actual reflect but also deny an underlying relationship to the ethically real. We get an unresolved dialectic of the ethically real, the ideal and the actual, and this provides us with an historical phenomenology of modern ethical standpoints. This phenomenology produces three typical modern ethical problematics for thinking of law: the ideal *in* the actual, the ideal *under* the actual, and the ideal *against* the actual.

The ideal in the actual and the problem of repetition

The ideal in the actual is the typically Kantian way of formulating the idea of freedom in modern society. In this view, human freedom is represented through law: law is the place where freedom exists since it is the home of the free individual, and his or her freedom of choice. The ability to think rationally and ethically, and thereby to self-legislate, is reflected in the ability to be a legal subject with responsibility for one's acts. In the classical retributive account of punishment, for example, the individual submits to the law as a rational agent who wills the consequences of his actions. This standpoint produces a critique of the relation between law and society in that it points to all those situations in modern social life where the free individual is not respected, and demands that he be so.

A Kantian standpoint is for that reason a natural home for legal analysis, for it seeks to go with the logic of the law, and to make the modern world better in legal terms. If individual freedom is not respected in the law, the courtroom or the police station, the lawyer, informed with a sense of Kantian individualist principle, is there to argue that what is happening disrespects human subjectivity and is therefore wrong.

This ideal in the actual standpoint is not to be dismissed lightly, although it sometimes is by critical thinkers (see eg Norrie 2005a: ch 9 on Adorno). Nonetheless, it suffers from deep-seated problems. Whilst it defends individual liberty in modern society, it does so in a social context (an actuality) that is liberty threatening, for that is the nature of modern society. Freedom is always under threat under modern social and economic conditions (conditions of 'structural violence') and this threat is always at least latent so that the Kantian lawyer is always needed but often disappointed as she becomes aware of the inherently repetitive nature of what she has to say: the same problems constantly recur. If the project of modernity is one that is inspired by Kantian thought (as in e.g. Habermas), that is why it is necessarily and endlessly 'unfinished'.

A response to this problem of repetition and permanent disappointment is to say that Kantian freedom nonetheless operates as a 'regulative ideal', which, even if it cannot transform the actual, at least operates as a permanent reminder of what ought to be. The ideal may not be able to transform the actual in its image, but the tense relationship between ideal and actual is better than no relation at all. Like the poor who are always with us, the ideal in the actual is a relationship that remains perpetually unresolved. But this is the nature of modern legal (and moral) experience, and we should soon feel the lack of 'the ideal' were it to be removed from the equation. Think, for example, of the role of judges in applying human rights standards. We congratulate judicial censure of governmental power, but are aware that legal victories often turn out to be hollow as the government refashions law to bypass judicial decisions or achieve its ends by other means.

The ideal in the actual is accordingly a difficult, critical, terrain on which little is resolved or achieved. It entails an ethical relation based upon respect for individual freedom in its juridical and negative forms which is always under threat. In this way, the ideal is frustrated and brought down by its relationship to the actual, in a state of permanent struggle, subject to repeated defeat, yet always keeping going. The accompanying practical attitude among civil liberty or defence lawyers at their Sisyphean task is ultimately one of disappointment, weariness and disillusion.

Instability in the ideal in the actual relation

A state of consistent disappointment can push one in two directions. On one hand, one may be drawn to the conclusion that where the ideal is only ever repeated in the context of an unremitting and recalcitrant actuality, the actual wins and the ideal becomes its epiphenomenon. Once one understands that the relationship between the ideal and the actual means that the ideal will always entail a negative repetition where a recalcitrant actuality disappoints or defeats, one may conclude that in upholding the ideal in its intrinsic relation to the actual, one is also accepting the actual, or the system in which the ideal and the actual are necessarily conjoined, as a whole. One is in truth endorsing the whole situation including not just the ideal, but the ideal's unhappy relation to the actual. One is in effect *accepting*, despite one's best intentions, the relation between the ideal and the actual. Accordingly, one becomes complicit in the actual in its ongoing relation to the ideal. From there, it is a short step to think that the ideal is itself complicit with the actual, that the ideal becomes no more than a way of sustaining the actual. In this line of thought, the ideal eventually is seen as subsumed *under* the actual.

On the other hand, to hold to the ideal can also take one in a different direction, for to uphold the ideal in its relation to the actual can lead to a form of utopianism in which one imagines a world could exist that really *did* reflect the preoccupations of the ideal. A world of free and equal individuals living in rational unity with each other could in fact exist. Hence, the relationship of the ideal to the actual pushes in two quite different directions, one insisting on the ideal and pitting it against the actual, the other accusing the ideal of complicity with regard to the actual with which it is inevitably associated. Hence, starting from the relationship of the ideal to the actual, we see that that relationship is a necessarily unstable one. It can move to a situation where the ideal is held to have been subsumed *under* the actual (the situation of repetition and complicity with the actual), or one in which the ideal is held to generate a transcendent possibility that lies *against and beyond* the actual (the ideal as utopian possibility). Thinking about the ideal in the actual thus moves one to thinking about how that relationship generates two conflicting alternatives out of the original relationship: a view of the ideal *under* the actual, and of the ideal going *against and beyond* the actual.

The ideal under the actual and the problem of subsumption

These two alternative ways of configuring the ideal and the actual are borne out by the development of the modern ethical field generally, and as it pertains to law. The thought that the ideal has been subsumed under the actual under modern social conditions is a dominant theme in modern critical thought, and especially about law. In the early writings of the Frankfurt School, it is the claim that reason, as the ideal, original, place and ground of modern freedom, has been subsumed as a technique of domination under modern social conditions (by the actual) that lies at the core of the dialectic of Enlightenment (Adorno and Horkheimer 1997). For Adorno, Kantian freedom becomes in his negative dialectic a site of unfreedom. Legal freedom becomes the means by which freedom is denied. For example, punishment becomes no honouring of individual freedom but rather a means of hardening the criminal, as Nietzsche (1967) had suggested. And similarly, the categorical imperative becomes a means not of self-legislation but of control in an oppressive environment (Adorno 1973).

This upturning of the relationship between law and freedom (law as unfreedom) is a common theme generally in critical legal thought. I initially took up something like it in writing of criminal law when I drew on the following quotation from Roland Barthes:

> And this universal language (law) comes just at the right time to lend a new strength to the psychology of the masters: it allows it always to take other men as objects, to describe and condemn at one stroke. It is an adjectival psychology, it knows only how to endow its victims with epithets, it is ignorant of everything about the actions themselves, save the guilty category into which they are forced to fit.
>
> (Barthes 1973: 45, quoted in Norrie 2014: 365)

Law (and legal subjectivity) not as a form of liberty, but of mastery of the subject: the theme is well-rehearsed in Nietzsche, in Foucault's work and, more recently, in Agamben's, where law becomes the means of instantiating a bare humanity, one that is stripped of all liberties. It is also present in any account of law that goes back to Carl Schmitt and his claim that law is purely decisionistic. For Agamben, rightlessness in a legal system, such as is exemplified in the creation of the Guantanamo prison camp, or in the idea of 'extraordinary rendition', reveals the fundamental nature *of law* as operating to instantiate the actualities of power

(Agamben 1998, 2005). Or, take the idea of 'humanitarian intervention', that is an intervention in the domestic affairs of foreign powers against international law, but in the name of liberal principle. For some, this reveals the way in which ideal liberal principles have become subsumed under actual power relations and operate to reproduce them (Douzinas 2007) – albeit with a utopian gesture to non-subsumption attached. Law in particular, despite its ideal principles, is a form of actual unfreedom.

The ideal against the actual and the possibility of transcendence

Opposed to this idea that the ideal has been subsumed under the actual is the alternative view that emphasises the utopian potential in the ideal. Here, human freedom operates as a moment of critique that is found in law in a limited and constricted way, and yet points beyond it. In my work on law and the beautiful soul, I sought to present law in such terms (Norrie 2005a: ch 9). Drawing on Hegel's account of the beautiful soul in his early theological writings and comparing this with his work from the *Phenomenology of Spirit* onwards, I argued that his early enthusiasm for a radical Enlightenment liberty gave way to a more cautious, constrictive, law-based conception of freedom. In the early account, there was a vision of humanity as living in a general state of freedom, in which each would live in harmony with herself, with every other individual, with society in general and with nature.

This was a radical conception of freedom which focused primarily on the possibility of universal flourishing, perhaps at the expense of more basic notions of liberty associated with law. It was therefore incomplete as an analysis of the different forms of freedom described previously, but its focus on the deeper forms set it at odds with modern civil or bourgeois society in which private property dominates and limits how we understand social and legal relations, and the possibilities for freedom and solidarity available to humanity.

When Hegel came to write his mature work (i.e. became 'Hegel'), this radical conception of freedom was ditched in favour of a freedom that integrated conceptions of private property and law into its development. In consequence, the early radical conception of freedom was rejected, and this was seen in the way that Hegel dealt with the beautiful soul. Whereas, in the early writings, this had been a figure of principle to be admired (examples were drawn from Christian doctrines such as Christ and the money-lenders in the temple), from the *Phenomenology* onwards, a much more critical view was taken. In modern-day parlance, the beautiful soul became a 'loser' who ought to 'get a life'.

However, there was still a sense, I argued, of a restless utopian spirit, such as the beautiful soul had originally involved, to be found in modern law, and this was seen in the antinomies that pervade its categories. Often these antinomies are ones of form and content, where questions of individual freedom and a broader social freedom and solidarity are seen as in tension with each other. Law focuses primarily on form and on formal, abstract, individual freedom, but is accordingly often reminded of the need to look beyond formal kinds of freedom to deeper substantive relations of freedom, solidarity and justice. Thus, there is an engagement with a utopian quality of freedom in law itself, secreted in the forms of individual freedom. The ghost of the beautiful soul stalks the corridors of the law (Norrie 2005a: ch 9).

In this way, human freedom in law operates as a moment of critique, and pointing at the same time beyond it. There are many examples of this in critical thought. Generally, it seems to me that efforts at Aristotelian critique of modernity seek to open up a terrain of freedom and justice that law does not express, for example, in the thought of Alasdair MacIntyre (2007). Marxian critiques of, for example, the 'narrow horizon of bourgeois right', which point out that every right of equality is a right of inequality, are in a different but parallel vein (Marx 1968c).

Deconstructionist critiques are interesting here too for, in their initial form, they are of the ideal under the actual form. Thus, in Nietzsche, stripping back our forms of law, justice and so on reveals the hidden genealogies of power that inform them; but at the same time, there is a need to configure an alternative ethics of the 'overman'. Post structuralism often looks at how constrictive, freedom-denying forms also generate or sediment utopian ideals which have a continuing validity. Hence, for Derrida, deconstruction examines the hidden historical genealogies of power, but is also a form of justice, albeit one that is 'mad' and 'messianic'. Here, Derrida is fusing together an ideal under the actual with an ideal in and against the actual strategy. A promise of transcendence exists in different forms in all these cases.

In legal practice itself, one also finds examples of the ideal operating as a critique of the actual. Here, one can think, for example, of restorative justice in comparison to legal, or penal, justice. The work of restorative justice may in part be a way of supporting and enriching the social relations that tend to be ignored by straightforward legal conceptions of punishment (Johnstone 2002). The state, the offender and the victim are seen to possess a potentially deeper relationship that goes beyond the crime and its punishment. Each is the means by which the other may become more whole and, in the process, the community itself is morally developed.

If legal justice in its usual Kantian form deals with abstract subjects enjoying agential and negative freedoms, restorative justice pushes into deeper forms of freedom such as well-being and flourishing, and that involve deeper relations of solidarity. There is something significantly eudaimonic and utopian in the conception of restorative justice – even if in a non-eudaimonic world it must always fall short, and may end up as authoritarian in practice. Pointing beyond the present with images of an ideal solidarity, and suggesting genuine possibilities for a better world, it is always in danger of instantiating actually existing relations of power so that its ideas of community become more invasive means of enforcement. Viewed by proponents as a means of promoting an ideal against the actual, its reality is often one of subsumption of ideal hopes under actual realities.

Conclusion

The socio has a double relationship to ethical being. On one hand, ethical issues lie at the core of those things that socio-legal studies examines. If we look at the killing of James Bulger, the murderous activities of the Nazis or, at the other extreme, the quality of mercy killing, we can see that explanation of these phenomena pivots around key ethical notions of good and evil, and behind them, of freedom and solidarity.

On the other hand, an understanding of modern ethics also draws on an understanding of freedom and solidarity. It depends on a grasp of how different kinds of modern ethics are historically shaped by a dynamic of the ideal and the actual which rests upon further underlying real ethical possibilities. The starting point here is the Kantian relation between the ideal and the actual, which is negotiated over time, and in the light of evolving historical circumstances. The resulting dynamic commences with an Enlightenment move to be found in Kant, and then, under the appreciation of evolving historical circumstances, turns towards the bleak, inversionary strategies of Nietzsche and the post structuralists. Yet a utopian possibility is still seen to exist: there is always something more in law than unfreedom, even for those who claim that as its essence. To grasp the 'something more' is to appreciate an unactualised possibility of universal human freedom and solidarity at much deeper levels than modern society permits. On the basis of a realist ethics of freedom and solidarity leading to the eudaimonic condition, we are able to develop a modern phenomenology of the ethical forms available to us, their limits and what lies within and beyond them.

Chapter 10

Responsibility and the metaphysics of justice

'we hybrids moulded from clay and spirit'

(Levi 2013: 71)

In this chapter, I consider the problems of guilt in connection with genocide discussed after the Second World War by Hannah Arendt, Karl Jaspers, Primo Levi and Jean Améry. I look at the different forms of guilt: of perpetrators, bystanders, victims who became perpetrators, and of collective guilt. The way in to understand the structure of guilt is to consider the idea of survivor guilt, and the chapter links this to an underlying metaphysics of guilt. It considers primarily Levi's account of survivor and accomplice guilt, and the 'grey zone' where judgment becomes problematic.

The aim is to consider the ethical structure that supports our understanding of specific guilt categories, and this links Jaspers and Levi to Roy Bhaskar's philosophy of metaReality.[1] There he argues for a sense of metaphysical unity or identity that operates at a deeper level than the difference, conflict and change that occupy his dialectical critical realist philosophy. The philosophy of metaReality rounds out and deepens his thought, and I explore it for the first time in this chapter, arguing that it represents a key to understanding the philosophical thoughts and thoughtful experiences of Jaspers and Levi. The chapter considers the shape and structure of ethical enquiry, and what it is that makes ethical enquiry possible. From that point of view, it becomes possible to understand better our concepts of guilt and justice.

With regard to critical realism, I wish to say something in the next section about the work of Roy Bhaskar,[2] its different levels, and how it is relevant to my own views on issues of guilt in the law and in moral thinking today. The three levels of

1 This was Bhaskar's 'term of art'.

2 Roy Bhaskar died in November 2014. Before his death, he was able to produce a final work which focuses on and integrates his developing account of ontology as the key to the three levels of his philosophy. It is published by Routledge in 2016 under the title *Enlightened Common Sense: an Introduction to the Philosophy of Critical Realism.*

critical realism are critical realism in its basic form, dialectical critical realism and metaReality. Bhaskar always said that people should take what they wanted or needed from his thought, but that there was an immanent logic that led from one level to another.

This chapter is in the spirit of that remark. My work has been particularly influenced by dialectical critical realism, but recently I have started to address what I see as a resistance in legal studies to think metaphysically about law. Another way to put this would be to say that I see increasingly the need to think metaphysically about issues of justice and guilt in order to understand our contemporary juridical practices, and this takes me to the third level of Bhaskar's philosophy on what he termed metaReality.

Most work in law has a secular and non-metaphysical cast, and the idea of overcoming resistance is significant. Bhaskar used to say that his clue as to how to proceed philosophically was to push against those points where he encountered most resistance to his argument. Broadly, we can say that his work tracks three such resistances in its different levels of development. In its first phase, the resistance was most obviously to arguing for ontology and depth realism in a world that was much more comfortable to talk of epistemology and empirical reality (Bhaskar 1975, 1979). In its second phase, it was the significance of absence or negativity that was key, and here the resistance was historical as well as modern (Bhaskar 1993, 1994).[3] The third resistance was to what became the 'spiritual turn' in Bhaskar's thought, in what he called metaReality. This is the thought that we can broadly identify as involving the significance of a metaphysical underpinning to the nature of reality (Bhaskar 2012a, 2012b). In speaking of identifying and addressing resistances, there is a parallel with the practice of psychotherapy, which also has a depth realist aspect. Bhaskar was keen to thematise his work around the idea of a 'reality principle' that is denied by modern thought in its epistemic and positivistic quality. For now, I make the simple point that there was courage in his willingness to follow 'the line of most resistance'.

In this chapter, I adopt a similar approach, in an area that is daunting even to the uninhibited. I organise my thoughts around two linked discussions. First, I look briefly at Bhaskar's work from critical realism to dialectical critical realism and on to metaReality. Second, I address issues of guilt and its judgment in the context of the aftermath of the Second World War. This starts with thinking about Hannah Arendt and Karl Jaspers, and their dialogue on the subject, and then moves on to consider Primo Levi's thoughts in *The Drowned and the Saved* (Levi 2013) and then Jean Améry's thoughts on collective responsibility in his *At the Mind's Limits* (Améry 1980). My aim will be to link ideas from metaReality with a metaphysics of guilt, which I will draw from Jaspers and Levi, and then apply to concepts of perpetrator, accomplice, bystander and collective guilt.

3 In his dialectical philosophy, Bhaskar traces the problems and therefore the 'metacritique' of western philosophy back to the Greeks Parmenides and Plato, where absence (real determinate non-being) is denied. See Norrie (2010: chs 6, 7).

The different phases of critical realism

The basic achievement of critical realism is the revindication of ontology over the imperialist ambitions of epistemology, and within that, the vindication of a particular, depth, ontology. The analysis of what scientists did in both the natural and social sciences was only explicable once you understood that the world was real and existed independently of thinking about it (Bhaskar 1975) (or at least this was relatively the case with regard to the social sciences: Bhaskar 1979).

More than that, the world was structured, deep, and with generative mechanisms at play that could be discovered by scientific investigation. A depth realist mode of enquiry into such mechanisms was required as the basis for understanding how the world worked. Particularly relevant to the social sciences was the existence of structures and, working to produce, reproduce or transform these, agency. The structure–agency couple, together with the hermeneutic circle that this engaged (Bhaskar 1979: ch 4), had to be understood. Once grasped, reasons could be seen as causes and, ultimately, a scientific naturalist attitude was as possible in the social as in the natural sciences *mutatis mutandis*. Depth realism in the social sciences recognised natural necessity, but it had also to deal with a particular kind of subject, the human being as agent.

These are the core ideas of basic or original critical realism and Bhaskar was to spend the 1980s and 1990s working to develop it first in the direction of dialectical critical realism, and then metaReality. In dialectical critical realism, the idea of a structured and differentiated world was developed in three moves. The first of these was the idea that central to our understanding of the world is the importance of change, and change is to be understood as involving the negation of what exists as it is transformed and becomes something else. The world is constantly changing and this 'becoming and begoing' is understood in terms of absenting what is there, the 'real determinate negation' of what exists. This recognition of absence as real determinate negativity was essential, and those who refused this move had a one dimensional, 'ontologically monovalent', attitude to the world (Bhaskar 1993; Norrie 2010: chs 2, 6, 7). At the same time, all change is geo-historically located and subject to its own spatio-temporal rhythms (Bhaskar 1993: chs 2.2, 3.6; Norrie 2010: 28–34).

Second, alongside this, the structure–agency dual was transformed into four-planar social being in which relations with nature, interpersonal relations, social (institutional, structural) relations per se and intrapersonal relations (individual psychic structures) all go to constitute the human being's concrete universality/singularity (Bhaskar 1993: ch 2.7, 2.9; Norrie 2010: 113–117). Putting the first and second points together, we can summarise the core perspective of dialectical critical realism as an understanding of the world as involving both structured being and becoming. Third, attached to these, there was a further move to integrate an ethical understanding of human freedom and solidarity with the socio-historical (spatio-temporal) understanding of the evolution of human being as a special kind of natural, anthropological, being (Bhaskar 1993: ch 3; Norrie 2010: ch 5).

What I have just described is sometimes referred to as the MELD structure of dialectical critical realism. The first Moment of basic, structural critical realism moves to a second Edge of negativity and is transformed thereby, before a third Level of seeing things as a whole, in their totality, emerges, and this leads to a fourth Dimension of ethical agency or praxis (MELD). Although not too much should be read into the MELD structure (it is as much descriptive of a particular journey as providing a necessary form for the theory), its end point, ethical agency or praxis, was already present in original critical realism. Now, however, it is thought through as a drive towards freedom in its various forms, which can only be achieved in solidarity with others. The logical and practical outcome of this drive to universalise the forms of freedom and solidarity is the latent, potential, tendential possibility of the eudaimonic condition, one in which the free flourishing of each depends on the free flourishing of all (Bhaskar 1993: ch 3.10; Norrie 2010: 144–56). This, it might be added, requires as its condition, the flourishing of the planet and other natural species as a whole.

Such a vision only needs to be stated in order to disclose the gulf between the actually existing world with its generic master–slave relations, and the immanent, real possibilities available to human being. Nonetheless, the message of dialectical critical realism is that the gulf is real only because both sides, the world that actually exists, and what is really possible within it, are both true, or 'alethic',[4] as Bhaskar has it. The vision of dialectical critical realism is of a world in which alienation, splits, contradictions and conflicts animate modernity alongside the inherent, latent possibilities that exist for human socio-natural being.

Bhaskar, however, was not to leave his argument there. There was a further development to occur, which involves the idea of metaReality. If the eudaimonic condition is a tendential, un- or under-actualised possibility for modernity, then it is real, true and alethic. What form does this condition take? Its emphasis on the universal, on connection and solidarity, and on the full flourishing of each and all, indicates a potential for universality, identity and oneness contained within the actually existing world of splits, contradictions, lacks and dualisms. Modernity exists as a world of conflict and structural violence: Bhaskar thematises the existence of what he called $power_2$ or generalised master–slave relations.[5] Underlying this, however, he began to see a deeper sense of identity, which he was to analyse in metaphysical terms at the level of metaReality.

In metaReality (Bhaskar 2002, 2012a, 2012b), Bhaskar builds this vision in his analysis of the ways in which moments of transcendental connection underpin social transactions that are conflicted and split – in the forms of human exchange where even simple communications disclose moments of real identity and connection, in the senses of community that exist even in communities that

4 The truth of, or real reasons for, or dialectical ground of things, as distinct from propositions: see Bhaskar 1993: 394; Norrie 2010: 126.

5 '$Power_2$' was another of Bhaskar's terms of art.

are split and contradictory, in the transcendental feeling that participating in nature or music, art, or literature provides, or in acts of kindness and love. In moments of creativity which overcome the split between subject and object we also find identity behind non-identity.

Such considerations led Bhaskar in this third phase of his thought to consider being as involving an ultimate unity that underlies difference and conflict, between oneself and the other, across time and place: a co-presence in human being of all the experiences open to human beings, for good and ill, and this co-presence lies at the core of metaReality. It involves a sense of universality in the human condition. Co-presence 'is where some other thing is enfolded or implicit within a being' and the claim of metaReality is that 'the alethic truth of all other beings' is enfolded within myself (Bhaskar 2012b: xlix). Beings remain distinct in their constitution and their location in space and time, but my potential ability to understand or identify with another stems from an ultimate underlying identity.

For myself, I resisted this third move in the initial ways that Bhaskar presented it. It seemed to me to abandon, or at least to downplay, the central importance of what he had achieved in his dialectics and original critical realism. I felt it led too quickly to an ethical 'call to arms', which de-emphasised the historicity and structuration of conflict. Yet I could not get away from the sense that there was something very important in what he was saying, and something that, *because it was true*, would have to come out in the working and therefore the thought of law. That something is found in the idea of metaphysical guilt, which I first encountered in Jaspers's thought, and which I now investigate in Levi and his and Améry's accounts of guilt.

Before moving on, however, let me give a brief centenary illustration of what I have in mind. In 1916, after the Easter Uprising in Dublin, Sir Roger Casement was hanged by the British for treason. Casement, who was born and raised in Ireland, had been knighted by the British in 1911 for his work in exposing the conditions of Amazonian Indians working in rubber plantations. In this work and earlier work relating to the position of native Africans in similar settings in the Congo, Casement had become convinced of the iniquities of Western colonialism, and he came to see the relationship of Ireland to Britain in similar terms. During the First World War, he sought to raise a regiment of Irish nationalist troops from those held prisoner by the Germans and also sought German arms for the rising. When he was arrested on landing on the Irish coast, he was charged with treason, sabotage and espionage and taken to the Tower of London. He was hanged in London in August 1916. A strong campaign was mounted against his execution, but this was countered by stories circulated in the press relating to a set of diaries that he had seemingly written which showed him to be a promiscuous homosexual.

Prior to his execution, Casement was received into the Catholic Church, and his last words were as follows: 'My final message for everyone is a *sursum corda.* I wish the best to those who will take my life and those who have tried to save it. All of you are now my brothers' (Vargas Llosa 2012: 388).

Mario Vargas Llosa has recently described Casement as a man of contradictions and contrasts, and, although no model of perfection, one where 'angels and demons combine inextricably in his personality'. In Ireland, he has 'gradually, though always with reluctance and prudery' begun to be accepted as 'one of the great anti-colonial figures and defenders of human rights and indigenous cultures of his time, and a sacrificed combatant for the emancipation of Ireland' (Vargas Llosa 2012: 398).

In light of this, it is the power and significance of those final words to which I point, and the sense of identity and co-unity between Casement and his enemies. Casement was to be executed by his enemies in the middle of a world war, after a violent uprising against a colonial power that he opposed, and that had been ruthlessly suppressed. When he had been tried by a British court, he refused to recognise it and, in order to promote his execution against significant opposition, his character had been dragged through the mud. A holy man, no doubt, as his late reception into the church makes clear, but the religious dimension is not central to the point. The point is that a human being could find the grace to see his enemies and executioners as his brothers prior to his death. How do we understand this moral quality to surface as it did in the end for Casement? It is the sense of identity beyond difference and conflict that lies at the heart of Bhaskar's non-religious philosophy of metaReality which I wish to pursue. In what follows, my focus will now turn to issues of war guilt.

The problem of war guilt: Arendt and Jaspers

If we now explore this sense of the metaphysical in relation to the question of guilt, I am interested in the idea of 'transitional justice'. This involves the problems thrown up for justice by transitions from one regime to another, where the transition involves dealing with figures in the old regime in terms of calling them to account for their actions. One sees this in many parts of the world, especially nowadays in Latin America, but also in Africa (Rwanda, South Africa). The *locus classicus* of the problem is the war crimes trials of the Nazis after the Second World War, and I have done some work on the views of Hannah Arendt in *Eichmann in Jerusalem* (Arendt 1964), and her engagement immediately after the war with Karl Jaspers (see Chapter 7 above).

Jaspers had written a book on German war guilt (Jaspers 2000), and Arendt had responded that Germany was saddled with a real problem. There were tens or hundreds of thousands of people who could not be adequately punished for their crimes. The problem was not just one of numbers or scale, but the widespread, systematic abandonment of its moral compass by whole swathes of a people. What had been done was carried out by 'civilised barbarians', who had no sense of the wrongness of their actions, despite their enormity. The problem was focused later in her consideration of Eichmann, who, she argued, could be executed but not on the basis of the normal moral understanding that he had done wrong, which his punishment could communicate. Eichmann, and many like him, was incapable of such communication, because he could not see that he had done wrong. He thought indeed that he had done his 'duty', that he had acted 'according to Kant'. Punishment would therefore lack the normal moral quality that was expected of it. There was no possibility of a moral dialogue with such a person.

The argument seems both logically persuasive and morally counter-intuitive. It makes sense in terms of the need to address Eichmann as a responsible moral agent, but it leads to the conclusion that the worse someone like him behaved, the less justice could make its claims upon him. In opposition to this, I pursued Jaspers's argument when he distinguished four different kinds of guilt – political, legal, moral and metaphysical – but I noted the problematic quality of this typology at the same time. Political guilt was an 'external' form of guilt involving for example reparations that were imposed on a people as a whole by a victorious power, regardless of their actual wrongdoing. Legal guilt, again an 'external' form, was imposed on individuals where a crime was formally identified, and where a formally free act had taken place.

Neither of these forms of guilt addressed the moral dialogue that a process of criminal justice is normally thought to involve. Moral guilt, on the other hand, was an 'internal' form of guilt, but in Jaspers's account, it was not appropriate for engagement in a public trial process. Instead, it involved a moral agent's private engagement with himself and with close family and friends. In any case, it was self-evident that the accused in the trials of Nazis felt no such guilt. That did, however, leave the fourth form of guilt, metaphysical guilt, and this intrigued me. What did Jaspers mean by this fourth category?

In this first quotation, morality's 'mundane purposes' are contrasted with the more transcendental quality of metaphysical guilt, which involves an absolute solidarity or unity with other human beings, one which goes beyond a 'morally meaningful' sense of duty. This, importantly, taps into the idea of 'survivor guilt', about which, more below:

> Morality is always influenced by mundane purposes . . . Metaphysical guilt is the lack of absolute solidarity with the human being as such—an indelible claim beyond morally meaningful duty. This solidarity is violated by my presence at a wrong or a crime. It is not enough that I cautiously risk my life to prevent it; if it happens, and if I was there, and if I survive where the other is killed, I know from a voice within myself: I am guilty of being still alive.
>
> (Jaspers 2000: 65)

In the following passage, this sense of absolute solidarity as an unconditional obligation to every other is articulated as follows:

> Somewhere among men the unconditional prevails – the capacity to live only together or not at all . . . Therein consists the substance of their being. But that this does not extend to the solidarity of all men . . . but remains confined to the closest of human ties – therein lies this guilt of us all.
>
> (Jaspers 2000: 26)

In considering Jaspers's account, one can identify perhaps five different meanings of the 'metaphysical' as it connects with guilt. These are, first, the lack of absolute solidarity with the human being as such, as above and, second, and closely connected, to identify but not live by the unconditioned in human relations. These fundamental metaphysical or transcendental elements represent the basis by way of negative contrast for a third meaning, to live in history and politics. In such a state, one does not live by the unconditional alone. A fourth meaning, closely linked to the third, is to live in relations of power given to one. Finally, a fifth meaning links to survivor guilt: to live after a crime, to survive it.

In terms of the debate between Arendt and Jaspers, the value of this conception of metaphysical guilt was that, in a world where the worst perpetrators felt no guilt, indeed felt vindicated in what they had done, here was a conception of guilt that could operate beyond the need for actual acceptance of, or capacity for, moral dialogue between perpetrators and those judging them. Of course, Jaspers was speaking at the highest level of abstraction, and he was not speaking of the guilt of those who were perpetrators, but either onlookers or survivors. Nonetheless, the conception of guilt here was non-actualist, and related to a deeper set of claims about universality and humanity, and what humans owe to each other, regardless of whether this was accepted in an agent's particular understanding or actual acceptance of responsibility.

My argument therefore was that one could take this formulation which Jaspers deployed to speak of universal guilt – of the survivor, the bystander and the collective group – and turn it on the perpetrators themselves. Metaphysical guilt, operating at a different level, was complexly related to, but in some way operated to underpin, the other forms of guilt, in the political, legal and moral spheres. In providing it with a fuller role in relation to Jaspers's typology, it was possible to see the limitations of Arendt's criticism of guilt attribution in the case of perpetrators of crimes against humanity.

This was the attraction of the idea of metaphysical guilt, but it seems on reflection to be vulnerable to a possible criticism (see above, pp 135–6). Jaspers himself had worried that his conception would be too abstract, too questionable, and would be seen as simply the crazy idea of a philosopher (Jaspers 2000: 68). His own background was in Christian pietism, and it might be thought that the idea of metaphysical guilt reflects too much his Christian worldview.

A further meaning he had given to metaphysical guilt involved the common guilt of mankind, by which he meant 'original sin'. The resolution of such guilt was to be sought by living in relation with God, and reflecting on the way to humble self-purification. Is it only from a religious point of view that metaphysical guilt appears valid, and if so, what persuasive power does it have for those who do not share it? In reaching into this domain, is one in danger of basing one's thought on a terrain that academics, legal and otherwise, will find hard to accept? We may be happy to strike a further blow against the 'positivist unconscious', that dominates much academic work, but are we reaching for a somewhat 'local' universal in pressing Jaspers into service? Alternatively, is it possible to align Jaspers's conception with the view advanced by Bhaskar in his philosophical, non-theological,[6] account of metaReality?

One way of reflecting on these concerns is to pose a more concrete question. It will be recalled that the fifth meaning of metaphysical guilt involved the person who survives a crime. It is with regard to that meaning that I will pursue my concern here. The question can be put as follows: is a conception like survivor guilt no more than a fancy name for psychological trauma, or does it deserve a different kind of understanding, as a form of metaphysical guilt? If it does, this would support the intuition that such a conception may be important to our understanding not just of the metaphysical, but of how the metaphysical manifests itself in worldly guilt and justice.

The nature of survivor guilt: reading Primo Levi

In this section, I begin with the understanding of survivor guilt in psychoanalytical accounts of survivor trauma, before considering how this conception of guilt as psychological mimesis is taken up and extended metaphysically by Levi. It is on this basis that the distinctions as well as the difficulties in his account of the different kinds of guilt emanating from the experience of the camp can be understood, including his account of the 'grey zone'.

Guilt versus shame: the nature of survivor guilt

Survivor guilt is a controversial topic in the psychoanalytical understanding of traumatisation, and it is also a topic taken up by Primo Levi in his account of life and survival in the concentration camp. A helpful intermediary between the two uses is the work of Ruth Leys on guilt and shame (Leys 2007), which analyses the psychoanalytical debate on survivor guilt and draws on Levi to do so.

Leys's book is a powerful analysis of evolving directions in the psychiatric analysis of trauma, and the use of the concept of survivor guilt in the treatment of trauma disorders. Her argument is that conceptions of *shame* have over the last 30 years tended to supplant conceptions of *guilt*, and this has meant ultimately a move to seeing trauma in terms of an external psychological assault on the victim, from the outside. In the approach associated with guilt, on the other hand, the analysis of traumatic disorder involves a sense of the potential for taking an internal view of the psychology of the victim. This may involve a process of mimesis, or imitation and identification with the person perpetrating the violence. It is mimesis, under the requirement of survival, that leads ultimately to the sense of guilt that we call survivor guilt, and which lies at the root of the way some victims experience their traumatic situation:

6 'What I wanted to do was to make spirituality compatible with secularism.' See Bhaskar and Hartwig (2010: 167).

> The concept of survivor guilt had been theorised within the terms of psychoanalytic ideas about the relationship – the imitative or identificatory relationship – between the victim and the aggressor. The claim . . . was that one characteristic, indeed primordial, mode of defense against violence was for the victim to save herself by giving in to power and identifying with the threatening other.
>
> (Leys 2007: 181)

Such identification leads in due course to feelings of guilt as the victim reflects consciously or unconsciously on her past thought processes and how she had identified with the perpetrator in the time when she had survived, but others had perished. According to Leys, the sense of trauma as survivor guilt draws on something of this more classical psychoanalytic understanding. The significance of this claim has in recent times been contested, but it is not my purpose to enter into the internal debate between psychiatrists and psychoanalysts, or between Freudians, post-Freudians and anti-Freudians. As we will go on to see, it is borne out by Levi's account of his own moral experience of the death and labour camp. Accordingly, Leys's analysis, which is sympathetic to the classical approach, is helpful in positing a material psychological mechanism that can underpin the idea of survivor guilt. The question for me now is whether it can help us in understanding the role of metaphysical guilt as deployed by Jaspers. Can we then develop the idea beyond the religious basis that might otherwise be our only way of understanding what he has to say?

From mimesis to metaphysics

In working through her defence of survivor guilt with regard to the internal, mimetic approach to guilt in the psychoanalytic/psychiatric literature, Leys had looked closely at Levi's experience of the death and labour camp, especially in his book *The Drowned and the Saved* (Levi 2013). If we follow her there, we find an analysis that substantially supports her argument about survivor guilt, but also takes us further, towards an ethical, metaphysical, conception.[7] In the camp, Levi writes, power was sought amongst others 'by the many among the oppressed who were contaminated by the oppressors and unconsciously strove to identify with

7 Giorgio Agamben (2002: 94–97) seeks to dismiss the idea of survivor guilt in Levi's account. Linking it to collective guilt and then to the analysis of guilt in Greek tragedy, he misses the ground I discuss below concerning metaphysical guilt. He wishes to side-line survivor guilt in order to promote a 'new ethics' located in Levi's grey zone, but based on shame as the focus of an existential ontology of subjectification and desubjectification. (2002: 104–35). The key link is Robert Antelme's account of a young Italian student whose face turns pink (flushes) when he is picked at random for execution on a death march. It appears, however, that Agamben has interpreted this event in his own way: see Leys (2007: 174–79).

them' (ibid: 45). Levi describes as mimesis the 'identification or imitation, or exchange of roles between oppressor and victim' (ibid: 45–46). He warned, however, that this idea 'has provoked much discussion', continuing that much of it has proved highly problematic (ibid: 46).

We will come to the difficulties in the next section but, for now, we should note the salience of the mechanism of mimesis for Levi. There is, however, an important difference in his approach from the analysis presented by Leys, and it involves the different – moral – register in which he thinks. For Levi, what was at stake was not simply a psychological, trauma-inducing, mechanism, although that was a crucial part. Beyond it was an ethical wrong that had been done that went to the heart of what it meant to be human. His comment that he does 'not believe that psychoanalysts . . . are competent to explain this impulse' (Levi 2013: 90) emphasises the difference in standpoints. Psychoanalytical knowledge had not been developed in the camp, and even where a psychoanalyst such as Bruno Bettelheim had experience of the camp, the analysis seems 'approximate and simplified, as if someone wished to apply the theorems of plain geometry to the solution of spheric triangles' (ibid: 90).

In seeking the correct ethical register, Levi observes that everyone in the camp 'suffered from an unceasing discomfort that polluted sleep and was nameless. To define this as a 'neurosis' is reductive and ridiculous' (ibid: 91). It would, he says, 'be more correct to see in it an atavistic anguish, [that] of a deserted and empty universe crushed under the spirit of God, but from which the spirit of man is absent: not yet born or already extinguished' (ibid: 91).[8] Earlier in the book, he had written, in the case of those who had collaborated, of 'the death of the soul' which yields and breaks under pressure (ibid: 60), and of being made to live 'at an animal level', in which 'our moral yardstick has changed' (ibid: 78). But there are two sides to the hybrids that we are, clay and spirit, and it is the spiritual side of humankind that needs to be attended to in thinking about survivor guilt. Here the psychoanalyst cannot help us.

In a number of passages, Levi returns to the need to think through the metaphysics of guilt. To return to normal life from the mental states imposed in the camp was not just to experience and work through psychological trauma; it was to experience and live with a sense of ethical abandonment that went to the very heart of what it meant to be human, and to possess a human spirit. Many of the precise comments made by Levi take these observations and give them a transcendental or metaphysical frame. In the following quotation, Levi points to the general capacity of humankind to turn the world into one of sheer pain, and the impact of knowledge of this on those who observed it:

> The just among us, . . . felt remorse, shame and pain for the misdeeds that others and not they had committed, and in which they felt involved, because

8 Levi writes that he 'entered the Lager as a non-believer, and as a non-believer I was liberated and have lived to this day' (2013: 163). The reference to God in this passage must be read in this light.

> they sense that what had happened around them in their presence, and in them was irrevocable. It would never again be able to be cleansed; it would prove that man, the human species – we in short – were potentially able to construct an infinite enormity of pain.
>
> (Levi 2013: 92)

More concretely, there is the failure to offer solidarity with a human being who is your companion, whom you fail to help. This is the nub of survivor guilt:

> Almost everybody feels guilty of having omitted to offer help. The presence at your side of a companion who is weaker, or less cunning, or older, or too young, hounding you with his demands for help or with his simply being there . . . The demand for solidarity, for a human word, advice, even only a listening ear was permanent and universal but rarely satisfied.
>
> (Levi 2013: 82)

And finally, there is again the guilt of the survivor, or perhaps just the observer, who now knows that humankind, and therefore the individual him or herself, may be capable of such things. In the following passage, Levi points to specific failures to act, but it seems that not acting or not acting adequately, is a further issue to the simple guilt at the existence of a crime. Here he speaks of

> . . . the shame which the just man experiences when confronted by a crime committed by another, and he feels remorse because of its existence, because of its having been irrevocably introduced into the world of existing things, and because his will has proven non-existent or feeble and was incapable of putting up a good defence.
>
> (Levi 2013, 75)[9]

However one reads these comments, it seems that they occupy similar territory to Jaspers's account of metaphysical guilt. An understanding of this deep layer of human being or experience is central to the nature of the judgment of guilt. On Levi's account, survivor guilt operates as living proof in the extreme or limit case of the significance of Jaspers's account. We have moved here beyond the understanding of such guilt as a material mental mechanism underlying traumatisation, although what we have is a deepening of the understanding of such things, rather than simply an alternative mode of explanation. The metaphysical, indeed, builds on the existence of the mental mechanism, but it is important to see that it is acknowledged by the testimony of the survivor as a sentiment generated by the reality of the camp experience, and not just as a metaphysical speculation. Survivor guilt was ingredient in the real structure and the actual events.

9 Levi uses the term 'shame' here, but he uses it interchangeably with 'guilt' in this work.

Perpetrators, victims, collaborators[10]

Now, however, we need to pause, and to be clear about the line of argument. We have seen that survivor guilt can operate to indicate a deep sense of metaphysical guilt in the human condition, and the argument has been that this conception can operate to ground a Jaspersian response to an Arendtian question. But I noted above that we move here between two forms of actual, worldly guilt: that of the camp survivor (the victim) and that of the war criminal (the perpetrator), and these are two very different people. As we noted above, Levi was both drawn to the theory of mimesis, to which he gave an ethical turn, and also concerned that it led to serious misunderstanding about the nature of guilt in the camp. We need to explore this point.

Perpetrators and victims

The problem with survivor guilt is that it can lead to the conclusion that all are complicit in guilt, and this can erase the important distinctions between different kinds of guilt. It is clear that people, perpetrators and victims, are not guilty in the same way, or for the same things, and some are not guilty at all. Here, Levi wanted to hold on to a sense of the universal guilt we share for the existence of the camp, whilst being clear about the distinctions we need to draw to identify the guilt of different classes of agents in relation to it. These included those in the 'grey zone' of collaboration that existed between the victim and the perpetrator. He adopts a subtle and nuanced line, which both acknowledges who the real perpetrators are, and assigns a degree of responsibility, or refuses to do so, to those who collaborated, but all this against the horizon of a general sense of universal responsibility.

With regard to collaborators, Levi cites the case of Rumkowski, the Chief Elder of the Jews of Lodz. He writes of Rumkowski's distorted view of the world, his dogmatic arrogance, his clinging to power, and his contempt for law. The man had been drugged by the power given him by the Nazis, but, Levi notes, this 'does not exonerate [him] from his responsibilities' (Levi 2013: 69). His own life was tragic but, still, although there were extenuating circumstances, 'no tribunal would have absolved him, nor certainly can we absolve him in the moral plane' (ibid: 70). However, Levi also describes this as a case of *impotentia judicandi*. Are many of us not just like Rumkowski?

> We are all mirrored in Rumkowski, his ambiguity is ours, it is our second nature, we hybrids moulded from clay and spirit; his fever is ours, the fever of our Western civilisation that 'descends into hell with trumpets and drums',

10 A further category that ought to be discussed here is that of the supporters and beneficiaries of systems premised on structural violence: see above, pp 147–8) and, generally (Meister 2012). Perhaps we should talk of 'beneficiary guilt' alongside that of the perpetrator, accomplice, bystander, survivor and the collective.

> and its miserable adornments are the distorting images of our symbols of social prestige (Levi 2013: 71).

Levi continues that, like Rumkowski, we are all dazzled by power and prestige so that we forget our 'essential fragility'. We all come to terms with power, 'forgetting that we are all in the ghetto, that the ghetto is walled in, that outside the ghetto reign the lords of death and that close by the train is waiting' (Levi 2013: 71). Despite this impotence in judging in the 'grey zone', Rumkowski stands as one who deserves to be held responsible.

There were, however, others who worked the system and should not be held accountable. Some were ready to compromise and, as 'grey, ambiguous persons', 'they are the rightful owners of a quota of guilt' (Levi 2013: 47). But others, for example the 'crematorium ravens', those who worked in the special squads in the crematoria in order to preserve their own lives for a few weeks – no one is authorised to judge them, and 'a judgement of them [should] be suspended' (ibid: 61). Here the language is important, since a judgment suspended is nonetheless one that can be made – but not carried out. *Impotentia judicandi* again, yet with a different outcome to that in the case of Rumkowski.

It should be repeated, however, that none of this counts against the full responsibility of the perpetrators, the men and women who ran the death camps. As Levi says, it is crucial not to conflate perpetrators, victims and collaborators. A sense of the universality of the human condition should not undermine these distinctions. As regards the different positions of the perpetrator and the victim, Levi says, 'I do not know . . . whether in my depths there lurks a murderer, but I do know that I was a guiltless victim and I was not a murderer' (ibid: 46). Confusing the two roles 'means wanting to becloud our need for justice'. Yet, it is having just said this that he then wishes to make a 'few more remarks' (ibid: 47) about the grey, ambiguous people: the crematorium ravens, those who cooperated in running the system, but also, it seems, himself who did not do enough, who failed to offer solidarity, who continued to live while a crime was committed, who witnessed the systemic rendering of the world as one of enormous pain.

There remains a commonality of guilt, but there are also victims, perpetrators and collaborators. Overall, it must be recalled, the three groups are located in the structure and context of the camp, which allows perpetrators to victimise, and turns some victims into accomplices. The 'greatest responsibility lies with the system, the very structure of the totalitarian state . . .' (Levi 2013: 40). It is that which establishes the setting in which the different kinds of actor operate. What it does not do is homogenise all guilt into a general category, although it complicates it beyond a simple account of perpetrators and victims.[11]

11 Compare Agamben's understanding that the Camp reduces all to a 'zone of irresponsibility' (2002: 21) 'in which victims become executioners and executioners become victims' (2002: 17). This is not Levi's position. See Leys (2007: 157–61) for a considered critical response to this.

Bystanders and collective guilt

Then there is the guilt of the bystander. Insofar as he or she is a camp inmate, the bystander is the person who may feel guilt at not having acted, in the ways described above. However, bystander guilt goes further than this, into the question of a general guilt that might exist for a people that has allowed genocide to occur. Here again, we should consider the positions of Arendt and Jaspers. For Arendt, a distinction is made between political and moral responsibility. With regard to the former, she agrees that every generation 'is burdened by the sins of the fathers as it is blessed with the deeds of the ancestors' (Arendt 2003b: 27), but this should not lead to a sense of personal responsibility for it is only metaphorically that we can say 'we feel guilty for the sins of our fathers or our people or mankind, in short for deeds we have *not* done'. Morally speaking, 'it is as wrong to feel guilty without having done anything specific as it is to feel free of all guilt if one actually is guilty of something' (ibid: 28).

From this standpoint, she neatly pins the tendency in post-war German debate to whitewash individual perpetrators for what they had done, since all were guilty anyway. But this was surely a consequence of political moves in favour of post-war reconstruction, rather than a necessary consequence of identifying both individual perpetrators and a general sense of a collective guilt as distinct moral phenomena.

Jaspers's approach to the same issue is intriguing and different (see above, pp 137–40). His initial view is that collective guilt exists only in the limited form of political liability, for 'there is no such thing as a people as a whole' so that the 'categorical judgment of a people is always unjust . . . and results in the debasement of the human being as an individual'. Accordingly, 'to pronounce a group criminally, morally or metaphysically guilty is an error akin to the laziness and arrogance of average, uncritical thinking' (Jaspers 2000: 35–36). Yet, later in his account, Jaspers becomes concerned that his fourfold typology, although 'correct and meaningful,' might have lost something in the process, which 'in collective guilt is always audible in spite of everything'.

In the end, he finds himself returning 'to the question of collective guilt' (Jaspers 2000: 69), and this leads him back to the formulations we encountered above relating to metaphysical guilt. People live under evolving conditions which determine the moral aspects of a nation's life and which 'help to determine individual morality'. The individual lives 'as a link in [a] chain' and there 'is a sort of collective moral guilt in a people's way of life which I share as an individual' (ibid: 70). The world of which the Germans were a part could produce a regime such as the Nazis, and this is a moral fact for which all Germans are at a certain level responsible:

> We . . . feel that we not only share in what is done at present—thus being co-responsible for the deeds of our contemporaries – but in the links of a tradition. We have to bear the guilt of our fathers. That the spiritual conditions

> of German life provided an opportunity for such a regime is a fact for which all of us are co-responsible . . .
>
> (Jaspers 2000: 73)[12]

Levi also confronts the question of collective guilt, in the shape of those who 'turn their backs so as not to see [the crime] and not feel touched by it'. This is 'what the majority of Germans did during the twelve Hitlerian years, deluding themselves that not seeing was a way of not knowing, and that not knowing relieved them of their share of complicity or connivance' (Levi 2013: 91).[13] How does Levi's view of bystander guilt relate to the metaphysical conception that we have seen underpins his account of survivor guilt? To speak of guilt as he does as a sin of omission involved in looking the other way suggests it is the failure of an aggregate (a majority) of actual agents that counts, so the way is not opened directly to a metaphysical conception. Where a metaphysical account would be needed, however, is in relation to those who did not look the other way, and who still feel guilt, or those in subsequent generations who express feelings of guilt for the tradition and the actions of the earlier generations.

Levi's approach to this can be discerned from the penultimate chapter of *The Drowned and the Saved*, where he reports on correspondence with Germans. To one he writes that he feels no hatred for the Germans as a whole, that hatred is only due to the perpetrators, and that any judge should only punish actual culprits and not those innocent of crimes (Levi 2013: 212). But this does not exclude for Levi a sense of collective guilt, in the manner expressed by Jaspers. Whilst it is 'dangerous, wrong, to speak about the "Germans", or any other people as of a single undifferentiated entity, and include all individuals in one judgement', at the same time, 'I don't think I would deny that there exists a spirit of each people (otherwise it would not be a people), a *Deutschtum*, an *Italianata*, an *Hispanidad*' so that one can expect 'one specific, collective behaviour rather than another', whilst dismissing caricature and allowing for individual exceptions (ibid: 210–211).

This is difficult territory, but Levi follows it by quoting a German physician who writes to him that he is 'conscious of being implicated in the greatness and culpability of my people' and that he 'stands before you as an accomplice of those who did violence to your destiny and the destiny of your people' (Levi 2013: 212–213). With regard to the generation to come, Levi quotes without comment but seemingly with approval the following:

> At the end of the war I was still a child; I cannot take upon myself any share of guilt for the frightful crimes committed by the Germans; and yet I am

12 Ultimately, Jaspers extends the claim of metaphysical guilt beyond the German context to a 'guilt of all', whilst insisting that this 'must not become a way to dodge German guilt' (Jaspers 2000: 94).

13 'I repeat: the true crime, the collective, general crime of almost all Germans of that time was that of lacking the courage to speak' (Levi 2013: 208).

> ashamed of them . . . You write that you cannot understand the Germans. If it is your intention to allude to the executioners and their helpers, then I too cannot understand them; but I hope I will have the strength to fight them if they should appear again on the stage of history. I spoke of 'shame': I meant to express this feeling – that what was perpetrated by German hands at that time should never have happened, nor should it have been approved of by other Germans.
>
> (Levi 2013: 213)

Behind this sense of historical resolve, there seems to stand a sense of collective responsibility in the Jaspersian sense. The line of argument is familiar, and it is also seen in the work of Jean Améry, whom Levi discusses in *The Drowned and the Saved*, and whose approach to blaming is rather different to Levi's. Yet, on this point, there is little difference. Améry too begins by taking an aggregative view. Collective guilt is, he says 'sheer nonsense if it implies that the community of Germans possessed a common consciousness, a common will, a common initiative to act' (Améry 1980: 72), but it is a useful hypothesis if it means 'the objectively manifested *sum* of individual guilty conduct'. From that point of view, there 'grows out of the guilt of individual Germans . . . a total guilt of the people'. Collective guilt must be demystified, but can then be seen as based upon a 'statistical statement' (ibid: 73).

Beyond this, however, there is also a further sense of collective guilt that is non-summative or aggregative, in the sense of sharing in a particular culture and history that has in some way produced Nazism, and to which all belong:

> It is understandable that the young people are free of individual guilt and of the collective guilt that results from its summation . . . [Yet] as long as the German nation, including its young and its youngest groups, does not decide to live entirely without history . . . then it must continue to bear responsibility for those twelve years that it certainly did not terminate itself. German youth cannot cite Goethe, Mörike, and Baron von Stein, and ignore Blunck, Wilhelm Schäfer, and Heinrich Himmler.
>
> (Améry 1980: 76)

To summarise and conclude this section, we might say that in Levi, the moral status of perpetrators and victims represent the more straightforward pivot on which hinges the guilt of survivors, bystanders and the collective group. Yet, if we are to answer Arendt's initial problem, the underlying structure of a metaphysical guilt is required in order to render that pivot straightforward. It is only, then, once we understand this position that we can move towards an understanding of the grey zone, wherein the complicity of victims in perpetration in the systematic context of the camp may lead to the impotence of judging. Lurking behind this ethical problematic is the guilt of the survivor, a guilt that is both with and without ground. Metaphysical guilt also underlies what is explicable and valid in the concept of collective guilt. The greatness of Levi's testimony of the camp is that he is able to reflect with clear moral vision on how guilt in its different forms could be experienced, described and differentiated.

What I have sought to do here is to think through the kind of ethical structure that would be necessary to ground Levi's judgments.[14] Taking my cue from his and others' reflections, especially on survivor guilt, it seems to me that the kind of meta-ethics, or ethical structure, necessary is one that can ground the distinctions between different guilt forms, and provide them with a deeper framing that structurally locates them. Such a framing is provided by the kind of metaphysical account of ethics I have discussed here.

Conclusion

My substantive starting point in this essay was the issue of survivor guilt. How do we understand it, what does it tell us about guilt in general, and how does it connect with Jaspers's account of metaphysical guilt? What we find in Levi is a subtle and nuanced series of judgments about guilt in the concentration camps, in which perpetrators remain perpetrators and victims remain victims, but between the two there stands a grey zone in which the two sides, whilst remaining apart, also blur together. To be a complicit victim is not the same as a perpetrator, but it is to participate in a way that can lead to an attribution of responsibility, or not. It may be a question of suspending a judgment, or recognising a quotient of guilt, or both, or neither. There is no question of denying key distinctions, but there are still questions to be addressed which run up against those distinctions.

The figure of Rumkowski, or the crematorium ravens, or the guilty survivor focuses the issue, but it also goes deeper into our sense of what it means to be human, and this is where the idea of metaphysical guilt comes in. From this standpoint, it is also essential to think through the issue of collective guilt. No doubt that notion should be freed of 'myth and mystification' (Améry 1980: 73), its 'Old Testament' connotations (ibid: 75), and of course it should not be manipulated for political ends. Once all that is said, there is still something that we should look at in both a summative and a deeper historical sense.

What are the vulnerabilities we share, and what do we owe to each other in terms of fundamental questions about solidarity and our moral being? The question of the right to live in the place of another, and what we may do, or should do, or owe to the other require an understanding of what it is that is universal in the human condition: the things we fundamentally share as human beings. These questions cannot be answered as a matter simply of psychological mechanism: they require an understanding of the deep ethics at the core of our being. It is that deep ethics that is brought out by confronting Arendt's vision of Eichmann,

14 For an alternative view which sees Levi as divided between Kantian and in effect Levinasian philosophical approaches, see Druker (2009).

Jaspers's account of metaphysical guilt and Levi's experience and nuanced judgment of the camp.

Relating this back to Bhaskar's journey through critical realism to its dialectical phase, and on to metaReality, if the first two are about understanding the working of natural necessity and the place of human, ultimately moral, agency in the world, then the issues surrounding agency as an emergent power of biological matter disclose important questions of human freedom. In these phases, questions concerning the historical, structural and organisational dimensions of a social phenomenon are central. Critical realism has its feet firmly planted in the social and historical understanding of the human world, but this then leads us in the direction of fundamental questions about the human condition that touch on our universality and what we owe each other. The questions at this third level are not separate from the first two, but are already present in them.

In what I have sought to explore in this essay about metaphysical guilt, and how it comes out of the most cruel experience, I have tried to indicate that the thought needed to understand the concentration camp, and its aftermath, leads us into the same area. In this way Bhaskar's understanding of metaReality underlabours for our understanding of some of the darkest moral experiences that have confronted human beings – by implication, all human beings.

An answer to the question of guilt takes us beyond the positive or actual realities of formal law, where agents are held responsible for their acts. The camp discloses the metaphysical substratum that underlies our understanding of individual responsibility. Bhaskar's work underlabours to this conclusion.

Bibliography

Adorno, T W (1973) *Negative Dialectics* London: Routledge

Adorno, T and M Horkheimer (1997) *Dialectic of Enlightenment* London: Verso

Agamben, G (1998) *Homo Sacer: Sovereign Power and Bare Life* Stanford CA: Stanford University Press

Agamben, G (2002) *Remnants of Auschwitz: the Witness and the Archive* New York: Zone Books

Agamben, G (2005) *State of Exception* Chicago IL: University of Chicago Press

Althusser, L (1969) *For Marx* London: Penguin Books

Améry, J (1980) *At the Mind's Limits* Bloomington: Indiana University Press

Arendt, H (1964) *Eichmann in Jerusalem* London: Penguin Books

Arendt, H (1968) *Origins of Totalitarianism* London: Harcourt Brace

Arendt, H (2003a) 'Auschwitz on Trial' in Kohn, J (ed) *Responsibility and Judgment* New York: Schocken Books

Arendt, H (2003b) 'Personal Responsibility Under Dictatorship' in Kohn, J (ed) *Responsibility and Judgment* New York: Schocken Books

Arlidge, A (2000) 'The Trial of Dr David Moor' *Criminal Law Review* p 31

Aschheim, S (ed) (2001) *Hannah Arendt in Jerusalem* Oakland: University of California Press

Ashworth, A (1996) 'Criminal Liability in a Medical Context: the Treatment of Good Intentions' in Simester, A P and A T H Smith (eds) *Harm and Culpability* Oxford: Oxford University Press

Ashworth, A (2005) *Sentencing and Criminal Justice* Cambridge: Cambridge University Press

Ashworth, A (2009) *Principles of Criminal Law* 6th edn Oxford: Oxford University Press

Ashworth, A and B Mitchell (2000) *Rethinking English Homicide Law* Oxford: Oxford University Press

Ashworth, A and J Horder (2013) *Principles of Criminal Law* 7th edn Oxford: Oxford University Press

Ashworth, A and L Zedner (2008) 'Defending the Criminal Law: Reflections on the Changing Character of Crime, Procedure and Sanctions' *Criminal Law and Philosophy* 2(1) pp 21–51

Ashworth, A and L Zedner (2013) *Preventive Justice* Oxford: Oxford University Press

Barnett, S (ed) (1998) *Hegel After Derrida* London: Routledge

Barthes, R (1973) *Mythologies* St Albans: Paladin

Beiner, R (ed) (1992) *Lectures on Kant's Political Philosophy* Chicago: The University of Chicago Press

Benhabib, S (2000) 'Arendt's Eichmann in Jerusalem' in Villa, D (ed) *Cambridge Companion to Hannah Arendt* Cambridge: Cambridge University Press

Berlin, I (1969) 'Two Concepts of Liberty' in Berlin, I (ed) *Four Essays on Liberty* Oxford: Oxford University Press
Bernstein, R (2002) *Radical Evil* Cambridge: Polity
Bhaskar, R (1975) *A Realist Theory of Science* Leeds: Leeds Books
Bhaskar, R (1979) *The Possibility of Naturalism* Brighton: Wheatsheaf
Bhaskar, R (1993) *Dialectic: the Pulse of Freedom* London: Verso
Bhaskar, R (1994) *Plato Etc* London: Verso
Bhaskar, R (2002) *Reflections on Meta-Reality* London: Sage
Bhaskar, R (2012a) *From Science to Emancipation* Abingdon: Oxford
Bhaskar, R (2012b) *The Philosophy of MetaReality* Abingdon: Oxford
Bhaskar, R with M Hartwig (2010) *The Formation of Critical Realism: A Personal Perspective* Abingdon: Oxford
Bosanquet, B (1919) *The Philosophical Theory of the Modern State* 3rd edn London: Macmillan
Bower, T (1997) *A Blind Eye to Murder* London: Warner
Brudner, A (2009) *Punishment and Freedom: A Liberal Theory of Penal Justice* Oxford: Oxford University Press
Brudner, A (2011) 'A Reply to Critics of *Punishment and Freedom*' *New Criminal Law Review* 14, 495–517
Buck-Morss, S (2009) *Hegel, Haiti and Universal History* Pittsburgh PA: University of Pittsburgh Press
Cesarani, D (2004) *Eichmann: His Life and Crimes* London: William Heinemann
Collier, A (1999) *Being and Worth* London: Routledge
Crown Prosecution Service (20 October, 2005a) 'CPS Decision in Henry (Harry) Stanley Case' http://wwwcpsgovuk/news/press_releases/153_05/indexhtml (last accessed 13 April 2016)
Crown Prosecution Service (2005b) 'Householders and the Use of Force Against Intruders: Joint Public Statement from the Crown Prosecution Service and the Association of Chief Police Officers' http://wwwcpsgovuk/publications/prosecution/householdershtml (last accessed 13 April 2016)
Crown Prosecution Service (17 July 2006) 'CPS Statement: Charging Decision on the Fatal Shooting of Jean Charles de Menezes' http://wwwcpsgovuk/news/press_releases/146_06/indexhtml (last accessed 13 April 2016)
Crown Prosecution Service (9 December 2008) 'Decision on Prosecution: the Death By Suicide of Daniel James' http://wwwcpsgovuk/news/articles/death_by_suicide_of_daniel_james/indexhtml (last accessed 13 April 2016)
Crown Prosecution Service (October 2014) 'Policy for Prosecutors in Respect of Cases of Encouraging or Assisting Suicide' http://wwwcpsgovuk/publications/prosecution/assisted_suicide_policyhtml (last accessed 13 April 2016)
Cuddon, J A (1992) *The Penguin Dictionary of Literary Terms and Literary Theory* London: Penguin
Deleuze, G (1993) *Difference and Repetition* New York: Columbia University Press
Dennis, I (1997) 'The Critical Condition of Criminal Law' *Current Legal Problems* 50, 1, 213
Derrida, J (1990) 'Force of Law: the "Mystical Foundation of Authority"' *Cardozo Law Review* 11 pp 920–1046
Derrida, J (1992) 'The Force of Law: the "Mystical Foundation of Authority"' in Cornell, D, M Rosenfeld and D G Carlson (eds) *Deconstruction and the Possibility of Justice* London: Routledge pp 3–67
Derrida, J (1994) *Specters of Marx* London: Routledge
Derrida, J (2001) *On Cosmopolitanism and Forgiveness* London: Routledge

Dews, P (2008) *The Idea of Evil* Oxford: Blackwell
Douglas, L (2001) *The Memory of Judgment* New Haven and London: Yale University Press
Douzinas, C (2007) *Human Rights and Empire: The Political Philosophy of Cosmopolitanism* London: Routledge-Cavendish
Druker, J (2009) *Primo Levi and Humanism After Auschwitz: Posthumanist Reflections* New York: Palgrave Macmillan
Dubber, M (2005) *The Police Power: Patriarchy and the Foundations of American Government* New York: Columbia University Press
Duff, R A (1990) *Intention, Agency and Criminal Liability* Oxford: Blackwell
Duff, R A (1996) 'Penal Communications: Recent Work in the Philosophy of Punishment' *Crime and Justice* 20 pp 1–97
Duff, R A (1998) 'Principle and Contradiction in the Criminal Law: Motives and Criminal Liability' in Duff, R A (ed) *Philosophy and the Criminal Law* New York: Cambridge University Press
Duff, R A (2007) *Answering for Crime* Oxford: Hart
Dworkin, R (1993) *Life's Dominion* London: Harper Collins
Dworkin, G, R G Frey and S Bok (1998) *Euthanasia and Physician-Assisted Suicide* Cambridge: Cambridge University Press
Eagleton, T (2010) *On Evil* Yale: Yale University Press
Fanon, F (1965) *The Wretched of the Earth* London: Penguin Books
Farmer, L (1997) *Criminal Law, Tradition and Legal Order* Cambridge: Cambridge University Press
Fine, R (2001) *Political Investigations: Hegel, Marx, Arendt* London and New York: Routledge
Finnis, J (1991) 'Intention and Side-Effects' in Frey, R G and C Morris, *Liability and Responsibility* Cambridge: Cambridge University Press
Fitzpatrick, P and B Golder (2009) *Foucault's Law* London: Routledge
Fletcher, G (1975) *Rethinking the Criminal Law* Oxford: Oxford University Press
Fletcher, G (1998) *Basic Concepts of Criminal Law* Oxford: Oxford University Press
Foucault, M (1977) *Discipline and Punish: The Birth of the Prison* Harmondsworth, UK: Allen Lane
Foucault, M (1991) 'Governmentality' in Burchell, G, C Gordon and P Miller (eds) *The Foucault Effect* Hemel Hempstead: Harvester Wheatsheaf
Gardner, J (2007) *Offences and Defences* Oxford: Oxford University Press
Garland, D (2001) *The Culture of Control: Crime and Social Order in Contemporary Society* Oxford: Oxford University Press
Glover, J (1977) *Causing Death and Saving Lives* London: Pelican
Goff, R (1988) 'The Mental Element in Murder' *Law Quarterly Review* 104, 30
Greasley, K (2010) 'R (DPP) v Purdy and the Case for Wilful Blindness' *Oxford Journal of Legal Studies* 30(2) pp 301–26
Greenawalt, K (1984) 'The Perplexing Borders of Justification and Excuse' *Columbia Law Review* 84(8) pp 1897–927
Grubb, A and I Kennedy (1994) *Medical Law: Text and Materials* London: Butterworths
Habermas, J (1992) *Postmetaphysical Thinking* Cambridge: MIT Press
Hart, H L A (1963) *Punishment, Responsibility and Justice* London: Oxford University Press
Hart, H L A (1968) *Punishment and Responsibility* Oxford: Clarendon
Hegel, G W F (1952) *The Philosophy of Right* Oxford: Clarendon
Hegel, G W F (1956) *The Philosophy of History* New York: Dover Publications

Horder, J (1990) 'Cognition, Emotion and Criminal Culpability' *Law Quarterly Review* 106 pp 469–86
Horder, J (1997) 'Two Histories and Four Hidden Principles of Mens Rea' *Law Quarterly Review* 113 pp 95–119
Horder, J (2000) 'On the Irrelevance of Motive in Criminal Law' in Horder, J (ed) *Oxford Essays in Jurisprudence: 4th Series* Oxford: Oxford University Press
Jaspers, K (2000) *The Question of German Guilt* New York: Fordham University Press
Johnstone, G (2002) *Restorative Justice: Ideas, Values, Debates* Cullompton: Willan
Kant, I (1948) *The Moral Law* London: Hutchinson
Kant, I (1965) *The Metaphysical Elements of Justice* Indianapolis: Bobbs-Merrill
Kant, I (1991) 'Perpetual Peace: A Philosophical Sketch' in Reiss, H (ed) *Political Writings* Cambridge: Cambridge University Press
Kant, I (1993) *Critique of Pure Reason* London: J M Dent pp 532–3
Kant, I (1996) *The Metaphysics of Morals* Cambridge: Cambridge University Press
Kelman, M (1981) 'Interpretive Construction in the Substantive Criminal Law' *Stanford Law Review* 33 pp 591–674
Kennedy, I and A Grubb (1994) *Medical Law: Text with Materials* London: Butterworths
Kohler, L and H Saner (eds) (1992) *Hannah Arendt/Karl Jaspers Correspondence, 1926–1969* New York: Harcourt Brace
Kutz, C (2000) *Complicity: Ethics and Law for a Collective Age* Cambridge: Cambridge University Press
Lacey, N (1998) 'Contingency, Coherence and Conceptualism' in Duff, R A (ed) *Philosophy and the Criminal Law* New York: Cambridge University Press
Lacey, N (2007) 'Space, Time and Function: Intersecting Principles of Responsibility Across the Terrain of Criminal Justice' *Criminal Law and Philosophy* 1(2) pp 233–50
Lacey, N, C Wells and O Quick (2003) *Reconstructing Criminal Law* 3rd edn LexisNexis
Lacey, N, C Wells and O Quick (2010) *Reconstructing Criminal Law* 4th edn Cambridge: Cambridge University Press
Law Commission (1989) *A Criminal Code for England and Wales* The Law Commission, No 177
Law Commission (1993) *Legislating the Criminal Code* The Law Commission No 218
Law Commission (2006) *A New Homicide Act for England and Wales? A Consultation Paper* The Law Commission, consultation paper No 177 https://wwwlawupennedu/cf/faculty/cfinkels/workingpapers/Report%20for%20British%20Law%20Commission%20cp177 pdf (last accessed 13 April 2016)
Lewis, P (2007) *Assisted Dying and Legal Change* Oxford: Oxford University Press
Leverick, F (2007) *Killing in Self-Defence* Oxford: Oxford University Press
Levi, P (2013) *The Drowned and the Saved* London: Abacus
Leys, R (2007) *From Guilt to Shame: Auschwitz and After* Princeton: Princeton University Press
MacIntyre, A (2007) *After Virtue* 3rd edn London: Duckworth
Mackay, R (2010) 'The New Diminished Responsibility Plea' *Criminal Law Review* p 290
Marshall, TH (1992) *Citizenship and Social Class London*: Plato Press
Marx, K (1968a) 'The 18th Brumaire of Napoleon Bonaparte' in Marx, K and F Engels (eds) *Selected Works in One Volume* London: Lawrence & Wishart
Marx, K (1968b) 'Manifesto of the Communist Party' in Marx, K and F Engels (eds) *Selected Works in One Volume* London: Lawrence & Wishart
Marx, K (1968c) 'Critique of the Gotha Programme' in Marx, K and F Engels (eds) *Selected Works in One Volume* London: Lawrence & Wishart
Marx, K (1975) *Karl Marx: Early Writings* London: Pelican Books

McMahan, J (2002) *The Ethics of Killing* New York: Oxford University Press
Meister, R (2012) *After Evil: a Politics of Human Rights* New York: Columbia University Press
Murphy, J (1979) *Retribution, Justice and Therapy* Dordrecht: D Reidel
Neumann, F (1953) 'The Concept of Political Freedom' *Columbia Law Review* 53(7) pp 901–35
Neumann, F (1957) *The Democratic and the Authoritarian State* Glencoe: Free Press
Neumann, F (1986) *The Rule of Law: Political Theory and the Legal System in Modern Society* Leamington Spa: Berg Publishers
Nietzsche, F (1967) *On the Genealogy of Morals* in *Basic Writings of Nietzsche* New York: Modern Library
Norrie, A (1991) *Law, Ideology and Punishment* Netherlands: Kluwer
Norrie, A (1998) '"Simulacra of Morality"? Beyond the Ideal/Actual Antinomies of Criminal Justice' in Duff, A (ed) *Philosophy and the Criminal Law: Principle and Critique* Cambridge: Cambridge University Press
Norrie, A (1999) 'After Woollin' *Criminal Law Review* 532
Norrie, A (2000) *Punishment, Responsibility and Justice* Oxford: Oxford University Press
Norrie, A (2001) *Crime, Reason and History* 2nd edn London: Butterworths
Norrie, A (2001a) 'Review of Ashworth and Mitchell', *Rethinking English Homicidc Law* (2000) *Legal Studies* 699
Norrie, A (2005a) *Law and the Beautiful Soul* London: The GlassHouse Press
Norrie, A (2005b) 'Theorising "Spectrality": Ontology and Ethics in Derrida and Bhaskar' in Dean, K, J Joseph and A Norrie (eds) *New Formations (Special Issue on Critical Realism Today)* 56 pp 96–108
Norrie, A (2007) 'Historical Differentiation, Moral Judgment and the Modern Criminal Law' *Criminal Law and Philosophy* 1(3) pp 251–57
Norrie, A (2010) *Dialectic and Difference: Dialectical Critical Realism and the Grounds of Justice* London: Routledge
Norrie, A (2014) *Crime, Reason and History* 3rd edn Cambridge: Cambridge University Press
Ormerod, D (2005) *Smith and Hogan Criminal Law* Oxford: Oxford University Press
Pidd, H (2010) 'Mother guilty of murdering disabled son' *Guardian* (20 January 2010) http://wwwtheguardiancom/uk/2010/jan/20/mother-guilty-murder-disabled-son (last accessed 13 April 2016)
Price, D (1997) 'Euthanasia, Pain Relief and Double Effect' *Legal Studies* 17(2) pp 323–42
Rabinbach, A (2001) 'German as Pariah, Jew as Pariah: Hannah Arendt and Karl Jaspers' in Aschheim, S (ed) *Hannah Arendt in Jerusalem* Oakland: University of California Press
Ramsay, P (2004) 'What is Anti-Social Behaviour?' *Criminal Law Review* pp 908–25
Ramsay, P (2006) 'The Responsible Subject as Citizen: Criminal Law, Democracy and the Authoritarian State' *Modern Law Review* 69(1) pp 29–58
Ramsay, P (2012) *The Insecurity State: Vulnerable Autonomy and the Right to Security in the Criminal Law* Oxford: Oxford University Press
Sachs, A and G Welch (1990) *Liberating the Law* London: Zed Press
Schaap, A (2001) 'Guilty Subjects and Political Responsibility: Arendt, Jaspers and the Resonance of the "German Question"' *Political Studies* 49(4) pp 749–66
Simester, A (1992) 'Mistakes in Defences' *Oxford Journal of Legal Studies* 12(2) pp 295–310
Simon, J (2007) *Governing Through Crime* Oxford: Oxford University Press
Smith, J C and B Hogan (1983) *Criminal Law* 5th edn London: Butterworths
Tadros, V (2005) *Criminal Responsibility* Oxford: Oxford University Press
Thornhill, C (2002) *Karl Jaspers: Politics and Metaphysics* London: Routledge
Vargas Llosa, M (2012) *The Dream of the Celt* London: Faber

Index